Perspectives on the Holocaust

Raul Hilberg

Perspectives on the Holocaust

Essays in Honor of Raul Hilberg

EDITED BY
James S. Pacy
and
Alan P. Wertheimer

Westview Press
BOULDER • SAN FRANCISCO • OXFORD

All rights reserved. No part of this publication may be reproduced or transmitted in any form or by any means, electronic or mechanical, including photocopy, recording, or any information storage and retrieval system, without permission in writing from the publisher.

Copyright © 1995 by Westview Press, Inc.

Published in 1995 in the United States of America by Westview Press, Inc., 5500 Central Avenue, Boulder, Colorado 80301-2877, and in the United Kingdom by Westview Press, 36 Lonsdale Road, Summertown, Oxford OX2 7EW

Library of Congress Cataloging-in-Publication Data
Perspectives on the Holocaust : essays in honor of Raul Hilberg / edited by James S. Pacy, Alan P. Wertheimer.
   p. cm.
 Includes bibliographical references.
 ISBN 0-8133-2034-8
  1. Holocaust, Jewish (1939–1945)—Congresses. 2. Holocaust, Jewish (1939–1945)—Moral and ethical aspects—Congresses.
3. Holocaust, Jewish (1939–1945), in literature—Congresses.
4. Literature, Modern—20th century—History and criticism—Congresses. 5. Jewish literature—20th century—History and criticism—Congresses. 6. Hilberg, Raul, 1926– —Congresses.
I. Hilberg, Raul, 1926– . II. Pacy, James S. III. Wertheimer, Alan.
D804.3.P487 1995
940.53'18—dc20   94-24851
                                                                                                      CIP

Printed and bound in the United States of America

The paper used in this publication meets the requirements of the American National Standard for Permanence of Paper for Printed Library Materials Z39.48-1984.

10   9   8   7   6   5   4   3   2   1

Contents

Acknowledgments — vii

Introduction, *James S. Pacy and Alan P. Wertheimer* — 1

PART ONE
Essays on the History of the Holocaust

1. Nazi Paperwork for the Final Solution, *Robert Wolfe* — 5

2. On the Purpose of the Wannsee Conference, *Eberhard Jäckel* — 39

3. Profits and Persecution: Corporate Involvement in the Holocaust, *Peter Hayes* — 51

4. Beyond Warsaw and Łódź: Perpetrating the Holocaust in Poland, *Christopher R. Browning* — 75

5. Nazi-Jewish Negotiations, *Yehuda Bauer* — 91

PART TWO
Philosophical and Literary Analyses of the Holocaust

6. Through a Glass Darkly, *George Steiner* — 109

7. Primo Levi: The Survivor as Victim, *Alvin H. Rosenfeld* — 123

8. Elie Wiesel and Primo Levi, *Richard L. Rubenstein* — 145

9. Raul Hilberg's "Minutiae": Their Impact on Philosophical and Religious Inquiries After Auschwitz, *John K. Roth* — 167

**PART THREE
Personal Tributes**

10 Raul Hilberg, Actor in *Shoah*, *Claude Lanzmann* 185

11 "Inescapable, and the Best": Tribute to Raul Hilberg,
    Herman Wouk 189

About the Contributors 193
About the Book and Editors 195

Acknowledgments

This volume had its origins in an international conference on the Holocaust honoring Raul Hilberg, "The Hilberg Symposium: Perpetrators, Victims, and Bystanders." The conference took place on the University of Vermont campus, April 14–16, 1991. Approximately 1,000 people attended. The editors, who were co-chairs of the Hilberg Symposium, wish to thank all the members of the University of Vermont community who worked to make the symposium possible. In particular, we wish to thank David A. Scrase and the late Samuel N. Bogorad, who served on the organizing committee, and Candace L. Smith, who served as the symposium coordinator. We also thank the alumni and friends of the University of Vermont, without whose support none of this would have succeeded.

James S. Pacy
Alan P. Wertheimer

Introduction

James S. Pacy and Alan P. Wertheimer

This volume has its origins in an international conference on the Holocaust honoring Raul Hilberg's retirement from the University of Vermont in April 1991. The volume contains all seven of the presentations delivered at the conference by Yehuda Bauer, Christopher R. Browning, Claude Lanzmann, Alvin H. Rosenfeld, Richard L. Rubenstein, George Steiner, and Herman Wouk and an additional four essays that have since been prepared by Peter Hayes, Eberhard Jäckel, John K. Roth, and Robert Wolfe.

Both editors of this volume were fortunate to have been colleagues of Raul Hilberg for some twenty-five years. We provide below some brief biographical information about Raul Hilberg and a few observations about his contributions to the University of Vermont.

Raul Hilberg has spent his entire scholarly life studying the Holocaust. His first edition of *The Destruction of the European Jews* (1961) was regarded as the definitive study of the Holocaust until he published a three-volume revised version in 1985. The (London) *Times Literary Supplement* described the book as "one of the great historical works of our time." Hilberg is also the author of *Sonderzüge nach Auschwitz* (Special trains to Auschwitz; 1981, 1987) and *Perpetrators, Victims, and Bystanders: The Jewish Catastrophe, 1933–1945* (1992). He edited *Documents of Destruction* (1971, 1972) and, with Stanislaw Staron and Josef Kermisz, *The Warsaw Diary of Adam Czerniaków* (1979). He has produced numerous articles in journals and encyclopedias and has presented papers at various fora around the world, including New York, Paris, Stuttgart, Nürnberg, Jerusalem, Haifa, and Lublin. His works have been translated into Dutch, French, German, Hebrew, Italian, and Spanish. He was a member of the President's Commission on the Holocaust from 1978 to 1979 and a member of the United States Holocaust Memorial Council from 1980 to 1988. He has also served as an expert witness for the United States in denaturalization and deportation cases and for other legal proceedings in Canada, Australia, and Scotland.

Born in Vienna, Hilberg came to the United States via Cuba. He served in the United States Army in 1944–1946, graduated from Brooklyn College, was a research specialist in the War Documentation Project at Alexandria, Virginia, in 1951 and 1952, earned his Ph.D. in public law and government at Columbia University in 1955, and in 1956 arrived at the University of Vermont, where he served for thirty-five years.

In 1978 Hilberg was appointed the John G. McCullough Professor of Political Science. In 1988 he received the university's highest teaching award, the George V. Kidder Outstanding Faculty Award, and, most fittingly, the University Scholar Award as well. The University of Vermont awarded him an honorary degree in 1991.

Raul Hilberg may be the most important scholar to have served on the faculty of the University of Vermont. He was also one of its greatest teachers. As some 10,000 students can attest, Hilberg was an awe-inspiring instructor, sometimes intimidating, always fascinating. His students were motivated and enthralled by his spellbinding lectures—shaped by a matchless sense of timing and climax—and challenged to the hilt by his demanding examinations. We know we speak for our colleagues and for our students in thanking Raul for the years he spent in our midst in Vermont. Mentor and dear friend, it was our great pleasure to have shared that time with you.

PART ONE

Essays on the History of the Holocaust

1

Nazi Paperwork for the Final Solution

Robert Wolfe

Some people—so-called revisionists—say that the Holocaust is a myth, a hoax, even a political instrument wielded by Jews in general and the state of Israel in particular. But most of us know that the Holocaust—dubbed *Endlösung der Judenfrage* (the Final Solution to the Jewish question) by its Nazi perpetrators—regrettably and terribly almost accomplished its fanatic project to murder all European Jews.

How do we know this? Survivors, Allied soldiers who liberated concentration camps late in the war, bystanders, and perpetrators themselves have told us so in courtroom testimony, oral history, memoirs, articles, books, and plays; in still and motion pictures, including documentaries, docudramas, and fictional works; and, most trustworthy, in scholarly monographs derived from the most direct contemporaneous sources, that genre in which Raul Hilberg excels.

Some day, however, survivors, liberators, bystanders—and perpetrators—will all be gone. A generation will disappear, and future generations will be left only with the documentary record to counter inevitable revisionist skepticism and denial.

Of what does that record consist? Memoirs, oral history, courtroom testimony, and sworn affidavits are indirect and unavoidably subjective. None of these is immediate, contemporaneous, objective, or unaffected by hindsight. However masked by scholarly apparatus and however indirectly derived through oral history, memoirs, or private papers—or even from contemporaneous official records—the imperfectly observed or remembered and recorded experiences of ac-

---

The documents shown in facsimile are held, as cited, on original paper or on microfilm by the National Archives and Records Administration. Original paper records from which the microfilm was copied have been returned to the Federal German Archives (Bundesarchiv) at Koblenz, which graciously furnished the author direct reproductions from the originals.

tors therein and eyewitnesses thereof are the ultimate sources of all written history.

Records, official or other, are most useful and reliable *if* they were created to accomplish short-range *administrative* purposes: to conduct programs, projects, or operations; to order, convince, persuade, influence, inform, or merely communicate; to document agreements, plans, or commitments for operational or legal purposes. Documents deliberately prepared for the historical record, including official records, must always be suspect of intent to influence the writing of favorable biographic or "house" histories. Final signed copies of treaties or capitulations, decorated with colored ribbon and seals in gold skippets, do not disclose (and sometimes conceal) complicated prior negotiations.[1] Record copies of impromptu speeches are usually polished in print for posterity.[2]

Isolated documents, such as textually undocumented photographs,[3] can be more convincingly fabricated than interrelated documents, which, even when partly contradictory in content, may be mutually supportive in context. To be sure, sound, visual, and audiovisual documents possess the greater impact of immediacy, but they are more easily misinterpreted, faked, or staged. The politically popular photo opportunity is the most obvious example of staging impressions often deliberately contrary to fact, particularly to delude a population already conditioned to gullibility by printed advertisements and televised commercials.[4]

In short, the most reliable sources are *primary textual* sources, contemporaneous in fact and purpose, provided they are authentic. Authenticity may be established in two ways: from external and internal characteristics. Analysis of external evidence involves not only determining the contemporaneity of paper and ink but examining contemporaneous agency, organizational or unit procedures, and paperwork practices such as the drafting, editing, signing, distribution, and initialing of memoranda and correspondence, as well as filing systems, letterheads, and "incoming," "outgoing," and "circulate" stamps. It also includes documenting the life cycle (the legal term is *chain of control*) of the records: identifying where, when, and by whom they were prepared; writers of signatures, initials, and marginalia; when and where the records were filed (the archival term for the act of systematic filing is *created*), and regulations for permanent retention or scheduled periodic destruction of records (especially classified records).

In archival parlance a document is created not necessarily by the person who prepares or even *signs* it but by the agency that (or individual who) *files* it. Thus, when Oswald Pohl wrote and signed a memorandum to Heinrich Himmler, whose staff filed it with other communications from Pohl and/or among file series on that or related subjects dated during a specific year or other time span, the signed, letterhead original deposited in the Persönlicher Stab Reichsführer SS, Schriftgutverwaltung (Personal Staff Reich Leader of the SS and German Police, Records Administration) is said to be created by that agency. Conversely, an unsigned carbon copy of the same document, retained among related records of Pohl's SS-Wirtschafts-Verwaltungs-Hauptamt (WVHA, or Economic Administration) according to contemporaneous correspondence practices of that agency, is said to have been created by *that* agency.

Internal analysis of documents consists not only of determining who drafted, edited, typed, and signed a document (the identification of signatures, initials, and marginalia already mentioned) but for what purpose, with what basis for knowledge, and with what ax to grind. A sharp eye must also be alert for anachronism: foreknowledge of events as differentiated from accurate prediction.[5]

To sum up, if documents are to be accepted as reliable primary sources, they must be examined not just for content but for context. This requires careful and knowledgeable analysis. All of us draw on our own experiences in reaching conclusions about the weight and interpretation of the available evidence. The only possibility of reaching a semblance of agreement about complex or controversial events of the past requires sharing, as a common point of departure, essentially accurate facts based on authentic documents contemporaneous in fact and purpose.

No complex enterprise conducted by an organization consisting of many people dispersed over a wide area can function without considerable paperwork. Not even so secretly held an undertaking as the Nazi Final Solution of the Jewish question, which relied as much as possible on oral communication, could avoid leaving a telltale paper trail in the files of the operating agencies of the Third Reich and of the SS in particular. The Holocaust was too vast and far-flung an enterprise requiring too much organization and communication to be accomplished without generating a great deal of paperwork.

Although much of the incriminating evidence was destroyed by the perpetrators, there was too much to destroy all of it as Hitler's Thousand-Year Reich accelerated toward its götterdämmerung. A probably preclusive deterrent, however, was that anyone destroying even top secret records without specific orders could be charged with defeatism in the waning weeks of spring 1945, sometimes with fatal consequences. But as usual, top executives, having belatedly issued instructions to destroy records, failed to follow their own orders, as in the case of Himmler, whose voluminous personal staff files, recovered from a salt mine at Hallein just south of Salzburg, provided prosecutors at Nürnberg and other war crimes trials with the most telling proof of the charges in the indictments.[6]

But this paper trail was disrupted by Allied Forces' shortsighted handling of captured records in otherwise legitimate exploitation for purposes of wartime military intelligence and postwar military government, the latter especially including war crimes prosecutions. Removing original records from their file context without replacing them with photocopies or at least noting their file locations, Allied analysts and prosecutors at Nürnberg and elsewhere vitally damaged the integrity of many files, in the process tainting both the evidentiary and historical value of some of the most significant documentation of the Holocaust. This unintended vandalism—to say nothing of the zealous but misguided attempts by many a "hot" Holocaust museum to "sensitize" its visitors by misconstruing or overplaying the import of some of the more "visual" exhibit pieces—has provided damaging grist for revisionist mills.

As noted above, an isolated short document is comparatively easy to concoct, particularly if the fabricator has letterhead or blank paper of the right provenance and vintage. To manufacture even one or two spurious supporting documents, however, magnifies the risks of detection; conversely, diverse documents that complement one another provide a fair warranty of authenticity.[7]

For several weeks in spring 1960, a team of investigators from the Zentrale Stelle der Landesjustizverwaltung (Central Office of the State Justice Administration) at Ludwigsburg, headed by Dr. Erwin Schüle, visited the Federal Records Center at Alexandria, Virginia, in search of documentary evidence against alleged Nazi criminals, some 400 of whom had been indicted before the twenty-year German statute of limitations expired. Before leaving Alexandria, the investigators briefed me on the subjects and units (not individuals) of interest to them since, as a member of an American Historical Association (AHA) team of historians, I was describing still classified SS records to be microfilmed for deposit in the National Archives and Records Service (NARS).

After the German prosecutors departed, I encountered in a seized SS file a voucher submitted by an SS corporal accounting for his damaged rifle (Document A).[8] Its historical and evidentiary import was immediately clear to me, but its signature—in the German style, last name only and without a typewritten version underneath—was uncertain, making it questionable for prosecution purposes. The one specific clue was a rifle number: 6682.

In another record (Document B)[9] of the same SS unit, a list of weapons and equipment issued to its personnel disclosed the typewritten name of the trooper to whom rifle number 6682 had been assigned. In the same file, a form (Document C) listing weapons rendered unserviceable by "combat damage" verified the discarding of that and ten other damaged weapons.[10] Thus supported, Document A possessed prosecutorial potential.

Unaccompanied by documentation, the heaps of corpses familiar to the public in photographs and motion pictures taken by liberators of Nazi concentration camps might depict any of hundreds of massacres in innumerable locations anywhere in the world since the invention of photography. But for all the horror in these visual records and in oral accounts of mass shootings of numbered but nameless Jews, they lack the stark impact and poignant immediacy of this brief but documented account of the fate of one desperately courageous unnamed Jewess as provided by her murderer in his prosaic response to charges for his damaged weapon.

Georg Miller *was* among Dr. Schüle's 400 or so indictees. The evidence I had discovered, which the U.S. government provided to the German court, secured Miller's conviction: He was sentenced to four years.

One of the most publicized records of the Holocaust is a 1978 embellishment of an aerial photograph of Birkenau taken by the crew of an Allied aircraft on Au-

Document A: Memorandum Regarding Rifle Damage

Lublin, den 31.1.44

An
II C b
im Hause .

Betr.: Waffenschaden – Gewehr Nr. 6682 .

Bei der am 3.11.1943 in Trawnicki stattfindenden Judenaussiedlung wurde ich von einer Jüdin durch einen Schlag in's Gesicht tätlich angegriffen und leicht verletzt. Da die Person Anstalten machte nochmals zum Schlage auszuholen, sah ich mich genötigt abzuwehren und schlug ihr mit dem Kolben meines Gewehres auf den Schädel, wobei der Kolben leicht beschädigt wurde. Der Schaden selbst ist unerheblich (leichter Riss am Kolben) und beeinträchtigt die Feuerkraft und Sicherheit nicht im geringsten, was durch den Gebrauch im Anschluss an diesen Vorfall unter Beweis gestellt werden konnte.

[signature]
SS-Hauptscharführer

[Translation of Document A]

Lublin, Jan. 31, 1944

To: IICb (in house)
Subject: Damaged Weapon—Rifle No. 6682

During the resettlement of Jews taking place in Trawnicki on November 3, 1943, I was slapped in the face, and slightly injured, by a Jewess. Since this person was preparing to strike me again, I found it necessary to defend myself and hit her on the skull with the butt of my rifle, whereby the butt was lightly damaged. The damage itself is negligible (the stock slightly split), and does not in the least interfere with fire power and safety [of the weapon], which was demonstrated by its discharge in concluding this incident.

[Georg] Miller, SS-Corporal

Document B: List of Weapons and Equipment Issued to an SS Unit

Name	Gewehr Nr.	Pistolen Nr.	Seiten gewehr	Brot beutel	Feldflasche	Stahl helm	MPi Nr.	Patronentasche
Buchaj	5358	K 314 47o	–	–	–	–	–	–
Bojda	–	K 249 181	–	–	–	–	–	–
Biegelmeyer	–	K 234 431					Nr.19 971	
Frommeyer	–	K 249 178						
Gangl	Nr. 49o5	–	–	1	1	1	–	2
Gehrmann	–	K 314 476	–	–	–	–	Nr. 11 7o2	–
Bohlmann	–	–	–	–	–	1	Nr.14 971	
Hoch	–	K 249 179	–	–	–		Nr. 14 964	–
Hryhorowicz	–	K 314 472						
Hackel	–	K 249 182	–	–	–	–	–	
Kamelski	Nr. 7o3o	K 314 478	–	–	–	–	–	1
Kirsch	–	Steyr_Pistole	–	–	–	–	Nr. 11 251	–
Klause	–	K 242 864	–	–	–	–	–	–
Miller	Nr. 6682	–	–	1	–	1	–	1
Müller	Nr. 27oo	–	–	–	–	1	–	1
Steenbock	Nr. 4o79	–	–	–	–	–	Nr. 116 22	–
Schwank	Nr. 51 8o6	K 314 479	–	1	1	1	–	1
Werk	Nr.	K 242 991	–	1	1	–	Nr. 11 762	–
Preshl	Nr. 2777C	–	–	–	–	–		
Hübner	Nr.	–	–	–	–	–	Nr. 14 935	–
Strecker	Nr. 2861 E 2	K 314 467	–	1	1	–	–	1
Bieber	Nr. kein	K 281 874	–	–	–	–	–	–
Kühn		K 249 174	–	–	–	–	–	–
Nunrich	Nr. 69967pol.		–	–	–	1	–	1
Greinert	–	–	–	–	–	1	–	–
Silbert	Nr. 6232	242 835	–	1	1	1	–	1
Leiwald	Nr. 64 54 V 1	K 344 477	–	1	1	1	–	1
Gst.III.	Nr. 22 71 K	K 314 473	–	–	–	–	–	–

gust 25, 1944. Prompted by resurgent public interest resulting from the 1978 Martin Green television docudrama, "The Holocaust," and aided by ground information derived after the fact from a variety of postwar sources, American aerial photograph analysts used modern microstereoscopes to reexamine precise photo enlargements of the original 1944 films. The result, undoubtedly a great bonus to Holocaust documentation, has nevertheless been a mixed blessing.

From early April 1944 continuing until mid-January 1945, the Mediterranean Allied Air Force (MAAF) Photo Reconnaissance Wing (and beginning in August, the 15th Air Force) regularly flew missions over the IG Farben industrial complex (Lager III) located in the Auschwitz (Polish Oswięcim) area of Upper Silesia, preparatory to bombing synthetic fuel and rubber (Buna) plants then under construction. In flying such photographic runs—which also covered several other targets en route—cameras were usually opened early and left running late in or-

Document C: Voucher of Damaged or Destroyed Weapons

Der Kommandeur der Sicherheitspolizei
und des SD für den Distrikt Lublin
SD-Verwaltung

Unbrauchbarkeitsnachweis
(Kriegssachschaden)

Bel. Nr. 89

Von den unterzeichneten Führern wurden heute folgende Gegenstände für unbrauchbar erklärt:

Durch die Rückführung des KdS Lublin gingen verloren :

Gewehr Nr. 6562
            2700
            6684
            5358   wurde seinerzeit durch Beleg 65
            1162   vereinnahmt.
            9943
            3434
            5943
            2970
            6682
            6390

sind insgesamt 11 Gewehre (98)

Liegnitz , den 31. Januar 1944

SS-Hauptscharführer
(ein Verwaltungsführer)

Dienstgrad:
(ein aktiver Führer)

Genehmigt:

Dienstgrad:
(der Führer der Einheit)

Verausgabt in der Bestandsnachweisung

für _____ unter Nr. _____ Seite _____

SSV V 63 H-Vordruckverlag W. F. Mayr, Miesbach (Bayer. Hochland)

der to ensure complete coverage of the target, in this case resulting in an unexpected bonus of exposures of the murder mill at Birkenau (Lager II) 8 kilometers away.

Some thirty-five years later, photoanalysts from the CIA's National Photographic Interpretation Center (NPIC), applying advanced technology not available during World War II, enlarged, cropped, and captioned reproductions from original 1944–1945 aerial photographs to reveal extermination and other activities under way in Auschwitz-Birkenau Concentration Camp. In early January 1979, while their findings were still a CIA classified document,[11] I was given a private presentation in a secure area.[12] My suggestions were twofold: (1) that the original uncropped, uncaptioned photographs be shown side by side with their NPIC embellishments lest the public draw the mistaken conclusion that the Allied analysts of 1944 could have detected the ongoing exterminations; (2) that *contemporaneous* Allied and *German* sources be cited lest revisionists accuse the CIA of concocting disinformation to exploit the conveniently revived attention to the Holocaust spurred by the 1978 docudrama.[13]

In the event, I regret to report, my admonitions were ignored and my fears confirmed: a high-level triple play from Admiral Stansfield Turner of the CIA to his Annapolis schoolmate, President Jimmy Carter, to Elie Wiesel, then chairman of the United States Holocaust Memorial Council, resulted in the appearance of the latter on international television, standing in the Capitol rotunda and complaining, without contradiction from the president, Cabinet, Supreme Court, and congressional leaders visible on screen behind him, that "we had the pictures, we knew, and did nothing!"[14] Revisionists perceive this as an example of employment of the "Auschwitz lie" to blackmail the Western allies as well as the Germans.

Shown here (Document D)[15] in the unretouched form in which it was first available to Allied photoanalysts in 1944, is frame 3185 from the left side of a stereo series photographed at approximately 10:15 A.M. from 30,000 feet by a Mosquito aircraft of the 60th (South African) Squadron based in Bari, Italy, during PR (photo reconnaissance) Sortie 694 on August 25, 1944. This information can be deduced from the legend unique to each sortie automatically imprinted at the bottom of each frame by a frisket device (the frame numbers were printed on the negative film during manufacture).

Alongside the original photograph is the widely publicized blowup therefrom (Document E),[16] as enlarged, cropped, and captioned by NPIC analysts in 1978. The prisoners labeled "GROUP ON WAY TO GAS CHAMBER" appear to be going from the railroad siding across the tracks to "GAS CHAMBER AND CREMATORIUM II," the gate of which is open, as shown by its shadow, while the gate to Crematorium III on the near side of the tracks is closed.

Interpretation Report No. DP.95 (Document G) of August 30, 1944, concerns imagery acquired by the 60th Squadron on August 23 (Sortie 60 PR 686) and August 25 (Sortie 60 PR 694). Noteworthy is analyst Technical Sergeant Fryer's near exclusive concentration on bomb damage inflicted by U.S. European Command

Document D: Original Photo of Birkenau, August 25, 1944

Document E: 1978 Enlarged and Annotated Portion of Document D

(USEC) Sortie R86 on August 20 against the Farben Monowitz Lager III, as is particularly evident in the notation on page 2 of the prints he analyzed from Sortie 694, frames 4172 to 4178. Overlooked were the three consecutive and overlapping frames covering Birkenau, numbered 3184-3186, which are not listed in DP.95 as among those frames analyzed.[17]

Neither Allied air crews nor photoanalysts had the equipment, time, or mission to recognize the unprecedented systematic murder being inadvertently recorded by these photographic sorties over Auschwitz-Birkenau. Nor, although noting the existence of "labor camps" and "concentration camps" enclosed by barbed wire, did they see anything unusual in queues of civilians (or soldiers, for that matter) entraining or detraining, a common occurrence throughout wartime Europe in those days.

Document F, a small-scale, nonstereo aerial photograph,[18] was taken on June 26, 1944, also by an aircraft of the South African 60th PR Squadron flying at 30,000 feet. Beside it (Document H) is the 1978 NPIC embellishment thereof showing the layout of all three parts of the Auschwitz Concentration Camp complex: the Main Camp (Lager) I, Birkenau Camp II, and the IG Farben Buna plant

Document F: Original Photo of Auschwitz Camps, June 26, 1944

MEDITERRANEAN ALLIED PHOTO
RECONNAISSANCE WING

CONFIDENTIAL
30 August 1944

INTERPRETATION REPORT No. DP.95

Photographs taken by 60 Squadron on 23rd & 25th August 1944.

SORTIES: 60 PR 686.
60 PR 694.

SCALES: 1/9,700 Approx. (F.L. 36")
1/10,000 Approx. (F.L. 36")

POLAND

LOCALITY: OSWIECIM (AUSCHWITZ)

I. G.F. Synthetic Rubber & Synthetic Oil Plant.

COVER: Prints are of good scale & quality.

ATTACKED: 20 August 1944 by 15th Air Force.

REPORTS: DB 189, of 23 August 1944.
DB 191, of 25 August 1944.

1. **DAMAGE.** (This report deals with the synthetic oil refinery, but the plan issued is of the whole works. It will be seen that the greater part of the damage was done in the synthetic rubber plant. Interpretation has been done mainly on sortie 60 PR 686. On sortie 60 PR 694, of 2 days later, some slight clearance & repairs are seen.)

    PRIMARY OBJECTIVES. (Numbers in parenthesis refer to plan distributed).

    a. Boiler house & generator hall, with switch & transformer house: No damage seen. (10 and 11)

    b. Water gas plant, with blower house: no damage seen. (8 and 58)

    c. H2S removal plant: no damage seen. (73)

    d. CO2 & CO removal plant: small installation partly wrecked. (80)

    e. Gas conversion plant: no damage seen. (81)

    f. Injector houses: no damage seen. (83 and 84)

2. SECONDARY OBJECTIVES

    a. Distillation units: 1 small building destroyed. (98)

    b. Compressor houses: the E. end of a compressor house is slightly damaged. (75)

3. OTHER INSTALLATIONS

    a. Probable methanol plant: the building is about ½ badly damaged. (61)

    b. The purified gasholder and another gasholder have been damaged by blast. (64 and 70)

    c. Several workshops, storehouses, living huts, and some buildings which are still under construction, have suffered varying degrees of damage.

    d. Several instances of further construction since 26 June are seen.

Cont'd page 2.

I.R. No.D.P.95 (Cont'd)

ACTIVITY

There are no signs of operational activity on the photographs of 23 August, but on 25 August signs of activity include steam issuing from 4 or 5 vents of the water gas plant. Smoke can be seen in various parts of the plant, but since several smoke generators are in action around the perimeter of the plant, it is believed that the source of smoke at most of the internal points is also the smoke generation system. There is the usual amount of M.T. and personnel activity. Rail activity however, is largely limited to to movement of cars other than tank cars, only 7 to 10 of the latter being seen.

SUMMARY

Apparently this plant has not as yet come into production. The damage received is not sufficient to interfere seriously with synthetic fuel production, and should not greatly delay completion of this part of the plant.

Prints: 60PR/686:- 3067 to 3075
60PR/694:- 4172 to 4178
Comparative: 60PR/522:- 4044 to 4048.
Prints distributed:- 60PR/694, 4173, 4176, 4178.
Plan distributed:- Copy of A.I.C.U. plan No. D.410, altered to show damage.

DISTRIBUTION 'D.P.'
External..........13
Internal..........7

IG/FFB/BO

Document H: 1978 Annotated Version of Document G

at Monowitz Camp III. A nearly contemporaneous memorandum (Document I)[19] describing this tripartite layout, sent to Himmler on April 5, 1944, by SS general Oswald Pohl, the administrator of all concentration camps, unwittingly provides an uncanny verification of the Allied photograph.

Among thousands of captured Luftwaffe aerial photographic prints are two[20] of Birkenau taken on December 27, 1944, possibly to determine the adequacy of SS dismantling and camouflage operations then under way, and three by a Lieutenant Lüthje on February 19, 1945, presumably to ascertain what the Soviet troops were discovering on the ground since they overran Auschwitz on January 25, 1945. A comparison of one of Lüthje's German aerial photographs (Document J) with one of Birkenau taken on December 21, 1944 (Document K) by the U.S. 15th Air Force's 5th Photographic Group—that is, by opposing enemy air forces—in their obvious alikeness and immediacy serve to authenticate all Allied photographs of Auschwitz.

If there is one distinct body of documentation, standing alone, that provides ample evidence that the Final Solution, whether planned or evolved, was neither myth nor hoax, it is the multiform records—holographs, typewritten papers, and

Document I: Pohl to Himmler Describing the Auschwitz Layout

NO 0219

Der Chef
des SS-Wirtschafts-Verwaltungshauptamtes
D II/1 Az.: 27/2 Ma./F.
Tgb. Nr. 236/44 geh.

Berlin, den 5. 4. 1944
Lichterfelde-West
Unter den Eichen 126-135
Fernsprecher: Ortsverkehr 765261
Fernverkehr 765101

Geheime Reichssache!
2 Ausfertigungen
1. Ausfertigung

Betrifft: Sicherungsmaßnahmen in Auschwitz.
Bezug : Dortg. Schreiben vom 24.3.44
         Tgb.Nr. 38/32/44 geh. Bra/H.
Anlagen : 2 Pläne

An den
Reichsführer-SS
Berlin SW 11
Prinz Albrechtstr. 8

Reichsführer!

Die Ausdehnung und die hohe Belegstärke des Konzentrationslagers Auschwitz veranlaßten mich, bereits im Oktober v.J. eine Dreiteilung des Lagers vorzuschlagen. Nach Erteilung Ihrer Zustimmung wurde sie mit Wirkung vom 10.11.1943 durchgeführt. Es bestehen seitdem somit in Auschwitz 3 Konzentrationslager.

Über die für den A-Fall getroffenen Sicherungsmaßnahmen berichte ich folgendes:

1.) Das Lager I umfaßt das massive Männerlager und hat zur Zeit eine Belegstärke von rund 16.000 Häftlingen.
Es ist mit einer Umzäunung und mit Drahthindernissen umgeben, die, wie in allen Konzentrationslagern, elektrisch geladen werden. Außerdem sind Postentürme vorhanden, die mit Maschinengewehren besetzt sind.

Das Lager II befindet sich von dem Lager I etwa 3 km entfernt. In diesem sind 15.000 männliche und 21.000 weibliche Häftlinge untergebracht. Von der Gesamtzahl mit rund 36.000 Häftlingen entfallen etwa 15.000 auf nicht einsatzfähige.

Das Lager II ist ebenfalls mit einer elektrisch geladenen Drahtsicherung umgeben, auch Postentürme sind vorhanden.

Das <u>Lager III</u> umfaßt alle in Oberschlesien bestehenden Aussenlager bei Industriebetrieben, die räumlich weit von einander entfernt liegen. Es besteht zur Zeit aus 14 Aussenlagern mit einer Gesamthäftlingsstärke von rund 15.000 Männern. Diese Arbeitslager sind ebenfalls mit der üblichen Drahtsicherung umgeben und haben gleichfalls Postentürme. Das größte dieser Arbeitslager befindet sich in Auschwitz bei der J.G. Farbenindustrie AG. Es ist zur Zeit mit etwa 7.000 Häftlingen belegt.
Die übrigen Aussenlager haben wesentlich geringere Stärken.

Zusammengefaßt ergibt sich folgendes Bild:

Auschwitz I	16.000 Männer	-	-
Auschwitz II	15.000 "	21.000 Frauen	
Auschwitz III	15.000 "	-	-
	46.000 Männer	21.000 Frauen	
	zusammen:	67.000	

Die größte Belegstärke hat das Lager II, wobei jedoch berücksichtigt werden muß, daß von der dort vorhandenen Gesamtzahl mit 36.000 Häftlingen etwa 21.000 auf Frauen entfallen.

2.) Von der Gesamthäftlingszahl mit 67.000 sind die in den Aussenlagern befindlichen und die stationärkranken Häftlinge abzusetzen, wenn die Frage der Gefährdung durch einen etwaigen Aufstand oder Ausbruch für Oberschlesien betrachtet werden soll.

Von der Gesamthäftlingszahl mit   67.000
werden die in den Aussenlagern (Lager III)
untergebrachten   15.000 abgesetzt.
Die Zahl der Stationärkranken und
Invaliden beträgt zur Zeit   18.000,
sodaß praktisch mit   34.000 Häftlingen

zu rechnen ist. Diese würden für Auschwitz für den A-Fall dann eine Gefährdung bedeuten können, wenn die Sicherungs-

brüchen eine Groß-Fahndung unter Leitung der Kripoleitstelle Kattowitz einsetzt.

Die in Auschwitz liegenden Luftwaffeneinheiten in Stärke von 1.000 Mann stehen zur Verfügung, wenn der Alarm nicht mit einem Luftangriff zusammenfällt. Es kann mit diesen Luftwaffeneinheiten jedoch nicht unbedingt gerechnet werden. Bei Ausarbeitung des Einsatzplanes ist diesem Umstand Rechnung getragen worden.

In Kürze werden Planspiele mit allen beteiligten Stellen durchgeführt.

Ich glaube, Reichsführer, daß die getroffenen Vorkehrungen und Sicherungsmaßnahmen im A-Falle ausreichen werden.

Heil Hitler!

SS-Obergruppenführer und
General der Waffen-SS

[Translation of Excerpts from Document I]
Subject: Security Measures in Auschwitz
To: Reich Leader SS

... Camp II is also surrounded by an electrified barbed wire fence, and guard towers are also on hand. ... Camp III includes all outcamps in industrial plants in Upper Silesia, situated in widely separated locations. ... The greatest of these work camps is at the I.G. Farben Industries in Auschwitz. ... Camp II [Birkenau] has the greatest number of inmates ... 36,000 inmates, of which 21,000 are women.

Document J: German Photo of Birkenau, February 19, 1945

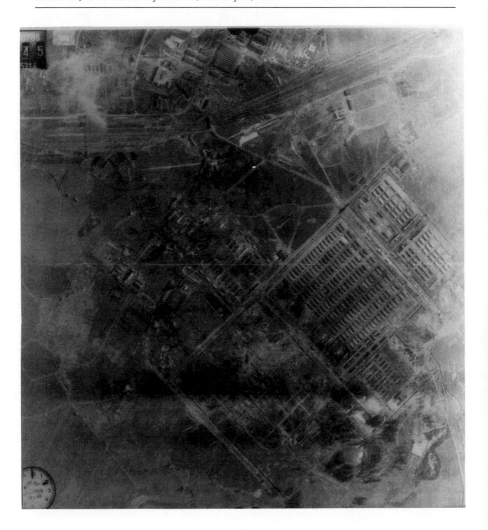

Document K: U.S. Photo of Birkenau, December 21, 1944

sound recordings—of Himmler's speeches seized by Allied troops from the salt mine at Hallein where they had been hidden only weeks before.[21]

In early October 1943 the Final Solution was already four years under way, with nineteen months still to go; perhaps one-third of the goal of 11 million contemplated in the Wannsee discussion had been reached, but about half of the actual total to be murdered had already been killed. Himmler—the administrator if not the architect[22] of the Holocaust—gave one of his habitual comprehensive periodic reports on the SS "war effort" to two high-level audiences. These two speeches contain Himmler's clearest statements on the Final Solution, although in earlier speeches he had briefly but directly referred to what his subordinates were doing to Jews.[23]

Among 130 Himmler speeches preserved in one or more textual or sound-recorded forms, the nine speeches that contain the most explicit passages on the Final Solution are extant in Himmler's holograph notes and/or typewritten transcripts for all but the earliest speech; full voice recordings on disk or tape of three speeches, partial recordings of two, and a fragment of one; direct transcripts from six recordings that were typewritten single space in normal size, with penciled editorial improvements; and full, edited texts, typewritten double space in large type of all but one.[24]

It was originally assumed, even among document experts, that Himmler read his speeches from the large-type[25] renditions; this remains a common misapprehension. Listening to this and other sound recordings[26] with copies of both their direct transcripts in standard type with penciled editing and large-type permanent copies in hand, however, makes it clear that Himmler habitually spoke at great length from keyword notes drafted in his own hand, although it is possible that he sometimes resorted to the large-type notes that are extant for some of his speeches.

On October 4, 1943, Himmler addressed nearly 100 of his chief SS subordinates during a luncheon in a lounge of the Hotel Posener Hof in Posen (Poznan) in Upper Silesia (annexed from Poland in 1939). Of 116 pages[27] of large-type edited text that constitutes his official record copy, fewer than four pages deal directly with the Final Solution. Extemporizing from one word on page 9 (Document L) of his seventeen pages of holograph notes, *Judenevakuierung* (evacuation of Jews), Himmler said:

> [p. 64] I want also to mention here ... a very difficult chapter. Among us it should be spoken out quite openly, but in spite of that we will never talk about it in public.... . [p. 65, Document M] I mean the evacuation of the Jews, the extirpation[28] of the Jewish people. It belongs to those things one says lightly: "The Jewish people will be extirpated" says every [Nazi] Party comrade, "Quite clear, it's in our program, exclusion of Jews, extirpation, can do." And then they all come, our 80 million good Germans, and each has his decent Jew. It is, of course, quite clear the others are swine, but this one is a first-class Jew. Of all who talk so, none has seen it, none has stuck it out. Of you, most will know what it means when 100 corpses lie together, when 500 lie there, or 1,000 lie there. To have held up through this, and meanwhile to have remained decent, that has made us hard. This is a never-written and never-to-be-written [p. 66, Document N] glorious page of our history... . We had the moral right, we had the duty toward our people to do away with this people who wanted to do away with us. But we have not the right to enrich ourselves with even one fur, one watch, one mark, one cigarette. ... .
>
> [p. 67] Because we extirpate a bacillus, we should not become sick from this bacillus... . All in all, however, we can say that we have fulfilled this most difficult task out of love for our people. And we have done no inner harm to our souls, to our character.[29]

Document L: Page 9 of Himmler's Notes for October 4, 1943, Speech

Document M: Page 65, Large-type Transcript of October 4 Speech

- 65 -

hatten, an die Wand zu stellen und zu erschießen, genau so wenig haben wir darüber jemals gesprochen und werden je darüber sprechen. Es war eine, Gottseidank in uns wohnende Selbstverständlichkeit des Taktes, dass wir uns untereinander nie darüber unterhalten haben, nie darüber sprachen. Es hat jeden geschaudert und doch war sich jeder klar darüber, dass er es das nächste Mal wieder tun würde, wenn es befohlen wird und wenn es notwendig ist.

Ich meine jetzt die Judenevakuierung, die Ausrottung des jüdischen Volkes. Es gehört zu den Dingen, die man leicht ausspricht. - "Das jüdische Volk wird ausgerottet", sagt ein jeder Parteigenosse, "ganz klar, steht in unserem Programm, Ausschaltung der Juden, Ausrottung, machen wir." Und dann kommen sie alle an, die braven 80 Millionen Deutschen, und jeder hat seinen anständigen Juden. Es ist ja klar, die anderen sind Schweine, aber dieser eine ist ein prima Jude. Von allen, die so reden, hat keiner zugesehen, keiner hat es durchgestanden. Von Euch werden die meisten wissen, was es heisst, wenn 100 Leichen beisammen liegen, wenn 500 daliegen oder wenn 1000 daliegen. Dies durchgehalten zu haben, und dabei - abgesehen von Ausnahmen menschlicher Schwächen - anständig geblieben zu sein, das hat uns hart gemacht. Dies ist ein niemals geschriebenes und niemals

-66-

Document N: Page 66, Completing Himmler's Reference to the Final Solution as a "Glorious Page of Our History"

- 66 -

zu schreibendes Ruhmesblatt unserer Geschichte, denn wir wissen, wie schwer wir uns täten, wenn wir heute noch in jeder Stadt - bei den Bombenangriffen, bei den Lasten und bei den Entbehrungen des Krieges - noch die Juden als Geheimsaboteure, Agitatoren und Hetzer hätten. Wir würden wahrscheinlich jetzt in das Stadium des Jahres 1916/17 gekommen sein, wenn die Juden noch im deutschen Volkskörper säßen.

Die Reichtümer, die sie hatten, haben wir ihnen abgenommen. Ich habe einen strikten Befehl gegeben, den 4-Obergruppenführer Pohl durchgeführt hat, dass diese Reichtümer selbstverständlich restlos an das Reich abgeführt wurden. Wir haben uns nichts davon genommen. Einzelne, die sich verfehlt haben, werden gemäß einem von mir zu Anfang gegebenen Befehl bestraft, der androhte; Wer sich auch nur eine Mark davon nimmt, der ist des Todes. Eine Anzahl 4-Männer - es sind nicht sehr viele - haben sich dagegen verfehlt und sie werden des Todes sein, gnadelos. Wir hatten das moralische Recht, wir hatten die Pflicht gegenüber unserem Volk, dieses Volk, das uns umbringen wollte, umzubringen. Wir haben aber nicht das Recht, uns auch nur mit einem Pelz, mit einer Uhr, mit einer Mark oder mit einer Zigarette oder mit sonst etwas zu bereichern. Wir wollen nicht am Schluss, weil wir einen Bazillus ausrotteten, an dem Bazillus krank werden und

This last passage reveals Himmler as the epitome of a mealy-mouthed moralist and murderer compatibly combined in one psyche.

Two days later,[30] on October 6, 1943, as the final speaker at a gathering of Nazi Party Reich and Gau (region) leaders in the Gold Room of the Posen city hall, Himmler made it perfectly clear that he was dead bent on genocide:

> [p. 16] I may refer here, in this context and in this most narrow circle, to a question that ... has become the most burdensome ... of my life: the Jewish question. You all take it as self-understood and gratifying that in your regions [*Gaue*] there are no more Jews. ... The sentence: "the Jews must be extirpated" ... is easily spoken. For those who must carry out what it demands it is the hardest and heaviest there is.
>
> [p. 17, Document O] ... I ask that what I say to you in this circle, you really just listen and never talk about it. The question arose for us, What about women and children? I decided here, too, to find a clear-cut solution. I did not believe I would be justified to root out the men—say, to kill them or to have them killed—and to allow their avengers in the form of their children to grow up [to confront] our sons and grandsons. The hard decision had to be made to make this people disappear from the earth. ...
>
> [p. 18] We have the obligation to our people, to our race, if we want to win the war—we have the obligation to our Führer, who has been given to our people only this once in a hundred years—not to be petty but to be consequent here. ... I feel obligated to speak to you as the leading bearers of authority, as the leading worthies of the Party, this political order, this political instrument of the Führer, to speak quite openly and to say how it has been.—The Jewish question in the lands occupied by us will be settled by the end of this year [1943].
>
> [p. 19] There will remain only remnants of individual Jews who have hidden themselves. ...
>
> I have cleared out big Jewish ghettos in the rear areas. In Warsaw we fought street battles in a Jewish ghetto for four weeks. Four weeks! We knocked out some 700 bunkers there. That entire ghetto made fur coats, clothing, and such things. When we wanted to intervene there earlier, it was said: "Halt! You are disturbing the war economy. Halt! War production!" Naturally, that has nothing to do with Party Comrade Speer; you [!][31] could do nothing about it. It is that portion of alleged arms factories that Party Comrade Speer and I will clean out together in the next weeks and months. We will do that exactly as unsentimentally as during the fifth war year all things will have to be done unsentimentally, but with great hearts for Germany.
>
> With that I would like to close the Jewish question. Now you are informed and will keep it to yourselves. Perhaps in much later times we can consider whether we can tell the German people more about it. I think it is better [p. 20] if we—we all together—having borne for our people the responsibility (for an activity, not an idea) take the secret to our graves.[32]

It is ironic that Himmler's "never-written and never-to-be written glorious page" has survived as the undeniable proof that the Holocaust is not a myth.

Document O: Page 17, Large-type Transcript, October 6, 1943, Speech

- 17 -

als überhaupt nominell vorhanden waren. In Deutschland haben wir nämlich so viele Millionen Menschen, die ihren einen berühmten anständigen Juden haben, dass diese Zahl bereits größer ist als die Zahl der Juden. Ich will das bloß deshalb anführen, weil Sie aus dem Lebensbereich Ihres eigenen Gaues bei achtbaren und anständigen nationalsozialistischen Menschen feststellen können, dass auch von ihnen jeder einen anständigen Juden kennt.

Ich bitte Sie, das, was ich Ihnen in diesem Kreise sage, wirklich nur zu hören und nie darüber zu sprechen. Es trat an uns die Frage heran: Wie ist es mit den Frauen und Kindern? - Ich habe mich entschlossen, auch hier eine ganz klare Lösung zu finden. Ich hielt mich nämlich nicht für berechtigt, die Männer auszurotten - sprich also, umzubringen oder umbringen zu lassen - und die Rächer in Gestalt der Kinder für unsere Söhne und Enkel groß werden zu lassen. Es musste der schwere Entschluß gefasst werden, dieses Volk von der Erde verschwinden zu lassen. Für die Organisation, die den Auftrag durchführen musste, war es der schwerste, den wir bisher hatten. Er ist durchgeführt worden, ohne dass - wie ich glaube sagen zu können - unsere Männer und unsere Führer einen Schaden an Geist und Seele erlitten hätten. Diese Gefahr lag sehr nahe. Der Weg zwischen den beiden hier bestehenden Möglichkeiten, entweder zu roh zu werden, herzlos zu werden und menschliches Leben nicht mehr zu achten

-18-

Notes

1. An outstanding example of a major working document is the initial order for *Fall Barbarossa*, the Nazi attack on the Soviet Union, dated December 12, 1940. The fourth of nine copies, although only a carbon, was signed by Hitler and initialled by his top military advisers and distributed to the Oberkommando der Wehrmacht/Wehrmachtführungstab (OKW/WFS, or Armed Forces High Command, Operations Staff). Captured by Allied forces and submitted as Prosecution Exhibit USA 331, Nürnberg Document PS 446 to the International Military Tribunal (IMT) at Nürnberg in 1945, it is now in National Archives Record Group (RG) 238, Collection of World War II War Crimes Trial Records. Despite its historical significance and highest-level origin and autographs, it is not a clean final copy intended for the ages but a practical working paper containing strike-outs and paste-overs that reveal significant changes during the course of planning this momentous operation.

2. For a prime example of such speeches, see the exposition of two Himmler speeches, parts of which are shown in Documents L, M, N, and O.

3. Cropping and montage of photographs have been effectively used for international as well as domestic political disinformation. Montage of textual documents, such as the Dreyfus case *bordereaux*, however, is more easily detectable by sharp and objective eyes.

4. The highly publicized photograph of Franklin Roosevelt and Winston Churchill, with French generals Charles de Gaulle and Henri-Honoré Giraud gazing at the camera in seeming harmony at Casablanca on January 24, 1942, might have misled historians were it not for Harry Hopkins's notes of that date describing the strained atmosphere; see Robert E. Sherwood, *Roosevelt and Hopkins* (New York: Harper, 1948), p. 692 (facsimile) and p. 693 (print).

5. For example, Hermann Göring's postwar attribution of Hitler's suicide to the latter's fear of suffering an end akin to Benito Mussolini's humiliating death is challenged as an anachronism by H. R. Trevor-Roper, *The Last Days of Hitler*, 3d ed. (Toronto: Collier, 1970), p. 256, no. 1, because the details of the Duce's death could not have reached the Führer's bunker before his suicide.

6. See RG 331, 7th U.S. Army, "T" Force Target No. 1003 of June 8, 1945, which reports the removal of twenty-three boxes containing RFSS Personal Staff files from the Wolf-Dietrich Stollen (mine shafts) at Hallein. These files had been hidden just a few weeks earlier, transferred presumably from Himmler's Feldkommandostelle Bergwald (one of several such field command posts of his) located in his Villa Trapp at Aigen near Salzburg. OSS Report XL 34777, dated November 8 (actually October 19), 1945 (RG 226, Records of the Office of Strategic Services), is a detailed but selective thirty-one-page secret analysis of these files, 200 copies of which were distributed among Allied intelligence and war crimes units. Personal Staff (2.5 tons) and other SS files aggregating over 7 tons, which had been assembled at the Berlin Document Center since early 1946, left Europe for the Pentagon on June 11, 1948 (Shipment No. 82). All were returned to the Federal German Republic for deposit in the Bundesarchiv in December 1961, after being microfilmed by the National Archives as Microfilm T 175, Records of the Reichsführer SS and Chief of German Police.

7. The *Wannsee Protokoll*, usually presented as a separate fifteen-page document, the only surviving copy (number 16) of thirty numbered copies distributed with covering letters typed on Reinhard Heydrich's CdS (Chief of Security Police) letterhead to those agencies that had sent representatives to the January 20, 1942, interagency meeting to coordinate the Final Solution, seems to skeptics too much of a smoking gun to be true. Its

authenticity becomes transparent, however, when it is seen as only one of many documents in a German Foreign Office file of 339 pages filed in two folders between January 1939 and November 20, 1943, under the file title *Endlösung der Judenfrage* (see NA microfilm T 120, Roll 780, frames 371885–372223), with earlier invitations (frame 372043) and postponements (372039) presaging the January 20, 1942, meeting, and follow-up meetings in March and October of that year referring back to the discussion summarized by the Wannsee protocol—to say nothing of corroborating references in the files of other Third Reich agencies such as Hans Frank's General Gouvernement and Otto Hofmann's SS-Rasse und Siedlungshauptamt.

    8. *Kommandeur der Sicherheitspolizei* (KdS) *Lublin/SD Verwaltung*, Item EAP 173-b-12/45, RG 242, National Archives Collection of Foreign Records Seized, Microfilm T 175, Records of the Reichsführer of the SS and Chief of German Police, Roll 248, frame 2739770.

    9. Ibid., 2739771.

    10. Ibid., 2739785. The title of the form is *Unbrauchbarkeitsbeweis*, or proof of unserviceability.

    11. It was eventually declassified and released; Dino A. Brugioni and Robert G. Poirier, "The Holocaust Revisited: A Retrospective Analysis of the Auschwitz-Birkenau Complex" (Washington, D.C.: Central Intelligence Agency, 1979).

    12. Colonel Roy S. Stanley, then deputy chief of the Defense Intelligence Agency (DIA), which had not yet released the aerial photographs to the National Archives, suggested that I be consulted before publication and also provided the secure site. His expertise on that subject is displayed in the monograph *World War II Photo Intelligence* (New York: Scribner's, 1981), pp. 340–351, p. 348 of which recounts my involvement in some detail.

    13. Brugioni and Poirier, "The Holocaust Revisited," states: "The 'intelligence collateral' for this paper was drawn mainly from O. Kraus and E. Kulka, *The Death Factory*, New York, 1966; N. Levin, *The Holocaust*, New York, 1973; and the official Polish government investigations, *German Crimes in Poland* 2 Vols., Warsaw, 1946–47, which draw on primary sources." Although the official Polish investigation drew on seized records and interrogations of the Auschwitz camp administration (including camp commander Rudolf Höss), as well as surviving inmates, none of these cited sources did or could provide any documentation on Allied air force procedures, missions, and analysis of aerial photography.

    14. The *Washington Post* of February 23, 1979, printed an article showing only the enlarged, cropped, and embellished NPIC photographs. In a joint CIA-NARA press conference held in the National Archives theater on that day, I attempted to rectify the misconception thus conveyed, but television reporters in particular were concerned that any complication of the oversimplified sensational effect of the story would benefit their competitors. Magazine reporters, especially those representing German "illustrateds," were more amenable to my suggestions. *Stern* (March 15, 1979), *Bunte* (April), and *Life* (April) not only published unretouched original aerial photographs side by side with their NPIC derivations, but the latter bore the additional caption that the National Archives has since added to all reproductions thereof: "Enlarged and Captioned in 1978 by the CIA." While a guest of the Polish National Archives in the Solidarity summer of 1979, I encountered several Polish archivists who assumed that the CIA (established in 1947) had captioned the aerial photographs of Auschwitz in 1944.

    15. RG 373, Records of the Defense Intelligence Agency, Mission Access 029283, Can F5637, frame 3185; Mission: 60PR/694, 60 Sq.; Scale 1/10,000; Focal Length: 36"; Altitude: 30,000'.

16. Brugioni and Poirier, "The Holocaust Revisited," p. 9, photo 4, available from the National Archives only with added warning caption about the 1978 date of the CIA embellishments.

17. RG 331, Records of Allied Operational and Occupational Headquarters (AFHQ), MAAF Mission Files, Roll 61D. As can be seen from the "Reports" entry immediately preceding Item 1 on DP.95, it draws on two earlier reconnaissance reports of bomb damage: DB 189 of August 23, 1944, and DB 191 of August 25, 1944. Roll 61D also contains a reproduction of the Target Information Sheet of July 18, 1944, which concentrates entirely on the IG Farben plants, obviously quite unaware that inmates of Auschwitz-Birkenau were being mass murdered as well as subjected to slave labor.

18. RG 373, Mission Access 039507, Can C1172, frame 5022; Mission: 60PR/522, 60 Sq.; Scale: 1/60,000; Focal Length: 6"; Altitude: 30,000'.

19. RG 238, Nürnberg Document NO-021, Prosecution Exhibit 357. Rudolf Vrba, who along with Alfred Wetzler, another young Slovakian Jew, escaped in early April 1944 after some two years of incarceration in Auschwitz-Birkenau, visited the National Archives not too long after the release of the aerial photographs in 1979. Shown a copy of the Pohl letter to Himmler for the first time, Vrba was astonished that the estimates of numbers of inmates and victims he and Wetzler had reported from haphazard observation and memory after reaching Hungary in summer 1944 (English translation in RG 226, XL 8883, OSS Field Memorandum 257) were astonishingly close to those reported at approximately the same time by Pohl, who certainly was in a position to obtain reasonably accurate figures. Shown the aerial photographs, which he also had not seen before, Vrba exclaimed, "Now I know why we were so confused during the dark night of our escape when we felt the sand of a river bank under our feet where we did not expect it. There are *two* rivers there [Sola and Vistula]!"

20. RG 373, Records of the Defense Intelligence Agency, GX 225, Nr. 127, and GX 12337, Nr. 145, respectively. The original Luftwaffe photographic negatives from which the NARA GX series directly derive were recently discovered in Germany and are now deposited in the Bundesarchiv.

21. See note 6, above.

22. Richard Breitman, *The Architect of Genocide: Himmler and the Final Solution* (New York: Knopf, 1991), (dis)credits the wrong culprit. Rather than Himmler, the bureaucratic ideologue, his henchman, the inventive Reinhard Heydrich, earned that infamy. For telling instances of Heydrich's role as the innovative planner of mass murder, see the stenographic record of the meeting for "Aryanization of the Germany economy" held in Göring's Air Ministry immediately after Kristallnacht (RG 238, Nürnberg IMT Document PS 1816, Prosecution Exhibit USA 261); the transcribed telegram, Reinhard Heydrich to chiefs of all operation commands of the Security Police, September 21, 1939, outlining the stages toward the "end goal" (*Endziel*) (RG 238, Document PS 3363, a carbon copy; or a ribbon copy of identical text but different format bearing the red-crayon marking "Anlage 4," Document EC 301-7); and as host and chairman of the Wannsee conference (see note 7, above).

23. These earlier speeches were to SS officer trainees at Bad Tolz and to SS corps commanders in Charkov, respectively, as well as five brutally frank later statements in December 1943 and the first half of 1944 during speeches in Posen, Weimar, and Sonthofen to generals and admirals (his military colleagues after Hitler appointed him commander in

chief of the Reserve Army in the aftermath of the July 20, 1944, assassination attempt, and commander in chief of Army Group Vistula in spring 1945).

24. See Bradley F. Smith and Agnes F. Peterson, *Heinrich Himmler Geheimreden 1933 bis 1945: und andere Ansprachen* (Frankfurt: Proplyläen Verlag, 1974), for a compendium of Himmler's speeches.

25. Typewriters producing such large letters were colloquially dubbed "Führer *Schreibmaschinen*" because Hitler purportedly preferred to read his speeches from text typed on them, as he was too vain to wear spectacles in public. This vanity seems plausible in view of such photographs stamped "not for publication" among the Heinrich Hoffmann Berlin Studio master copies held by the NA (RG 242 HLB).

26. Disk and tape recordings of speeches by Himmler, Grand Admiral Karl Dönitz, Air Marshal Erhard Milch, and Reich Minister for Armament and Munitions Albert Speer were confiscated from the farm of an SS man in Hof, according to a notation of June 25, 1946, by Captain E. E. Winn in the Daily Log of the U.S. Forces, European Theater Document Control Section. Apparently, these other recordings were commingled with the Himmler collection because they also were recorded, presumably by SS technicians, during the Reich and *Gau* leaders' meeting of October 6, 1943.

27. Actually, there are only 114 pages, numbers 62 and 68 having been omitted inadvertently, but there are no gaps in the text, as can be verified from the sound recordings. The numbers stamped on the document (at either the American "German Foreign Office Document Center" in Berlin or at Nürnberg to facilitate specific reference and perhaps for microfilming) are consecutive and complete. The document is also marred by blue-pencil markings (pp. 64, 65, and 67) almost certainly perpetrated by some German-speaking American analyst concerned with his immediate search for incriminating evidence on behalf of the non-German-speaking prosecution staff and apparently unaware of the indelible taint he was putting on that very evidence.

28. Himmler's term is *Ausrottung*, literally, to tear up by the roots, or uprooting. The closest English dictionary term is the seldom-used *extirpation*.

29. This is my near literal translation (hence its Teutonic cadence) of the bulk of pp. 64–68 of the large-type text, RG 238, Nürnberg IMT Document PS 1919, Prosecution Exhibit USA 190. Not only are these and the passages quoted below from Himmler's October 6 speech the most explicit about the purpose and extent of the Final Solution, they also reflect his suspicion that even the "synchronized" (*gleichgeschaltet*) and intimidated German people might balk at public acknowledgment of the mass murder of European Jewry being conducted in their name.

30. Himmler also spent October 5, the day between these two Posen speeches, at the Hotel Posener Hof with his entourage of SS generals, as can be seen from a list of meeting participants, their hotel room assignments, and a calendar of his appointments for that day found in his captured files (T 175, Roll 113, frame 2638042 ff.). For the fifty or so SS general officers not in attendance, Himmler prescribed circulation of copies of his October 4 speech to require each absentee to sign acknowledgment that he had read it (Roll 138, frames 2665923–2665924).

31. Presumably having caught the eye of Speer, who, now seated in the audience, had spoken earlier that day (at 10:05 according to the printed program), Himmler was concerned not to offend a Hitler favorite. Until his death, however, Speer could not recall hearing Himmler speak, although the sound recording and text of his own speech earlier that

day (RG 242-223, reels 5–8) attest otherwise. A copy of the program for the October 6 meeting, number (*Ausführung*) 79, marked "ORR [Oberregierungsrat] Stossberg [SS Obersturmbannführer Karl-Heinz Stossberg, head of Gestapo Leitstelle Posen]," bears the injunction that programs are not to be removed from the room but left on each attender's seat. How that particular copy of the program ended up in Himmler's Hallein files (Himmler File, orange folder, Drawer #8, Folder #342, T175, Roll 55, frames 2569605–6) is a matter of conjecture. Most likely, Himmler subsequently asked Stossberg, who as Posen SS commander would have been responsible for local arrangements, to furnish a copy for RFSS Schriftgutverwaltung permanent files.

32. RG 242, T 175, Roll 85, frames 152–242. For this entire speech, there exists a full transcript in standard type (27 pages, frames 201–227); shown here p. 10 (Document P) made directly from the sound recording; p. 17 of the large-type edited version thereof (49 pages, frames 152–200), from which the parallel passages of Document Q were edited; and handwritten notes (10 pages, frames 233–242), of which page 1 shown here (Document Q) contains the word *Jews;* and typewritten notes (5 pages, frames 228–232), from which is shown here the parallel page (Document R). Only a small, verifiable passage of the sound recording has thus far been retrievable. The recordings of Bormann, Dönitz, Milch, SA Chief Wilhelm Schepmann, and Speer and five of his deputies are intact. Documents O, P, Q, and R, although cited to National Archives microfilm for research convenience, are reproduced here from negatives of the original records furnished by the *Bundesarchiv.*

Document P: Page 10 of Direct Transcript of October 6 Speech

(RF-SS) -10-

Ich habe mich entschlossen, auch hier eine ganz klare Lösung zu finden. Ich hielt mich nämlich nicht für berechtigt, die Männer auszurotten - sprich also umzubringen oder umbringen zu lassen - und die Rächer in Gestalt der Kinder für unsere Söhne und Enkel groß werden zu lassen. Es mußte der schwere Entschluß gefaßt werden, dieses Volk von der Erde verschwinden zu lassen. Für die Organisation, die es tun mußte, der schwerste Auftrag, den wir bisher hatten. Der schwerste Er ist durchgeführt worden, ohne daß - wie ich glaube sagen zu können - unsere Männer, unsere Führer einen Schaden an Geist und Seele erlitten hätten. Das lag sehr nahe. Die Grenze, hier den Weg zu finden zwischen den beiden Polen, zwischen den beiden Wällern, die hier festgesetzt sind, entweder zu roh zu werden, herzlos zu werden, menschliches Leben nicht mehr zu achten, oder dem anderen, weich zu werden, durchzudrehen bis zu Nervenzusammenbrüchen, der Weg zwischen dieser Scylla und Charybdis ist entsetzlich schmal.

Wir haben das ganze Vermögen, das wir hier bei den Juden beschlagnahmten - es ging in unendliche Werte - bis zum letzten Pfennig abgeführt, dem Reichswirtschaftsminister übergeben. Ich habe mich immer auf den Standpunkt gestellt: wir haben die Verpflichtung unserem Volke, unserer Rasse gegenüber, wenn wir den Krieg gewinnen wollen, wir haben die Verpflichtung unserem Führer gegenüber, der nun in zweitausend Jahren unserem Volke einmal geschenkt worden ist, hier nicht klein zu sein und hier konsequent zu sein. Wir haben aber nicht das Recht, auch nur einen Pfennig davon zu nehmen. Ich habe von vornherein festgesetzt, daß SS-Männer, auch wenn sie nur eine Mark davon nehmen, des Todes sind. Ich habe in den letzten Tagen deswegen einige - ich kann es ruhig sagen, es sind etwa ein Dutzend-Todesurteile - unterschrieben. Hier muß man hart sein, wenn nicht das Ganze darunter leiden soll.

Ich habe ich für verpflichtet gehalten, Ihnen als den obersten Willensträgern, als den obersten Würdenträgern der Partei, dieses politischen Ordens, dieses politischen Instruments des Führers, auch diese Frage einmal ganz offen darzutun, wie sie gewesen ist.

Die Judenfrage in den von uns besetzten Ländern wird bis Ende d.J. erledigt sein. Das andere werden Restbestände von einzelnen Juden sein, die untergeschlüpft sind. Die Frage der noch mit nichtjüdischen Teilen verheirateten Juden und die Frage der Halbjuden werden sinngemäß und vernünftig unter-

Document Q: Himmler's Notes for October 6 Speech

Abschrift

Rede des Reichsführers-⹀ vor den Reichs- und Gauleitern, Posen, Rathaus, 6. Oktober 1943.

Einzelne Probleme:

1.) Ostfront - Partisanen-Banden
   General W l a s s o w
   Art der Slawen.

2.) Sabotage und Spionage des Gegners
   Weltanschauliche Gegner
   Juden, Freimaurer, Bolschewisten, Demokratie, Plutokratie
   nationale Völker
   Fallschirmspringer
   kein Überschätzen der Gefahr
   Arbeit der Sicherheitspolizei
   Verbrecher im Konzentrationslager
   Rüstungsarbeiter
   Stadtwacht - Landwacht
   "Gaudivisionen"
   Hereinbefehlen von Polizei und Waffen-⹀
   kein Über- und Durcheinanderorganisieren

3.) Judenfrage
   einzelne
   verheiratete
   Halbjuden

2

On the Purpose of the Wannsee Conference

Eberhard Jäckel

The most remarkable thing about the Wannsee conference, the controversial meeting that came to be known by that name only after the war, is that we do not know why it took place.

The most widespread and generally accepted explanation, namely, that the decision on the Final Solution to the Jewish question—that is, the murder of the European Jews—was reached there, is quite certainly the most inappropriate. In the Hitler state, such important decisions were never arrived at in conferences and certainly not by bureaucrats. And, incidentally, there is nothing in the minutes about such a decision. Moreover, the Final Solution could not have been decided there for the simple reason that it was already in full swing.

The murder of Jews had begun in the German-occupied portions of the Soviet Union in June 1941. By the end of the year, some 500,000 human beings had already been killed. The deportation of Jews from Germany had begun on October 15, 1941; the first of them were shot on November 25. The first death camp was already operating—Chelmno, where primarily Polish Jews from Łódź and its environs were killed in gas trucks from December 8 on. In this regard there was no decision to be taken at Wannsee.

Among scholars, therefore, the prevalent explanation is that the conference served to coordinate the activities of the various bureaucracies. When it comes to details of the conference, there are some interesting differences of opinion to be sure. In Gerald Reitlinger's classic book of 1953 (*The Final Solution,*) which was the first complete study, Reitlinger stated that it "was no more than a luncheon party."[1] In *Judenpolitik im Dritten Reich* (1972), Uwe Dietrich Adam saw the "purpose of the discussion"[2] as the inclusion of Jews from non-German states

---

Translated from the German original by David A. Scrase, professor of German, University of Vermont.

and the question of mixed marriages. The latter was also, according to Dieter Rebentisch, "the real topic."[3]

In fact, the purpose of the discussion has never yet been fully examined. Nor is it easy to do so, because, as is generally the case in such a highly secret area, only a few sources have come down to us: the minutes (a single extant copy out of the original thirty),[4] three invitations (with very revealing marginal notes),[5] one response to the invitation,[6] and a few brief notes in other files. In addition, there are a few later statements by participants (all now dead), especially by Adolf Eichmann.[7] That is all. And yet historians can reconstruct a considerable amount if they study these sources patiently, compare them to others, and place them within the greater context of other events.

It all began on November 29, 1941, when Reinhard Heydrich, the chief of the Security Police and the Security Service (SD), invited thirteen men to a conference. The number of delegates and their names can be ascertained because Heydrich stated in each letter of invitation whom he had invited. The discussion was to have taken place on December 9 beginning at noon but was "postponed indefinitely" one day before, apparently by telephone—the postponement was noted on the invitation to Under Secretary of State Martin Luther by a Foreign Office official on December 8. As to the reason, we know only what Heydrich wrote when he sent out his second invitation, that he "at that time unfortunately had to call off the meeting at the last minute owing to suddenly announced events and the attention they demanded on the part of a number of the gentlemen invited."

Which "suddenly announced events" claiming the attention of several participants might come into consideration? The only possibility is the Japanese attack on Pearl Harbor, news of which had been received in Berlin on the evening of December 7 (a Sunday). As a result, Hitler left his East Prussian headquarters on December 9 for Berlin (where he arrived at 11:00 A.M.) and announced on December 11 before the Reichstag that Germany had declared war on the United States. Since Heydrich and two of those invited were deputies, it is possible that they had been told that the Reichstag session could conceivably take place already on the ninth, because Hitler feared the United States might beat him to a declaration of war. It is unfortunate that all the relevant files of the Reichstag administration seem to be lost, so it has not yet been possible to clarify the matter.

The conference cannot have been urgent because Heydrich allowed himself a considerable margin of time after the postponement. It was not until a month later, on January 8, 1942, that he repeated his invitation, this time for January 20, when the conference actually took place. Between the first invitation and the conference there were seven weeks. Heydrich was, to be sure, extraordinarily busy during this time. But if the meeting had been urgent, he would certainly have found the time for it.

Heydrich clearly took pains to set the occasion apart. He invited the participants to "a discussion to be followed by a luncheon" (*Frühstück*).[8] This was unusual—especially in the third year of the war. It sounded almost like a state occasion for diplomats, who would have used *Frühstück* in the sense of luncheon as opposed to the more common word *Mittagessen*.

The venue was also unusual. Heydrich had at this disposal the lavish Prince Albrecht Palace situated on the Wilhelmstrasse in a spacious park. This palace had been regally converted around 1830 by no less an architect than Friedrich Schinkel for a Hohenzollern prince. It would have been an obvious place for a discussion—if there was meant to be one. But it was precisely this that Heydrich seems not to have wanted.

Rather than to the palace, the invitation was to the International Criminal Investigation Department in the exclusive residential suburb of Berlin-Wannsee. Strangely enough, this choice of venue has never been scrutinized. The International Criminal Investigation Department (IKPK, known generally as Interpol) had been founded in 1923 by twenty nations and served to combat international crime.[9] Its headquarters were in Vienna, Austria having pressed most energetically for its foundation. According to its constitution, its president was the current president of police in Vienna. The headquarters remained in Vienna even after the Anschluss in March 1938, when Austria was incorporated into the German Reich and ceased to exist as a nation. At this point a National Socialist, SS Colonel Otto Steinhäusl, became president of the Vienna police, and he was also the president of Interpol until his death in June 1940.[10]

Only then, it seems, did it occur to the Germans that the headquarters of Interpol should be in the capital of a member nation and that Berlin had replaced Vienna in this respect. It was accordingly announced in September 1940 that Heydrich had taken over the presidency of Interpol and that its headquarters had been moved to Berlin.[11] Heydrich was of course president of neither the Vienna police nor the Berlin police. But his ambition was such that he may have felt the urge to take on one more office, even if Interpol had diminished in importance because of the war.

At the same time it was announced that "the first item of importance ... would be the search for worthy quarters in Berlin."[12] And Heydrich did indeed acquire for this purpose in November 1940 a splendid villa in Art Nouveau style at 16 Am Kleinen Wannsee.[13] Because the building was not immediately available and then had to be renovated, it was not until November 1941 that it could be announced that Heydrich had put "a worthy home"[14] at the disposal of the IKPK, which seems to have moved in on December 8.[15]

So the official opening could have been celebrated on the ninth. Was it not, as Heydrich might have thought, an appropriate place? Was not the Final Solution a case of combating international crime?

But then he changed his mind. On December 4 he informed the participants by telephone that the conference would not take place at number 16 Am Kleinen Wannsee but at number 56–58 Am Grossen Wannsee. Once again we learn this from a marginal note ("on December 4, 1941, street changed"), after which officials added the new address in two invitations. The announcement was, however, by no means the correction of an inadvertent error in the first address given, as one of those invited insisted[16] (and many historians followed him in this regard).

The house Am Grossen Wannsee was not the headquarters of the IKPK but a guest house belonging to the SD. Heydrich likewise bought it in November 1940 in the name of a foundation whose purpose was "the creation and maintenance of rest and recreation homes for the Security Service and their families"; once it was handed over, probably in April 1941, he had the house renovated so that it was ready to be moved into at this precise time.[17]

We do not know what caused Heydrich to change the venue. We can only ascertain that the second house, a villa built directly on the lake in 1914 by an industrialist, was three times larger and more opulent than the nearby headquarters of the IKPK. Perhaps the facilities needed for the subsequent luncheon were better there. Contrary to what one reads again and again, neither of the two houses ever belonged to a Jew, nor was either requisitioned.

The festive setting and the care with which it was sought out do not suggest that it was intended as a backdrop for a discussion of factual matters. There was little time for such a discussion because the conference began at noon and the luncheon could not take place much later. It seems that the setting was more important than the content of the talks.

On this point Heydrich himself made a few comments in his first invitational letter. It began as follows:

> On July 31, 1941, the Reichsmarschall of the Greater German Reich commissioned me, with the participation of the appropriate other central agencies, to complete all the necessary organizational, functional and material preparations for a complete solution to the Jewish question in Europe and to submit to him in the near future an overall plan in this regard. I am enclosing a photocopy of this order.

This was essentially the wording of the much-quoted memo that Heydrich himself, as we now know, drafted and had Göring sign.[18] Now he presented it as if it were a legitimation and continued:

> In light of the extraordinary significance accorded to these questions and in the interests of attaining a consensus among the relevant central agencies regarding the remaining work relating to this final solution, I propose to make these problems the subject of a general discussion, especially since Jews from the Reich, including the Protectorate of Bohemia and Moravia, are already being evacuated in continual transports to the east.

There was, then, no talk of resolutions. The purpose was, rather, "attaining a consensus." This was remarkable enough, since Hitler's Germany generally did not find consensus particularly important. For officials who were subject to directives, in particular, orders and obedience prevailed.

The designation "central agencies" (which were to attain the consensus) was a term Heydrich likewise took from Göring's directive. In fact, however, he did not invite agencies but individuals. His letters of invitation began, for example, "Dear Hoffmann (sic)" and "Dear Party Member Luther."

It was a conference at the level of state secretaries, and in later correspondence it was indeed called the "conference of state secretaries." If there were several state secretaries in a ministry, Heydrich invited the one responsible for Jewish questions. In the case of the Foreign Office, he even invited the *under*secretary, Luther, although he was, to be sure, the appropriate person.

In two cases Heydrich went above the rank of state secretary and found his invitations declined. He invited the governor general in Poland, Hans Frank, who was, however, at the same time a Reichsminister and who declared already on December 16, 1941, that he would be sending his state secretary, Josef Bühler (who indeed did attend).[19] Franz Schlegelberger, who also received an invitation, was a state secretary but at the same time, since the death of Minister Franz Gürtner, was the acting Reich justice minister. He did not attend either but sent his state secretary, Roland Freisler. Thus the hierarchic order was reestablished.

If one assigns the invited participants to the agencies they represented, then the following "central agencies" seem to be the ones deemed relevant to the Final Solution: the General Government and the Ministry for Eastern Affairs (i.e., the occupied Soviet territories), each with two representatives; in addition the Ministries of the Interior, Justice, and Propaganda; the Office of the Four-Year Plan; the Foreign Office; the SS Office of Racial and Settlement Affairs; as well as the Reich Commissariat for the Preservation of the German National Identity, which was likewise under the control of the Reichsführer of the SS, the Party Chancellery, and the Reich Chancellery.

One is immediately struck that several agencies were missing that one might have expected to see there. Nobody from the Wehrmacht was invited. Why not? Of the ministries, those of Finance, the Economy, Labor, Post, Transport, and Food, as well as a few of lesser importance were missing. Particularly striking is the absence of the Ministry of Transport, under whose control was the railroad system, which had to provide the trains for deportation. Of the agencies controlling the occupied territories, only those for Poland and the Soviet Union were invited, although the collaboration of the others would be equally necessary.

If one ignores the military administrators, it is particularly striking that the *Reichskommissare* for Norway and the Netherlands, who reported directly to the Führer, were not considered. Most of the main SS offices were absent; especially noteworthy is the absence of the Inspector of Concentration Camps. Of the supreme Party offices, the Chancellery of the Führer was absent, although it was actively engaged in the Final Solution. Of the twenty-five higher SS and police leaders, only one was invited.

One way to explain this curious choice is to match the invited individuals to their chiefs. In this case, using the same order as the above-listed "central agencies," the following were represented: Hans Frank, Alfred Rosenberg, Wilhelm Frick, Franz Schlegelberger, Joseph Goebbels, Hermann Göring, Joachim von Ribbentrop, Heinrich Himmler, Martin Bormann, and Hans Heinrich Lammers. Not represented were Wilhelm Keitel (Supreme Command of the Wehrmacht), Erich Raeder (Navy), Lutz Graf Schwerin von Krosigk (Finance), Walther Funk (Economy), Franz Seldte (Labor), Wilhelm Ohnesorge (Post Office), Julius Dorpmüller (Transport), Richard Walter Darré (Food), and a few other ministers, as well as Josef Terboven (Norway), Arthur Seyss-Inquart (Netherlands), Richard Glücks (Concentration Camps), and Philipp Bouhler (Führer Chancellery).

The names make the choice more readily comprehensible. By means of the state secretaries, Heydrich had taken into account all politicians of influence and ignored those of lesser influence. It seems reasonable to conclude that he was gathering around him the leadership of the Reich at the level that was possible for him. What he said would be relayed to the highest political levels.

Only now do we come to the minutes. They are not written down in shorthand and hardly convey what took place. It is, for example, hardly conceivable that Heydrich read out the thirty countries with their Jewish population figures listed on page 6. His expert for Jewish affairs at the time, Adolf Eichmann, testified in Jerusalem that Heydrich had carefully edited the minutes, and that seems plausible.[20]

The text does not give the impression that this was a discussion. It was predominantly Heydrich himself who spoke. Only on the question of the German *Mischlinge,* or mixed races—whether *Halbjuden,* or half Jews, should be treated as Jews or not—did it come to a discussion, but neither at that point nor later was there a "consensus." And with the clearly emphasized extension of the Final Solution to the whole of Europe, this question was of relatively little importance; if 11 million Jews were to be seized, then the approximately 70,000 *Mischlinge* in Germany amounted to about half of 1 percent.

It seems reasonable to suspect a different purpose. This purpose is perhaps revealed in the first informative sentence of the minutes: "Chief of the Security Police and SD, SS Obergruppenführer Heydrich, began by stating his appointment by the Reichsmarschall as the person in charge of preparing the final solution of the European Jewish question." At first glance that sounds enormously presumptuous. Göring had simply given him a commission. *Appointment* (*Bestellung*) was an unambiguous term. It meant in the administrative jargon of the time the highest form of appointment, appointment to a newly created function. Ministers and *Gauleiters,* for example, were "named" (*ernannt*). When, however, Hitler bestowed upon subordinates the highest political offices for the first time, he used the term *appoint* (*bestellen*). It had been this way especially with regard to the *Reichskommissare* for the occupied territories, and on November 17, 1941, for example, the official news agency had announced that the Führer had "appointed" (*bestellt*) the *Gauleiter* Hinrich Lohse and Erich Koch *Reichskommissare* for the East and the Ukraine.[21]

This was now what Heydrich was claiming for himself. On July 1, 1941, in an internal memorandum, Theodor Dannecker, his deputy in France, had already called him the "European *Judenkommissar*,"[22] and on February 22, 1942, he called him the "*Judenkommissar* for Europe."[23] That was probably exactly what Heydrich had long wished to be: *Reichskommissar* for the Final Solution of the Jewish question in Europe.

But had anyone "appointed" him to this position? Would Göring have been able to do such a thing? Was that not the Führer's prerogative? As one of the participants (Luther) soon after, on August 21, 1942, informed his minister, Heydrich had declared at the meeting "the Reichsmarschall Göring's commission to him was at the direction of the Führer."[24] But this declaration had not been recorded in the minutes.

Since it is inconceivable that Heydrich could refer to a directive from the Führer if Hitler had not given one, the only conclusion possible is that Hitler had indeed issued it—but not in writing. Hitler did not want to be linked officially with the Final Solution. Heydrich had no other choice, therefore, than to refer to Göring's memo, to expand it verbally so that it was not then presumptuous to speak of an "appointment."

But if someone was going to be appointed to the position of *Reichskommissar* for the Final Solution, would that not then have to be Himmler? Was he not Heydrich's superior? In this regard another sentence in the minutes takes on a deeper meaning. It runs: "The overall control in dealing with the final solution of the Jewish question would remain, regardless of geographical borders, centrally located with the Reichsführer SS and the chief of the German Police (chief of the Security Police and the SD)." That was Heydrich's way of showing his consideration for Himmler: Formally he gave him precedence, but in fact he claimed the central authority for himself.

There are a number of indications that the relationship between Himmler and Heydrich was fraught with rivalry. When Heydrich became chief of the Security Police in 1936, there was not much else that he could become; above him was only Himmler. But Heydrich was ambitious, and he was young (thirty-seven in 1941). Himmler, however, was only three and a half years older. He could remain Reichsführer SS and chief of the German Police for another twenty-five years, but at that point Heydrich would also have reached retirement age.

It is therefore easy to imagine that he was looking for tasks that would enable him to climb higher next to Himmler. He knew, of course, the importance Hitler ascribed to the Jewish question. If Heydrich could succeed in outdoing Himmler in this area, this might mean promotion and an increase in power.

And indeed Heydrich had long been a mover in this regard. Himmler preferred to busy himself with other things. In May 1940 he had even sent Hitler a memorandum in which he repudiated "the Bolshevist method of physically wiping out a people out of a deep conviction that this was un-Germanic and impossible."[25]

Heydrich was quite different. When, after the November pogrom of 1938, Göring held a major meeting in which the participants outdid one another with suggestions as to how one might get the Jews out of the railroad sleeping cars and public swimming pools, Heydrich emphasized repeatedly that the basic problem remained "to get the Jews out of Germany," and he proposed setting up a central office for emigration.[26]

Three months later, on January 24, 1939, he become head of just such a *Reichszentrale*.[27] It was the first commission he received not from Himmler but from Göring, and certainly not without a directive from Hitler. Heydrich understood better than the others what the Führer wanted, and he had been rewarded accordingly.

Directly thereafter, on February 11, 1939, he had held a session that demonstrated a remarkable similarity to the Wannsee conference. He had invited fifteen fairly low-level representatives of various agencies to the modest quarters of the Gestapo. But he did most of the talking there, too, and the minutes reveal little more than the announcement that he was now responsible for Jewish emigration.[28]

After the outbreak of war, he continued to act. He wrote one memo after the other about how one could push forward with the Final Solution, whereas Himmler was rather restrained in this regard. In spring 1941 Heydrich set up the mobile units—the *Einsatzgruppen*—of the Security Police and the SD for the Russian campaign, and on July 31, 1941, he received that second commission from Göring that was described as an "expansion" of the commission of January 24, 1939.

The next decision must have fallen between September 22 and September 24, 1941. During these three days, Himmler and Heydrich were with Hitler at his headquarters. After this it was announced that Heydrich, in addition to his previous duties, was to carry out the duties of the *Reichsprotektor* in Bohemia and Moravia and that he was promoted to the rank of *SS-Obergruppenführer*. It was his first promotion since June 1934.[29] He now had a rank that corresponded to that of general in the army and state secretary in the government administration. And he had a territory such as only *Reichsminister* or *Gauleiter* had hitherto received. He immediately moved to his new province and arranged for official quarters in the Hradshin and a private palace on the outskirts of Prague.

It was also during these days that the decision to deport Jews from Germany was taken. We know this from the diary of Goebbels and can deduce it above all because preparations began immediately afterward. On September 30 Heydrich's representative in Vienna informed the leader of the Israelite Religious Community there that the first transport would leave on October 15.[30]

Now, one has to put oneself in Heydrich's position. Everyone knew that he had become *Reichsprotektor* and general. It was, however, not known that he had also become the *Judenkommissar* for Europe. That may also not have been so clearly expressed. Hitler certainly had no cause to demote Himmler. But the responsibility for the deportations, now not just from Germany but from other European countries, too, he had given to Heydrich. Hitler liked to play off his satraps against one another.

It must have been important to Heydrich that this somehow become official, not only because of vanity but also because others might otherwise dispute his competence. What could he do? In October 1939, when Himmler had been put in charge of resettlement (especially that of the so-called ethnic Germans from the Eastern European areas claimed by the Soviet Union), he had pompously announced in his first directive that he had "been named *Reichskommissar* for the preservation of the German national identity,"[31] although Hitler had never expressly named him such.[32] Heydrich may well have thought of this precedent. But to repeat it was out of the question because the Final Solution was top secret, and Hitler did not wish to be too obviously linked with it.

The solution was the Wannsee conference. It was the only possible way to make things known; it was at the same time a typically presumptuous gesture to announce and celebrate his "appointment" (*Bestellung*) in an unambiguous manner with an appropriate event, a collegial luncheon (after all, when you've been promoted, the drinks are on you!). The factual questions were in comparison simply distracting details. The decisive element was the attainment of the "consensus" among the central agencies; he, Heydrich, now had the central responsibility in the most central area of the Nazi state.

He probably reckoned with dissent. That may have been the reason why he was in no hurry to hold the conference. The more events that had taken place, the safer his position. In any case he seems to have been very much relieved at the end, indulging in a cognac, which Eichmann had never known him to do.

His expansion of power was successful. No one had objected to his "appointment." Heydrich stood at the peak of his career. Six months later he was dead. What has been obscured for posterity is that it was not Himmler but Heydrich who was the true architect of the Final Solution.[33]

Asked (unfortunately not very precisely) about the Wannsee conference, Eichman, in Jerusalem, first said it had marked "the beginning of the killing stories." When the objection was raised that there had already been killings before, he added: "Oh yes, that's right. This was a conference where Heydrich announced his appointment."[34]

Notes

1. Gerald Reitlinger, *The Final Solution* (London: Vallentine, Mitchell, 1953), p. 100.

2. Uwe Dietrich Adam, *Judenpolitik im Dritten Reich* (Düsseldorf: Droste, 1972; reprint, 1979), p. 314.

3. Dieter Rebentisch, *Führerstaat und Verwaltung im Zweiten Weltkrieg* (Stuttgart: Steiner, 1989), p. 439.

4. This copy is to be found in the Political Archives of the Foreign Office in Bonn.

5. Two were addressed to Luther in the Foreign Office (November 29, 1941, and January 8, 1942) and one, dated November 29, 1941, was to Hofmann of the SS Office of Racial and Settlement Affairs (*Nürnberger Dokument* PS-709).

6. From Hofmann, dated December 4, 1941 (*Nürnberger Dokument* PS-709).

7. Compare Kurt Pätzold and Erika Schwarz, *Tagesordnung: Judenmord. Die Wannsee-Konferenz am 20. Januar 1942. Eine Dokumentation zur Organisation der "Endlösung"* (Berlin: Metropol, 1992).

8. The word *Frühstück* means breakfast in normal, everyday German.

9. Hans J. Hoeveler, *Internationale Bekämpfung des Verbrechens* (Hamburg: Verlag Deutsche Polizei, 1966), p. 32 ff.; Manfred Teufel, "Aus der Polizeigeschichte. Vor 75 Jahren wurde der Grundstein für die INTERPOL gelegt," in *Die Kriminalpolizei*, June 1989, p. 93 ff.

10. *Die Deutsche Polizei*, No. 14 (July 15, 1940), p. 237.

11. Ibid., No. 18 (September 15, 1940), p. 305.

12. Ibid.

13. Information about the buildings is based on the unpublished land register documents, copies of which the Schöneberg district court kindly made available to me.

14. Described thus in the official organ of the IKPK, *Internationale Kriminalpolizei*, on November 14, 1941. Quoted from Hoeveler, *Internationale Bekämpfung*, p. 40.

15. This can be deduced from the fact that the move and the address were announced in a circular of this date from the SS general and the chief of the German Police; *Mitteilungsblatt des Reichskriminalpolizeiamts* No. 6 (June 1942), p. 55.

16. Namely, Hofmann in his above-mentioned response, in which he expressed his thanks for the "invitation to the conference to take place at the offices of the International Criminal Commission, Berlin, Am Grossen Wannsee 56/58, on December 9, 1941."

17. This can be determined from the above-mentioned land register documents. As regards the history of this house, there is now a thorough investigation by Johannes Tuchel: *Am Grossen Wannsee 56–58. Von der Villa Minoux zum Haus der Wannsee-Konferenz* (Berlin: Edition Hentrich, 1992).

18. *Nürnberger Dokument* PS-710.

19. Werner Präg and Wolfgang Jacobmeyer (eds.), *Das Diensttagebuch des deutschen Generalgouverneurs in Polen 1939–1945* (Stuttgart: Deutsche Verlags-Anstalt, 1975), p. 457.

20. Eichmann's testimony before the regional court in Jerusalem in the 106th session on July 21, 1961, Pätzold and Schwarz, *Tagesordnung*, p. 197 ff.

21. Max Domarus (ed.), *Hitler. Reden und Proklamationen 1932–1945* (Neustadt a.d. Aisch: Schmidt, 1963), p. 1782.

22. The memorandum is to be found in the Centre de Documentation Juive Contemporaine, Paris, XXVI-I.

23. *Nürnberger Dokument* RF-1210, IMT (German edition), Vol. 38, p. 741.

24. *Akten zur deutschen auswärtigen Politik 1918–1945* (ADAP), Series E, Vol. 3, p. 355.

25. Himmler's memorandum about the treatment of foreign peoples in the East, dated May 28, 1940, in *Vierteljahrshefte für zeitgeschichte* 5 (1957), p. 197.

26. *Nürnberger Dokument* PS-1816, IMT (German edition), Vol. 28, p. 532.

27. *Nürnberger Dokument* NG-341.
28. *Akten zur deutschen auswärtigen Politik 1918–1945* (ADAP), Series D, Vol. 5, p. 786 ff.
29. Personalakte, in Shlomo Aronson, *Reinhard Heydrich und die Frühgeschichte von Gestapo und SD* (Stuttgart: Deutsche Verlags-Anstalt, 1971), p. 311.
30. Fortieth weekly report of the Israelite Religious Community of Vienna of October 7, 1941, in Jonny Moser, *Die Judenverfolgung in Österreich 1938–1945* (Vienna: Europa Verlag, 1966), p. 28.
31. *Nürnberger Dokument* NO-3078.
32. Hitler's decree of October 7, 1939, *Nürnberger Dokument* PS-686, IMT (German edition), Vol. 26, pp. 255–257.
33. In this regard I am diametrically opposed to the view of Richard Breitman, *The Architect of Genocide: Himmler and the Final Solution* (New York: Alfred A. Knopf, 1991).
34. Questioning of Eichmann by Avner Less on June 5, 1960, quoted according to an edited version in Jochen von Lang, *Das Eichmann-Protokoll* (Berlin: Severin and Siedler, 1982), p. 82. Verbatim text in Pätzold and Schwarz, *Tagesordnung*, p. 166.

3

Profits and Persecution: Corporate Involvement in the Holocaust

Peter Hayes

Half a century after the onset of the Nazi assault on the European Jews, we sill lack a systematic and comprehensive study of the role of German big business in this terrible process. Despite important recent works on the complicity of the German professions in Nazi crimes, the steady economic persecution of the average Jewish citizen in Germany during the 1930s, the history of key families within the German Jewish economic elite, the unfolding of particular commercial takeovers, and the ubiquity of slave labor, the basic works of reference concerning corporate behavior toward the Jews remain Helmut Genschel's admirable but dated book of 1966 on Aryanization and Joseph Ferencz's report of 1979 on attempts to obtain compensation for slave laborers from German firms after 1945.[1] Worse, some of the most widely read or recent publications on these topics are quite unreliable.[2]

Among the reasons for this situation, the problem of sources is paramount, and its form is familiar to students of the Holocaust and readers of Raul Hilberg's work. In some respects historians have frustratingly little to work with; in other respects they have too much. The most glaringly sparse sort of documentation is that which might have emerged from the files of the private enterprises that acquired the property or exploited the labor of Jews or that played important intermediate roles in the transfer of assets. At the end of World War II, relatively few such records came to light, partly because of wartime destruction and postwar chaos and partly because the Allies treated such matters as secondary issues, even when they put German industrialists on trial. Thereafter, the firms involved or their successors proved reluctant to acknowledge their deeds and open their records to scholarly scrutiny, fearing legal claims, damage to their corporate images, and embarrassment to some of their leaders.[3]

The official record also has turned out to be remarkably spotty. Only one truly serviceable set of papers of the thirty-one Nazi *Gauwirtschaftsberater*, the regional

Party officials charged with supervising the dispossession of German Jews, appears extant, and that collection covers the *Gau* Westfalen-Süd, where few Jewish-owned entities were big enough to interest large German firms.[4] More valuable but equally rare are the files of the former Finance Ministry in Baden, which contain extensive material on the spoliation in that corner of Germany.[5] Assiduous workers in municipal and state archives in Germany and Austria have brought other patches of documentation to light over the past three decades, and the first serious study of the Reich Finance Ministry records also has appeared.[6] Yet enormous gaps persist, not least because Communist regimes long concealed or neglected substantial quantities of evidence concerning events in Berlin (the home of about one-third of German Jews in the 1930s), the parts of the Reich assigned to the DDR and Poland after 1945, and the occupied and satellite states.[7] Meanwhile, it is small wonder that researchers have barely sampled the almost hopelessly vast and dispersed stores of information in German tax and court records and in the postwar denazification and restitution proceedings. Even without the vagaries of the West German Law for the Protection of Personal Data (*Datenschutzgesetz*), going through these records would be a daunting process.[8]

A second barrier to a comprehensive synthesis is the diversity of Jewish experience at the hands of German corporations. Varying in intensity and impact from month to month and place to place between 1933 and 1939, the Nazi assault also sometimes affected German Jews differently according to whether they belonged to long resident or newly immigrant families, continued as at least nominal members of their community or had been baptized, did or did not possess non-Jewish relatives, were associated with economically strong or weak firms, and ranked among the rank and file or the *erste Garnitur* (elite) of an enterprise. To arrive at a historical account that neither over- nor understates these variations is not an easy matter, either intellectually or emotionally. Variety of experience with German firms continued for some German Jews even after 1939, depending on whether they got out of the country and to where, were able to hide, or ended up in a labor battalion. And here the problem of sources impedes even overall description, since the continued payment of pensions and the like (when it occurred) was perforce conducted secretly, and the mere figures for the numbers of Jewish slave laborers at specific firms are often both poor and problematic.[9] Finally, differences in postwar experiences in reacquiring property may have colored retrospective accounts, with those who succeeded perhaps inclined to refer more generously to the arrangements made with the erstwhile purchasers than the actual events may have warranted or than less fortunate survivors were wont to do.[10]

Probably a third explanation for the absence of a work of this sort is that few people have thought there is much left to unravel, much of a problem to be solved by inquiry. Most observers believe we know the essentials of the story, namely, as Avraham Barkai recently stated in reference to events in Germany during the 1930s, that "fundamentally, the distinguished and well-educated 'Aryan' big businessmen proceeded no differently than the little lower-middle-class Nazis; when it came to snatching Jewish property, they were not, in the final analysis, squeamish in their choice of methods."[11] That such people would and did extend their rapacity first to conquered Europe then to "annihilation through labor" requires no explanation. Not only, however, does so categorical a description blind us to the ambiguity and change over time of corporate conduct toward Jews, but it also begs the important question of *why* German businessmen behaved as they did from 1933 to 1939 and prevents us from recognizing exactly how Aryanization set a precedent for the ghastly forms of exploitation that followed. As has been the case with regard to Hitler's rise and the development of the program of arms, autarky, and aggression, close reexamination of the available evidence on this aspect of the relationship between big business and Nazism suggests that it has more complicated and disturbing things to tell us than the received image of unrelievedly biased and ruthless German capitalists would indicate.[12] This essay attempts, following the spirit and methods of Raul Hilberg's magnificent work, to outline what those things are and to point out, at least, issues and sources that may improve our knowledge of this still cloudy subject.[13]

Understanding the role German big business played in the so-called Aryanization of the German economy begins with an accurate appreciation of the relative economic position of Jews at the outset of the Third Reich. On the whole, that position had been declining for at least twenty years, both in prominence and distinctness, both within the country as a whole and within the leading ranks of the corporate world in particular. The national trends after roughly 1910 were all sharply downward: The Jewish proportions of the overall population, of the wealthiest taxpayers, of the citizens engaged in trade and commerce, of the students at universities and particularly in the law and medical faculties—all these fell by one-quarter to one-half during the two decades preceding the Nazi takeover.[14] These developments were mirrored in the corporate sector, where the number of major enterprises owned or led by Jews dropped, along with the staying power of the family-centered firms that remained. For example, several famous Jewish-owned companies, such as the Agfa and Cassella chemicals firms, disappeared into larger entities during the 1920s; the last Jew to head the great AEG corporation that the Rathenau family had built retired in 1927; the Jewish financiers who presided over the nation's three largest banks in 1929 all departed during the depression; and even the celebrated publishing enterprises, Mosse in Berlin and Sonnemann-Simon in Frankfurt, fell on such dark days before the republic collapsed that the former went into receivership and the latter was all but taken over by IG Farben.[15]

The causes of these patterns need not detain us here—on the whole, they resulted from an absolute and relative drop in the Jewish birthrate, itself a product of earlier prosperity and rising rates of intermarriage; from a "catch-up" effect, as non-Jewish Germans increasingly conformed to the demands of a modern economy; and from a secular decline in the fortunes of independent proprietors during World War I, the great inflation that followed, the merger wave of the 1920s, and the depression.

More relevant to the subject at hand are the consequences of what had happened. Chief among these was that the appeal of anti-Semitism and the appetite for Aryanization in Germany immediately before and after 1933 were concentrated among the gentile participants in those middle ranges of economic life where Jews remained conspicuous as competitors or middlemen, for example, wholesale and retail trade, the scrap metals business, milling and livestock dealing in rural areas, textiles, and the free professions, notably law and medicine. This was the core constituency—the old German *Mittelstand* of largely self-employed shopkeepers, artisans, peasant proprietors, and professionals—around which the Nazis gradually built their following, to which they directed their most anti-Semitic propaganda, and from which welled up agitation to drive the Jews from the German economy. It was this level of German society that looked most resentfully and covetously on the approximately 100,000 Jewish-owned economic operations in Germany at the time Hitler took power.[16]

Conversely, the leaders of German big business seem to have had little in the way of a collective personal or economic interest in Aryanization at the outset of the Third Reich. Not only were very few Jewish enterprises (about 1 percent of the total) of sufficient size or importance to attract the avarice of the nation's major firms, but also most of the corporate barons had served with Jews in the war, rubbed elbows with them in professional life, found them loyal and cooperative in cartels and interest groups, had first- or secondhand experience with intermarriage, and generally had come to recognize the absurdity of group vilification.[17] Of course, there were bigots among them, but they were usually of the country-club type and not up to Nazi standards. The prevailing tendency was to complain against allegedly corrupting Jewish influences in cultural rather than economic life, to distinguish sharply between supposedly uncouth immigrant or lower-class Jews and the native-born or well-educated ones, to cite acquaintances and colleagues as exceptions to prevalent derogatory stereotypes, and to draw a line between acceptable restrictions on the future activities of Jews—usually in the form of some sort of *numerus clausus,* or quota system—and impermissible assaults on their current livelihoods and status.[18] Narrow-minded by the standards of our day, the leaders of the nation's largest enterprises were generally moderate, sometimes even liberal, by the standards of their own. But they were also prepared on the basis of such views only to decry discrimination against particular individuals, not to refute the general practice.

Perhaps the best indication of the disinterest of German big business in anti-Semitism is the scrupulousness with which Hitler avoided that theme in addressing corporate executives. His experience with Emil Kirdorf, a retired coal magnate with long-standing and warm ties to the Salomonsohn family of bankers, may have convinced the Führer of the need for prudence in this connection. When Kirdorf joined the Party in 1927, he told Hitler personally that he had done so only *despite* the Nazis' anti-Semitism, and several of the fourteen industrialists whom Kirdorf assembled to speak with the Führer a few months later also explicitly challenged him on this point.[19] By the time Hitler met with Wilhelm Cuno, the head of the Hamburg-America Shipping Line, in September 1930, the Nazi had learned his lesson. He went out of his way to sanitize the Party's racial program, promising that once in power he would proceed against the "Jewish predominance in the state," not Jewish persons as such, and that there would be no violent persecution of Jews in Germany. Just over two months later, Hitler addressed the elite Hamburg National Club and ducked the subject of the Jews altogether, thus setting a pattern characteristic of his speeches to industrial audiences from then until even several months after his accession in 1933.[20]

Nonetheless, the Führer continued to encounter opposition to racial persecution. Early in 1932, Albert Vögler of the nation's largest steel company made so bold as to reproach both Hitler and Göring on the subject, and a few months later, Paul Reusch of the large Gutehoffnungshütte combine ordered his newspaper in Nürnberg to editorialize against Nazi racialism. Such deviation from the Party line persisted following the Nazi takeover. Even before the chairmen of IG Farben, Krupp, Siemens, and the United Steelworks began routing funds to the Reichsvertretung der Deutschen Juden under Rabbi Leo Baeck, several of them spoke up in defense of Germany's Jews.[21] Once more Kirdorf protested, this time not only in writing to Hitler but also in an open letter published in the *Rheinische Zeitung* denouncing the "stab in the back of a large number of men who have served Germany." Meanwhile, Robert Bosch, the founder of the famous automotive parts company in Stuttgart, dispatched a representative to Berlin to complain; his nephew Carl Bosch, the head of IG Farben, delivered his dissent to the Führer in person; and both Gustav Krupp von Bohlen und Halbach and Carl-Friedrich von Siemens allegedly made vain efforts to take up the matter with the new chancellor.[22] Simultaneously, Kurt Schmitt, the top man in the Allianz insurance corporation who became economics minister in June 1933, and Hjalmar Schacht, the president of the national bank, began trying to use their offices to limit infringements on the economic activities of Jews.[23]

To be sure, these men and their spokespersons usually made their cases in pragmatic terms, as they themselves were not immune to certain forms of prejudice and had learned that arguments of morality and decency cut no ice with the Nazis. They therefore paid some form of lip service to the Party's rationales for discrimination before stressing that neither the German economy nor an insecure new German government could afford the material losses that persecution and foreign reprisals to it would entail. But all of these figures, reinforced by others such as Hermann Bücher, the head of AEG, initially stood firm in rejecting attacks on Jewish entrepreneurs and the dismissal of employees or board members at home or abroad on grounds of their descent.[24]

Similarly revealing of opinion in the upper reaches of the corporate world on the so-called Jewish question at the outset of the Nazi Reich was a project devised under the auspices of Max Warburg, a Jewish banker from Hamburg, and a group of Jewish and gentile businessmen he had assembled, including Krupp von Bohlen, von Siemens, and Carl Bosch, as well as Kurt Schmitt until he became economics minister. Between April and August 1933, they reached agreement on a plan that they intended "to forward to a responsible office when the participants thought the moment had arrived."[25] Its central feature, a proposal to funnel Jewish young people increasingly into preparation for manual rather than mental labor, especially in agriculture, echoed the ideas various Jewish groups had been advancing since the early 1920s as antidotes to declining urban incomes and enduring German prejudice.[26] Though the scheme met the Nazis halfway by admitting that German Jewry's occupational distribution required some sort of remedy, it also challenged Party ideology and intentions in several ways. First, the plan posited that the existing distribution was a product of culture and history, not race and conspiracy, hence that changing it would lessen differences between gentile and Jewish Germans and lay the basis for long-range harmony. Second, the businessmen stipulated one precondition for the success of their proposal: that each "patriotic non-Aryan" should continue in his profession to "enjoy the same rank and the same respect as every man." Third, the group's final memorandum stressed the indivisibility of "Aryan" and "non-Aryan" economic interests, since attacks on the latter were bound to have adverse effects in both principle and practice on the former.[27]

Warburg's initiative had an ambiguous fate. On the one hand, scarcely had it taken agreed-upon form when the Nazi government literally cut the ground out from under the plan by promulgating the Hereditary Farm Law of September 29, 1933, which contained a ban on Jews owning or working on German farms.[28] That, and because the gentile participants wished to avoid giving ammunition to the rampaging Nazis whom Hitler had only recently reined in or to advocates of the much-feared "ständishe Wirtschaft," helps explain why there is no evidence that the group's memo ever went to any "responsible office." On the other hand, Schmitt's appointment as economics minister made overt delivery of the document superfluous, since his official behavior accorded with the objectives of the executives. Indeed, for a time, national policy as a whole seemed to do so. The Cabinet specifically rejected in mid-1933 various suggested means of pressuring Jewish firms out of business, such as denial of access to assorted forms of credit, to government contracts, and to the stock markets, and banned inquiries into the ethnic backgrounds of managers and owners doing business with government agencies.[29] At the end of the year, the Economics and Interior Ministries jointly issued a decree exempting commercial activities from all racial regulations passed to govern other walks of life during the preceding year.[30]

These decisions were, however, neither adhered to uniformly nor attributable simply to the influence of German corporations and their leaders' arguments. The enactment of the Hereditary Farm Law and the experiences of the Tietz department store chains and the Ullstein publishing house in 1933–1934 all make clear that when the Nazis invested a particular economic activity with political importance, as they did in the cases of owning land, large retail outlets, and newspapers, they did not hesitate to insist on prompt Aryanization at confiscatory prices.[31] They were only slightly less direct and more patient in targeting Jewish-owned military contractors.[32] Otherwise, the new regime consciously chose to stay its hand, regarding a massive assault on the "commanding heights" of Jewish property in Germany as unnecessary for the moment. After all, according to chapter 11 of *Mein Kampf*, economic power was but the most ancient means by which Jews had corrupted Germans and not nearly as insidious as the influence the racial enemy had later acquired in the political and cultural domains.[33] The same scale of priorities was reflected in the Nazi Twenty-Five-Point Program of 1920 and in the principal internal Party documents on the Jewish question that were prepared prior to January 1933, which called for numerous limitations on the rights of Jews but said scarcely anything of commercial curbs.[34] Neither ideology nor pragmatism took pride of place in Nazi policy toward Jews in the German economy during the initial phase of Hitler's rule in Germany; they went hand in hand.

This observation is essential to understanding why the assault on the economic bases of Jews' existence in Germany could be so uneven during the first years of the Third Reich, and why, at first, the involvement of German big business in Aryanization could be both limited and, in some cases, decent compared to what happened later. From the opening days of Hitler's rule, the Nazis ruthlessly but more or less surreptitiously drove small-scale Jewish proprietors out of business, with the result that more than 60 percent of them went under by the end of 1937, including five of every six Jewish-owned retail establishments.[35] Determined to satisfy their lower-middle-class following, sure that the economy would not suffer from the liquidation or takeover of most of these shops, and confident that foreign reporters and observers would pay little mind to what was happening, the Nazis did not shrink from this sort of Aryanization. But at the upper levels of the German economy, matters were different. Here fewer competitors grasped at possible gains, and extortion tended to arouse more sympathy than cupidity; here competent substitute owners and managers were harder to find; and here foreigners might notice and react negatively to what transpired. Since the ownership of banks and factories by Jews for the most part presented no dangers comparable to the holding of office or the influencing of public opinion, removing it for the present entailed higher costs than benefits. The Nazi regime therefore opted against taking the offensive.

Thus, from 1933 to 1937, if advancement to the upper ranks of major German companies became increasingly out of the question for Jews, many of those who were already prominent could remain at their posts. To be sure, those firms that aroused the ire of the *Mittelstand* (Karstadt), were state-owned (Viag), relied heavily on government contracts (Osram), or had been driven by the depression into subordination to official agencies (Mosse Verlag, most of the major banks) or dependence on government aid or goodwill in some respect (notably Mansfeld and the auto companies like Daimler-Benz and the Adlerwerke) conducted what bordered on purges in 1933–1934.[36] But most of the better-established enterprises refused to behave in this fashion. Mannesmann did not drop Oscar Altmann from its managing board until the end of 1936, and Max Steinthal remained chairman of its supervisory board until May of that year and a member until 1938.[37] The supervisory board of IG Farben continued to count five "racially" Jewish Germans, even offsetting the death of one by the election of another, Richard Merton, in 1935, and that of the concern's Rheinstahl subsidiary renewed Julius Flechtheim in 1934 and retained him until 1938.[38] Samuel Ritscher kept his seat on the managing board of the Dresdner Bank into 1937, and the Feldmühle paper concern came under attack from the SS for still having two Jews among its managing directors and one on the supervisory board as late as December of that year.[39]

When it proved awkward to keep prominent Jewish executives, usually because their functions involved them with government agencies that refused to work with them, many were evacuated to posts abroad, as in the cases of Ernst Schwarz, Carl Bosch's personal secretary, who took over the American Agfa-Ansco branch of Farben, and Edmund Pietrkowski, who became that concern's representative in Switzerland.[40] Whether a majority of the larger firms showed such solicitude or extended it to lower-ranking employees is a matter for further research, but there is scattered evidence at Yad Vashem that even the major banks were forthcoming in this regard.[41]

Similarly, only about one-quarter of the major Jewish firms, about 260 in all, sold out between 1933 and fall 1936, and only toward the end of this period did private Jewish banks begin to be swallowed up.[42] Moreover, it appears that rather few of these transactions amounted to takeovers by German big business. From contemporary newspapers and archival records, I have been able to document only fifteen such acquisitions in this period. Probably the majority fell under two headings: (1) shakedowns by local opportunists and Party bosses and (2) arrangements by which trusted gentile colleagues fronted for the Jewish owners.[43] When one of the 100 largest German firms was involved, the terms of sale seem to have come closer to what was commercially fair than did most other transfers at the time, let alone later, not least because in the context of the still fledgling economic upturn, some major firms wished to shelter their new profits from taxation or a possible devaluation of the mark without constructing new plants. The easiest and safest way to put their earnings to work was to acquire tested, perhaps complementary, and certainly depreciable operations.[44] Thus, the three substantial Aryanizations accomplished during 1933–1936 by Degussa AG, involving the Chemische-Pharmazeutische Fabrik Bad Homburg AG, the Degea AG (Auergesellschaft) of Berlin, and the Dr. L. C. Marquart AG of Beuel, all provided for the payment of well over the face value of their shares and for the retention of the existing Jewish personnel.[45] The Siemens group's two acquisitions in 1935 had simular financial provisions—it bought 60 percent of the Heliowert Werke, Elektrizitäts AG of Berlin at 85 percent of par and all of the stock in Dr. Cassirer and Company, Berlin, at 140 percent—but the Jewish board members all departed within months.[46]

In sum, though one cannot speak of adamant resistance on the part of German big business to the penetration of anti-Semitism into economic life, one can assert that among corporate leaders there was little rush and some reluctance to participate in the process. Prior to 1938, their behavior may have prolonged illusions among Jewish employees and entrepreneurs of being able to hold out until sanity returned to Germany.[47]

In November 1937 almost all of the circumstances that had insulated German big business from the full force of Aryanization changed rather abruptly.[48] To be sure, there was still no groundswell of corporate agitation for the elimination of the remaining Jewish-owned banks, factories, and trading companies. But three key shifts clearly occurred in comparison with earlier years: (1) governmental pressure for Aryanization at the upper levels of the economy rose, (2) resistance to cooperation on the part of major companies declined, and (3) both the willingness and capacity of corporate buyers to make fair sales offers also shrank.

The government's new adamance appears to have stemmed largely from Hitler, who in November convened his principal advisers in the famous Hossbach conference to inform them that war for lebensraum was in sight and that the preparations for it had to be accelerated. He thereupon did several things that had immediate bearing on the economic position of Jews. He fired Schacht, who had succeeded Schmitt as economics minister, thus removing the principal protector, however legalistic, of Jewish economic rights. He temporarily replaced him with Göring, whose intense and genuine anti-Semitism and desire to seize Jewish wealth for the purposes of the Four-Year Plan promptly resulted in a series of decrees enacting the measures rejected five years earlier for defining "Jewish influence" over firms, detecting it, and punishing it economically. And he authorized Julius Streicher, the crudest anti-Semite among the Nazi leaders, to launch in Nürnberg during the Christmas season the first organized boycott of Jewish shops in Germany since April 1, 1933.[49]

That the renewal of the offensive against the Jews, this time against the last substantial vestiges of their economic position, occurred when Hitler was preoccupied with the prospect of war is not coincidental. It is important to remember in this connection that the most infamous pronouncement in *Mein Kampf* on the subject of the Jews, namely, the one regretting that 12,000 to 15,000 of them had not been subjected to poison gas during World War I, appears in a section alleging their guilt for ideological sabotage and war profiteering.[50] By the same token, the ghettoization order of 1939, the directives to the *Einsatzgruppen* of early 1941, and the decision later that year to extend the murders to all of the Jews of Europe were all justified by the regime as security measures. For Hitler, the war against the Jews was always bound up with the war against external enemies, whom the

Jews allegedly instigated and served. Thus, it is not surprising that the moment when Hitler accelerated the pace of expansionism was also the moment when he escalated his attack on the Jews; and it is no surprise that he now chose to overrule timorous corporate concerns about adverse economic or political effects. In his mind, the time had come to batten down the hatches.[51]

The result over the next fifteen months was a sustained onslaught against Jewish firms and executives more far-reaching, inclusive, and cruel than all that had gone before. Against this, such corporate resistance as remained proved unavailing, since new laws first cut off government contracts and raw material allocations to firms with Jewish board members, senior managers, and owners, then required their removal.[52] By the middle of 1938, virtually all Jewish board members of major firms had lost their posts. As for large companies still owned by Jews, the most that could be achieved was damage containment, which took either of two forms. One consisted of trustee arrangements, such as those involving the Oppenheim Bank of Cologne, the Warburg Bank of Hamburg, and the Schocken department store chain based in Leipzig, by which reliable Christian associates of the Jewish owners took over the properties in question and their true possessors got out of the country.[53] The second was exemplified by the Aryanization of the Metallgesellschaft in Frankfurt, where Carl Bosch could not save the Merton family's position but succeeded in at least preventing local Nazi potentates from acquiring domination over the firm.[54]

But there was a good deal less of this sort of help extended to Jewish German entrepreneurs in this period than earlier.[55] Changes in the commercial world and its operating environment account for the deterioration in solidarity. By early 1938, newly ascendant enterprises in key industries and managers in many of the more ancient companies were opting to hitch their individual wagons to the star of Nazi policy far more firmly than their elders had been inclined to do. Thus, up-and-coming heavy industrial firms like Flick, Wolff, and Mannesmann engaged more extensively in Aryanization than Krupp or the Vereinigte Stahlwerke, and the relatively capital-poor Dresdner Bank quickly seized the chance to overtake the more restrained Deutsche by becoming the nation's leading broker of Aryanizations, usually at a 2 percent commission on the sales prices, which aggregated to an income of several million reichsmarks between 1937 and 1940.[56] At the same time, government control of the German economy had become so nearly complete that not only did growth, profits, and protection from more cooperative competitors depend almost entirely on satisfying the regime, but also increased allocations of key materials often could be obtained only by annexing another firm's quotas through complete acquisition.[57]

In this context, with massive Aryanization a given ordained from Berlin and sellers' bargaining positions weakened, many large firms gave up their scruples and plunged into the scramble for the spoils lest old or new rivals come away with more. Even so ready an Aryanizer as Friedrich Flick mobilized only after Party officials in Berlin egged him on in November 1937, and then partly in order to preserve the material advantages that flowed from serving the interests of Hermann Göring.[58] In other words, Aryanization within Germany in 1938, as in the occupied lands later, became an illustration of one of the key motivating methods of Nazism, "the threat in cases of recalcitrance," as Hans Mommsen has put it, "to entrust the dirty work to another."[59] Personal ambition and corporate competition produced a striking decline in human sympathy once the Nazi regime made its determination to dispossess Germany's remaining Jews unmistakable. As a result, between January and October 1938, according to the listings in the *Jüdische Rundschau*, the Aryanization of some 747 substantial producers and twenty-two private banks took place.[60] After the Nazi government decreed on December 12, 1938, that properties could be seized and sold by the state, the last restraints fell away.[61]

As for the downward pressure on purchase prices, it resulted not only from the number and desperation of the sellers but also from the illiquidity of some of the largest firms in consequence of the drives for armaments and autarky and from the regime's oversight of the sales.[62] The relevant Party and state agencies were generally hostile to both the Jewish owners and the "big concerns," hence determined to prevent either from "profiting" by transactions. In this context, corporate negotiators had to walk a fine line between offering too much or too little, lest they incur political challenge on either ground.[63] In rare instances, usually resulting from the international connections of the seller, some degree of generosity seemed advisable; thus the Reich was willing to smooth Flick's takeover of the Julius Petschek coalfields by permitting a rare and substantial, if not a fair, payment in scarce foreign exchange.[64] Always a possibility, however, was a case such as that of the Moos blouse factory in Buchau, when the responsible government officials halved the reichsmark figure on which the parties had agreed.[65]

Under these circumstances, the acquisitions from summer 1938 on were often the equivalent of fire sales, and the buyers knew it. Their only real choice, however, was *whether* to participate, not on what terms, and that choice came down to a matter of corporate self-interest in a particular commercial and political setting.[66] Similarly, that whatever they paid in marks was soon stripped from the Jewish seller by the regime was beyond the practical concern of the buying firms.[67] No thorough tabulation has ever been made of how many and which of the 100 largest firms in Germany bought what Jewish-owned properties for how much in this period, let alone an analysis of how much of this loot remained Aryanized after 1945.[68] When one is finally pieced together from contemporary publications, public and corporate archives, and the postwar restitution proceedings, the resulting picture is likely to be depressing on many grounds.

Once one recognizes that the key turning point in Nazi policy toward the Jews occurred in November 1937, when Hitler, Streicher, and Göring moved in concert against the remains of Jewish presence in the German economy, the intentionality of Nazi policy, which has been obscured by concentration on the improvised nature of the pogrom of November 1938, comes into focus. Moreover, the events that followed from Hitler's decisions assured that German business would prove less resistant to future forms of exploiting Jews than to past ones. The Aryanization program of 1938, which at first glance appears the less dramatic and frightful part of the history of corporate involvement in the Holocaust, in fact threw the switches for what came later. It demonstrated that the practical grounds for noninvolvement had been removed, the competitive ones for participation greatly increased, and the role of government decisions in channeling choices toward vicious outcomes solidified. The Nazi government had succeeded in transforming Jewish colleagues from people many of the nation's business magnates thought it in their interest to protect to people it was in their interest to exploit. Within another four years, the transformation had gone further: to people it was in business's interest to use up like any other factor of production.

It is, I think, remarkable how little we know of German corporate profiteering from the onslaught against the Jews of Europe after 1939. With regard to acquisitions of property, probably the most economically lucrative dimension of the Holocaust, scholars have barely begun to tally the booty, much of which passed through the hands of the two banks favored by the Nazis, the Delbrück, Schickler and the Dresdner, some of whose records lie, largely unexamined, in the U.S. National Archives.[69] Whether we will ever find out how much of the plundered foreign exchange, stocks, and bonds of Jews ended up in private corporate hands is questionable. Meanwhile, almost no one has paused to remark on, let alone to calculate, the proceeds from a particular service that Degussa performed for the German government from 1939 on: the conversion of billions of marks worth of gold and silver taken from Jews into negotiable ingots.[70] A converse example of our ignorance concerns something painful we are inclined to forget. Since the sales figures exist for the Degesch company, the subsidiary of Degussa and IG Farben that made Zyklon B, we can say with remarkable assurance that total receipts from selling the substance to Auschwitz were only about 40,000 marks.[71] This figure reminds us shockingly of how cheaply people could be enlisted in mass murder.

Yet the SS had expenses, which created the nexus of interests that produced another form of robbery about which we still know too little. The surviving documents provide only a sketchy accounting of the use of slave labor by major German firms during the war. To be sure, among the hundreds of corporations that employed nearly half a million camp inmates at the end of 1944, the greatest offenders were either the state-owned firms—like Brabag, the Hermann Göring works, and Volkswagen—or the munitions and arms makers in the narrowest sense: Dynamit Nobel, Rheinmetall-Borsig, Krupp, Messerschmitt, Heinkel, and Junkers. But by 1943 almost every major firm in Germany was woven into the military economy, so it is not surprising that BMW, AEG-Telefunken, Siemens, Daimler-Benz, and IG Farben were also among the principal exploiters. All of these enterprises put Jewish inmates to work in existing factories as well as new ones erected near the concentration camps. A Krupp subsidiary was even installed in the Łódź ghetto until its liquidation in August and September 1944.[72] In every case the laborers were not paid; their so-called wages of 3 to 8 marks per eleven- to twelve-hour day, depending on sex, age, and skills, went directly to the SS, and the companies' additional costs came to some fraction of a mark per worker per day for food and the overhead charge for the unheated, overcrowded, verminous barracks and the surrounding fences in which the workers were caged. While the SS pocketed the substantial sums, the companies engaged in a vicious circle of maltreatment and low labor productivity. IG Farben's factories 3 miles east of Auschwitz cost the lives of nearly 25,000 Jewish inmates; we will probably never be able to get accurate figures for the deaths at other installations.[73]

But if one looks away from the horrible consequences of corporate enslavement to concentrate on why it happened, the pattern of behavior that emerges is not unlike that typical of the history of Aryanization. Initial rejection by every major company of Himmler's attempts to lease camp labor to them ever since 1934 was followed—after 1940 in some quarters, after 1943 almost universally—by a conviction that the alternatives to accepting inmate labor had been exhausted, then by a general rush by firms to get their share. Once more, as in the Aryanization cases of 1938–1939, it appeared that firms were trying to outdo each other in rapacity, and once more they were. But the Nazi regime had structured events in such a way that nonparticipation seemed both disloyal and self-destructive, hence unthinkable to a competitive capitalist. With scarcely an exception, every major German firm acceded to the apparent imperatives of a situation in which 11 million workers had been called into uniform, a higher percentage of German women were already working in 1939 than was ever the case in the United States and Britain during the war, and 7.5 million conscripted foreigners were insufficient to generate the necessary production.[74] With Himmler's SS economic administration eager for the income, German industrialists clamored for workers. Practical, patriotic, and preoccupied men, these executives appear to have asked themselves few if any questions about what they were doing. Having once recognized the moral and economic defects of the opportunity Himmler offered, they came by 1943 to discern neither.

What does this dreadful tale of corporate complicity tell us? Can we conclude anything from it that reaches beyond the historical details? No one can examine the Holocaust and ignore the causal importance of anti-Semitism, for it alone, in the end, provides an answer to the fundamental question, Why the Jews?[75] But no researcher can rest content with an explanation of the Holocaust that goes no further, since such an explanation cannot tell us why *this* descent upon Jews was so much worse than any other. Avraham Barkai is no doubt right to claim that the massacre is inconceivable without the existence of a broad anti-Semitic consensus in German, perhaps in European, society, to which the German big business world was by no means immune.[76] Yet Peter Gay is also right to point out that the problem with the word *anti-Semitism* is that it is a single name for widely varying beliefs about and behavior toward Jews, all of them ugly but only some of them menacing.[77] And Michael Marrus is right to remind us that the menacing views become decisive only in certain contexts.[78] How can our understanding incorporate all of these sound perceptions? By recognizing, I think, what the sordid role of big business tells us in microcosm: that if hatred was the fuel that propelled Nazi Germany on the road to the Holocaust, that road was paved not just by indifference, as Ian Kershaw has remarked, but by self-interest.[79] The subject of corporate involvement in the Holocaust would be easier to dispense with if that self-interest had been of business's own making.

Notes

1. See Ingo Müller, *Hitler's Justice* (Cambridge: Harvard University Press, 1990); Michael Kater, *Doctors Under Hitler* (Chapel Hill: University of North Carolina Press, 1989); Avraham Barkai, *From Boycott to Annihilation: The Economic Struggle of German Jews, 1933–1943* (Hanover, N.H.: University Press of New England, 1989)—though some citations below are to the German paperback edition, *Vom Boykott zur "Entjudung"* (Frankfurt: Fischer, 1988); W. E. Mosse, *Jews in the German Economy, 1820–1935* (Oxford: Clarendon Press, 1987); Johannes Ludwig, *Boykott. Enteignung. Mord* (Hamburg: Facta Oblita, 1980); E. Rosenbaum, and A. J. Sherman, *M. M. Warburg & Co., 1798–1938* (New York: Holmes & Meier, 1979); Wilhelm Treue, *Das Schicksal des Bankhauses Sal. Oppenheim jr. & Cie. im Dritten Reich* (Wiesbaden: Steiner, 1983); Konrad Fuchs, *Ein Konzern aus Sachsen* (Stuttgart: Deutsche Verlags-Anstalt, 1990); Horst A. Wessel, *Kontinuität im Wandel: 100 Jahre Mannesmann 1890–1990* (Düsseldorf: Mannesmann-Archiv, 1990), pp. 229–238; Ulrich Herbert, *Fremdarbeiter* (Bonn: Verlag J.H.W. Dietz Nachf., 1985); Helmut Genschel, *Die Verdrängung der Juden aus der Wirtschaft im Dritten Reich* (Göttingen: Musterschmidt, 1966); Joseph Ferencz, *Less Than Slaves* (Cambridge: Harvard University Press, 1979).

2. In English the foremost example is William Manchester, *The Arms of Krupp* (New York: Little, Brown, 1968). Among German works, see Angelika Ebbinghaus (ed.), *Das Daimler-Benz-Buch* (Nördlingen: Greno, 1987), and Karl Heinz Roth and Michael Schmid (eds.), *Die Daimler-Benz AG 1916–1948. Schlüsseldokumente zur Konzerngeschichte* (Nördlingen: Greno, 1987), vols. 3 and 5 of the *Schriften der Hamburger Stiftung für Sozialgeschichte des 20. Jahrhunderts;* as well as the translations of the investigative reports drawn up by the Finance Division of the American occupation authorities in 1945–1947, prepared for publication and outfitted with new introductions by the Hamburger Stiftung: *O.M.G.U.S. Ermittlungen gegen die Dresdner Bank* (Nördlingen: Franz Greno, 1986). For a powerful critique of the volumes on Daimler-Benz, see Volker Hentschel, "Daimler-Benz im Dritten Reich," *Vierteljahrschrift für Sozial-und Wirtschaftsgeschichte*, v. 75 (1988), pp. 74–100.

3. A recent exception is the Degussa AG; see Peter Hayes, "Fritz Roessler and Nazism: The Observations of a German Industrialist, 1930–37," *Central European History*, v. 20 (1987), especially pp. 76–78. Among the other signs that such reticence is finally diminishing are the access given by BMW and MTU GmbH for Zdenek Zofka, "Allach-Sklaven für BMW," *Dachauer Hefte*, v. 2 (1986), pp. 68–78, and by Volkswagen and the Deutsche Bank to Hans Mommsen and Harold James, respectively, for their forthcoming volumes on these

enterprises during the Nazi period. Concerning the heretofore widespread lack of candor among German companies on this subject, see "Arisierung: 'Keiner hat hier was zu feiern,'" *Der Spiegel,* no. 52 (1987), pp. 58–72.

4. Nordrhein-Westfälisches Staatsarchiv Münster (hereafter NWSM), Gauleitung Westfalen-Süd, Der Gauwirtschaftsberater, Findbuch C12. See Gerhard Kratzsch, *Der Gauwirtschaftsapparat der NSDAP. Menschenführung—'Arisierung'—Wehrwirtschaft im Gau Westfalen-Süd* (Münster: Aschendorff Verlag, 1989). There is, however, a less complete collection of Gauwirtschaftsberater records at the Hessisches Hauptstaatsarchiv, Wiesbaden.

5. See Badisches Generallandesarchiv Karlsruhe (hereafter GLAK), Abteilung 505, Arisierungen.

6. The most useful municipal studies include Arno Weckbecker, *Die Judenverfolgung in Heidelberg 1933–1945* (Heidelberg: C. F. Müller Juristischer Verlag, 1985); Hans-Joachim Fliedner, *Die Judenverfolgung in Mannheim 1933–1945,* 2d ed. (Stuttgart: Kohlhammer, 1991); Hans Witek, "'Arisierungen' in Wien," in E. Talos, E. Hanisch, and W. Neugebauer (eds.), *NS-Herrschaft in Oesterreich 1938–1945* (Vienna: Verlag für Gesselschaftskritik, 1988), pp. 199–216; Roland Flade, *Die Würzburger Juden* (Würzburg: Freunde Mainfrankischer Kunst und Geschichte, 1987); Ulrich Knipping, *Die Geschichte der Juden in Dortmund während der Zeit des Dritten Reiches* (Dortmund: Ruhfus Historischer Verein, 1977); Regina Bruss, *Die Bremer Juden unter dem Nationalsozialismus* (Bremen: Staatsarchiv der Freien Hansestadt Bremen, 1983); Peter Hanke, *Zur Geschichte der Juden in München zwischen 1933 und 1945* (Munich: Buch- und Kunstantiquariat Wolfe, 1967); and Marie Zelzer, *Weg und Schicksal der Stuttgarter Juden* (Stuttgart: Klett, 1964). Among the regional accounts, see Johannes Simmert, "Die nationalsozialistische Judenverfolgung in Rheinland-Pfalz 1933 bis 1945," and Hans-Walter Herrmann, "Das Schicksal der Juden in Saarland 1920 bis 1945," in *Dokumentation zur Geschichte der jüdischen Bevölkerung in Rheinland-Pfalz und im Saarland von 1800 bis 1945,* v. 6 (Koblenz: Landesarchivverwaltung Rheinland-Pfalz, 1974); and Kurt Düwell, *Die Rheingebiete in der Judenpolitik des Nationalsozialismus vor 1942* (Bonn: Rohrscheid, 1967). I have not yet seen the new study of the Finance Ministry prepared by the Freie Universität, Stefan Mehl, *Das Reichsfinanzministerium und die Verfolgung der deutschen Juden 1933–1943* (Berlin: Zentralinst. für Sozialwiss. Forschung, 1990).

7. Illustrative of the limited usefulness of Eastern European historiography in this regard are the works of Kurt Pätzold, *Faschismus, Rassenwahn, Judenverfolgung* (East Berlin: Deutsche Verlag der Wissenschaften, 1975), and *Verfolgung, Vertreibung, Vernichtung* (Leipzig: Reclam, 1983). The materials now coming to light include not only those being released from archives in the former Soviet Union, which are likely to disclose considerable new information about industrial employment of slave labor in Eastern Europe during the war years. Also quite revealing are those of the Industrie- und Handelskammer, firms, and banks in the former Stadtarchiv Berlin (hereafter LAB [STA]), the Brandenburgisches Landeshauptarchiv Potsdam (BLHA), the Staatsarchiv Dresden (SAD), and the Bundesarchiv Potsdam (BAP).

8. For a hint of what such sources can reveal, see the admittedly hasty and journalistic work of Ludwig, *Boykott,* especially chapters 1–2.

9. With regard to pensions, see the interesting information regarding IG Farben's payments, which continued through 1943, in BAP, 31.01/15302/1. Concerning slave labor, see,

for instance, the divergent findings of Peter Hayes, *Industry and Ideology: IG Farben in the Nazi Era* (New York: Cambridge University Press, 1987), p. 343; and Gottfried Plumpe, *Die I.G. Farbenindustrie AG: Wirtschaft, Technik und Politik 1904–1945* (Berlin: Duncker & Humblot, 1990), pp. 629–631.

10. Something like this may have shaped the attitudes of Max Warburg, as expressed in his *Aus meinen Aufzeichnungen* (New York: Privately printed, 1952); Richard Merton, as conveyed in Hans Achinger, *Richard Merton* (Frankfurt: Waldemar Kramer, 1970); and Rudolf Hahn in 1955, as quoted in Wessel, *100 Jahre Mannesmann*, pp. 213–232.

11. Barkai, *Vom Boykott zur "Entjudung,"* p. 86.

12. For examples of how close empirical analysis can yield more complex and disturbing conclusions, see Henry Turner, *Big Business and the Rise of Hitler* (New York: Oxford University Press, 1985); Michael Geyer, "Zum Einfluss der nationalsozialistischen Rüstungspolitik auf das Ruhrgebiet," *Rheinische Vierteljahrsblätter*, v. 45 (1981), especially pp. 207, 214–219; and Hayes, *Industry and Ideology*, passim.

13. See Raul Hilberg, *The Destruction of the European Jews*, rev. ed. (New York: Holmes & Meier, 1985), v. 1, pp. 94–144, for an overview of the process of economic persecution in Germany during the 1930s.

14. On the demographic and economic distribution of German Jews, see Donald Niewyk, *The Jews in Weimar Germany* (Baton Rouge: Louisiana State University Press, 1980), pp. 13–20, 41–42; Monika Richarz (ed.), *Jüdisches Leben in Deutschland*, v. 3: *Selbstzeugnisse zur Sozialgeschichte 1918–1945* (Stuttgart: Deutsche Verlags-Anstalt, 1982), pp. 14–25; Genschel, *Verdrängung*, pp. 19–31, 274–287; Barkai, *Vom Boykott zur "Entjudung,"* pp. 11–18; and Sarah Gordon, *Hitler, Germans, and the "Jewish Question"* (Princeton, N.J.: Princeton University Press, 1984), pp. 9–15.

15. See Niewyk, *Jews in Weimar Germany*, p. 14; W. E. Mosse, *The German-Jewish Economic Elite, 1820–1935* (Oxford: Clarendon Press, 1989), pp. 97, 167–168; Hayes, *Industry and Ideology*, pp. 28, 55–56; Mosse, *Jews in the German Economy*, pp. 325–333; Peter de Mendelssohn, *Zeitungsstadt Berlin* (Frankfurt: Ullstein, 1982), pp. 398–402, 463, 499–500; and Modris Eksteins, *The Limits of Reason* (London: Oxford University Press, 1975), pp. 105–106, 287–288, 301–303.

16. See Barkai, *Vom Boykott zur "Entjudung,"* pp. 19–21; Wolfgang Benz (ed.), *Die Juden in Deutschland 1933–1945* (Munich: C. H. Beck, 1989), pp. 304–305.

17. See Mosse, *Jews in the Gemran Economy*, pp. 373–374. Intermarriage is one of the underresearched aspects of German Jewish history. The available data concerning the offspring of such marriages suggest that they were less frequent than often thought at the time and since; see Benz, *Juden in Deutschland 1933–1945*, pp. 686–687; and Jeremy Noakes, "Nazi Policy Toward German-Jewish 'Mischlinge,'" *Leo Baeck Institute Yearbook*, v. 34 (1989), pp. 291–292. With regard to intermarriage at upper socioeconomic levels, see Mosse, *German-Jewish Economic Elite*, pp. 161–185, 338, 339, 342. For contemporary attempts to establish the number of mixed marriages and their descendants, see Ernst Kahn, "Wieviel 'Nichtarier' gibt es in Deutschland?" *Jüdische Rundschau*, v. 38, no. 59 (25 July 1933), the reply by Dr. Ludwig Herz in no. 63 (8 August 1933), and the report of the study by Dr. H. Göllner of the Reichsgesundheitsamt, in v. 40, no. 93 (19 November 1935), p. 4.

18. For example, see Hayes, "Fritz Roessler and Nazism," p. 73; Paul Kleinewefers, *Jahrgang 1905* (Stuttgart: Seewald, 1984), p. 69.

19. Mosse, *Jews in the German Economy*, p. 343; Turner, *Big Business and the Rise of Hitler*, pp. 90–91, 94.

20. Turner, *Big Business and the Rise of Hitler*, pp. 129–131; Hayes, *Industry and Ideology*, pp. 83–84.
21. Turner, *Big Business and the Rise of Hitler*, pp. 469–470, note 99.
22. Ibid., p. 337; Reinhard Neebe, *Grossindustrie, Staat and NSDAP 1930–1933* (Göttingen: Vandenhoeck & Ruprecht, 1981), p. 194; Hayes, *Industry and Ideology*, p. 92; Leonard Baker, *Days of Sorrow and Pain* (New York: Oxford University Press, 1978), p. 249; and Hans Schäffer, "Meine Zusammenarbeit mit Carl Melchior," in *C. Melchior, Ein Buch des Gedenkens und der Freundschaft* (Tübingen: Mohr, 1967), p. 103.
23. Willi A. Boelcke, *Die deutsche Wirtschaft 1930–1945* (Düsseldorf: Droste, 1983), pp. 118–120, 124–128. For a specific instance of Schmitt's intervention to protect Jews, see Yad Vashem Archive (hereafter YVA), R-4/27, Wirtschaftsarchiv Baden-Württemberg, Schmitt to Deutsche Industrie-und Handelstag, Berlin, 8 September 1933. For examples of Schacht's stance, see Michael Kater, "Everyday Anti-Semitism in Prewar Nazi Germany: The Popular Bases," *Yad Vashem Studies*, v. 16 (1984), pp. 153–154; Uwe Dietrich Adam, "Wie spontan war der Pogrom?" in Walter H. Pehle (ed.), *Der Judenpogrom 1938* (Frankfurt: Fischer Taschenbuch Verlag, 1988), p. 86; YVA, R-4/27, Schacht to Reichwirtschaftskammer Berlin, 9 August 1935; NWSM, Gauleitung Westfalen-Süd, Gauwirtschaftsberater, Nr. 139, Schacht's Schnellbrief of 28 December 1935; and BAP, 25.01/6789, "Auswirkungen der Massnahmen zur Regelung der Judenfrage auf die Wirtschaft 1936," especially the memo by the Volkswirtschaftliche Abteilung of the Reichsbank, 2 January 1936, Bl. 181–190.
24. See Siemens-Archiv, SAA 4/Lf676, the letter prepared for circulation by Carl-Friedrich von Siemens in the aftermath of the boycott, dated 8 April 1933, and his exchange of letters with Fritz Kranefuss, 28 November–4 December 1933; on Bücher and Bosch, see the letters collected in BASF-Archiv, Sig. W1, as well as Hayes, *Industry and Ideology*, pp. 93–94. For other gestures of solidarity with Jewish entrepreneurs, see Mosse, *Jews in the German Economy*, pp. 376–377.
25. See BASF-Archiv, Sig. W1, Max Warburg to Carl Bosch, 18 May 1933, listing the members of the group, and the first draft of its report, 19 June [1933]; Siemens-Archiv, SAA 4/Lf676, the second draft, with a cover letter from Rudolf Löb to C.-F. von Siemens, 5 August 1933, from which the quoted words come; and Leo Baeck Institute Archive (hereafter LBIA), New York, Tagebuch Hans Schäffers, 1933, pp. 44, 47–49, 65–67, as well as AR 7177, Box IA, Schäffer to Melchior, 20 August 1933. Avraham Barkai, "Max Warburg im Jahre 1933. Missglückte Versuche zur Milderung der Judenverfolgung," in Peter Freimark, Alice, Jankowski, and Ina S. Lorenz (eds.), *Juden in Deutschland. Emanzipation, Integration, Verfolgung and Vernichtung* (Hamburg: H. Christians Verlag, 1991), pp. 390–405, provides a generally accurate account of this episode but requires a few amendments based on the eyewitness information in Schäffer's diary, which Barkai did not consult. The participating executives convened twice, not once—in May as well as June 1933; Carl Bosch did attend the second meeting; both Albert Vögler and Kurt Schmitt were kept apprised of what was going on; and while von Siemens's comments at the meetings fit Barkai's suppositions about the self-interested caution of the executives, those of Krupp and Bosch indicate a determination to keep pressing the government.
26. See Niewyk, *Jews in Weimar Germany*, pp. 21–24.
27. For the quoted passage, Siemens-Archiv, SAA 4/Lf676, p. 4 of the final draft enclosed with Löb to Siemens, 5 August 1933.

28. Karl A. Schleunes, *The Twisted Road to Auschwitz* (Urbana: University of Illinois Press, 1970), p. 112.

29. Boelcke, *Deutsche Wirtschaft*, pp. 118–120. On the enforcement of these and related policies, see YVA, R-4/27, letters from the Treuhänder der Arbeit, Karlsruhe, 1 and 12 June 1934.

30. Schleunes, *Twisted Road to Auschwitz*, p. 114.

31. Ullstein, for example, was forced to part with 60 million marks worth of stock for one-fifth that amount; see Avraham Barkai, "Die deutschen Unternehmer und die Judenpolitik im 'Dritten Reich,'" *Geschichte und Gesselschaft*, v. 15 (1989), p. 235 (also in English as "German Entrepreneurs and Jewish Policy in the Third Reich," *Yad Vashem Studies*, v. 21 [1991], pp. 126–153). The Hermann and Leonard Tietz department store chains became, respectively, the Hertie and Kaufhof AGs, which are still ubiquitous in Germany.

32. For example, the Waffenfabrik Simson, Suhl; see Genschel, *Verdrängung*, pp. 99–104.

33. Adolf Hitler, *Mein Kampf*, trans. by Ralph Manheim (Boston: Houghton Mifflin, 1943), pp. 308–326.

34. See Uwe Dietrich Adam, *Judenpolitik im Dritten Reich* (Königstein i.T.: ADTV, 1979), p. 31; and Schleunes, *Twisted Road to Auschwitz*, p. 70. Similarly, the draft "Law for the Regulation of the Position of Jews," which was prepared by an interministerial working committee in April 1933, probably at Göring's behest, and which anticipated much of what the regime enacted piecemeal over the next five years, proposed to exclude Jews from decisive positions in the media and finance and to subject them to quotas in the professions but contemplated no other economic restrictions; see Adam, *Judenpolitik*, pp. 35–37.

35. Schleunes, *Twisted Road to Auschwitz*, pp. 143–146, 148, 157; Barkai, *From Boycott to Annihilation*, chapters 2–3; Barkai, "Unternehmer und Judenpolitik," p. 232.

36. In general, see Genschel, *Verdrängung*, pp. 73–76. On the dismissals at Karstadt, Mosse, and Osram, see LBIA, AR 7177, Hans Schäffer papers, Box 1A, "Einzel-fälle von Massnahmen gegen jüdische Angestellte." On Daimler-Benz, see Hans Pohl et al. (eds.), *Die Daimler-Benz AG in den Jahren 1933 bis 1945* (Wiesbaden: Steiner, 1986), pp. 42–45. On the banks, whose troubles during the depression already had resulted in considerable reductions in the number of Jews among the leading personnel, see Mosse, *Jews in the German Economy*, pp. 331–333, 374–375; and Hamburger Stiftung, *Dresdner Bank*, pp. xxvii, xxxii–xxxiii, xxxiv, 86. On the Adlerwerke's repeated pleas for tariff protection and similar forms of government help, see the Geschäftsberichte in Stadtarchiv Frankfurt, Amtsgericht, Sig. 11195, 11205, 11220. On the Aryanization of that firm's management, see Sig. 11220, the notarized copy of the protocol of the stockholders' meeting of 31 July 1934; and Hayes, *Industry and Ideology*, p. 104. Also on Osram's purge, see LAB(STA), Rep. 231/424, Bekanntmachung 33/19, 19 May 1933 (concerning departing directors), and Rep. 231/449, Memo to Dr. Meyer, 9 June 1933, listing twenty-six employees dismissed "because of non-Aryan descent."

37. See Wessel, *100 Jahre Mannesmann*, pp. 210, 212, and the data in the Geschäftsberichte for Mannesmann AG for the years 1936–1940, which I have followed here.

38. On IG Farben, see Hayes, *Industry and Ideology*, p. 127; and Jens Heine, *Verstand und Schicksal* (Weinheim: VCH Verlagsgesellschaft, 1990), which provides brief biographical sketches of all of Farben's board members and shows that of the nine Jews on the supervisory board as of 1933, four resigned during the first year of Nazi rule and five remained.

See also Mosse, *Jews in the German Economy,* pp. 377–379, which also notes that among the 108 board seats held by the partners of M. M. Warburg & Co., eighteen were vacated during 1933, ten during the next two years, and the remaining eighty only after 1936.

39. On Ritscher, see Hamburger Stiftung, *Dresdner Bank,* p. xxxii; on Feldmühle, *Das Schwarze Korps,* no. 25 (23 June 1938).

40. Hayes, *Industry and Ideology,* p. 93. Such transfers hardly amounted, of course, to defiance of government policy. Indeed, in cases of Jewish employees with foreign citizenship, the Party favored such transfers; see LAB(STA), Rep. 231/449, Knauer of the Reichsleitung in Munich to Osram AG, 16 June 1933.

41. See, in particular, the informative contribution of Richard Glaser, formerly of the Commerzbank, to the Ball-Kaduri collection of oral testimonies, YVA, O-1/196, dated 18 November 1957. On the gradual departure of the six Jewish members of Degussa's supervisory board between 1933 and 1937, see Degussa-Archiv, Biographische Unterlagen Fritz Roessler, "Zur Geschichte der Scheideanstalt 1933–1936," dated January 1937, Abschrift, p. 98. On Degussa's treatment of Jewish employees, see Hayes, "Fritz Roessler and Nazism," p. 77, concerning ones transferred abroad; and Degussa-Archiv, Sig. D3.2, Dr. Ernst Baerwind, "Auszüge aus meinen Tagebuchnotizen, 1 Juni 1925–14 März 1953," p. 54, concerning Dr. Theodor Pohl, whom the firm kept on until the end of 1938.

42. See Barkai, *Vom Boykott zur "Entjudung,"* pp. 86–87, and BAP, R25.01/6790, "Verzeichnis der jüdischen Privatbankierfirmen. Stand Ende Mai 1938," which shows that as of the end of 1935, 345 private banks in Germany were still owned by Jews, that they constituted 38 percent of all such banks and held 57 percent of their capital, and that the five largest single private banks in the country at the time, with 29 percent of the stock capital, were all still Jewish owned. A few major industrialists apparently made a point of continuing to do business with "non-Aryan" banks into the mid-1930s. Among them was Paul Reusch, according to A. J. Sherman, "A Jewish Bank During the Schacht Era: M. M. Warburg & Co., 1933–1938," in Arnold Paucker et al. (eds.), *Die Juden im nationalsozialistischen Deutschland 1933–1943* (Tübingen: J.C.B. Mohr, 1986), pp. 170–171. Concerning the conduct of heavy industry in general, see the report of a former official at the Gebr. Arnhold Bank in Berlin that such customers remained loyal for several years and "left only under duress"; YVA, O-1/137, A. P. Michaelis, "Die jüdischen Banken in Deutschland von 1933 bis 1938," dated January 1957.

43. See Benz, *Juden in Deutschland,* pp. 306–307; and, on the "good cop/bad cop" method frequently applied in the shakedowns, Hermann Göring to Reinhard Heydrich, 27 July 1935, in Pätzold, *Verfolgung,* Doc. 56, p. 98.

44. On the motives behind acquisitions in this period, see Degussa-Archiv, Roessler's "Zur Geschichte der Scheideanstalt," Abschrift, pp. 121–122.

45. See Hayes, "Fritz Roessler and Nazism," pp. 76–78, and the documents cited there, as well as Bayer-Archiv, Sig. 6/14, IG Firmen Beteiligungen, Chemiewerk Homburg. Degussa (in partnership with IG Farben) paid 784 percent of the face value of Bad Homburg's stock (1.9 million marks, two-thirds in Swiss francs) in September 1933, 133 percent of Degea's (9 million marks) between mid-1933 and mid-1934, and 187 percent of Marquart's (1.5 million marks) in August 1936. Of course, under normal conditions the nominal value of the stock would have understated its value on the exchanges, and Fritz Roessler thought that of the Degea shares was closer to 14 million marks; see Degussa-Archiv, Roessler's "Zur Geschichte der Scheideanstalt," pp. 123–124. But in 1933–1934, at the end of the de-

pression, the two values were closer than usual. Both in this period and later, purchases of firms organized as partnerships (GmbH or KG) were effected in a lump sum, not through the acquisition of stock. As a rough rule of thumb in assessing the fairness of prices paid for such firms, the procedure followed by both the Nazi regime (in calculating whether a buyer owed the state an "equalization payment" as a result of having bought a firm at below value) and by at least one restitution proceeding after the war, was to compute the median between (1) the sum of the average profits of the firm over the preceding three years, capitalized at an assumed interest rate (the *Ertragswert*), either before or after deduction of the annual wage paid to the owner; and (2) the worth of buildings, inventory, and supplies on hand (the *Substanzwert*). See Genschel, *Verdrängung*, p. 98, note 7; and LAB(STA), Rep. 200-02/163/55-53, Zetsche of the Industrie- und Handeslkammer Berlin to Polizeipräsidenten Berlin, 22 November 1941.

46. See Pätzold, *Verfolgung*, excerpt from an article in the *Kölnische Zeitung*, 13 October 1935, Doc. 73, pp. 116–117, on the purchases; on the managers, see the 1935 and 1936 editions of the *Adressbuch der Direktoren und Aufsichtsräte*, and *Berliner Börsen-Zeitung*, no. 3 (3 January 1936) and no. 24 (15 January 1936), p. 10. I have not yet been able to establish the buyers and terms for the two other significant Aryanizations referred to in the *Kölnische Zeitung* article, those of Orenstein & Koppel AG of Berlin and of the Gebrüder Ritter AG, or the price paid for the takeover of the Frankfurter Eisengrosshandlung Hirsch & Co. by a newly founded firm owned by the Vereinigte Stahlwerke, mentioned in the *Jüdische Rundschau*, v. 41, no. 9 (21 January 1936), p. 6, and the *Berliner Börsen-Zeitung*, no. 43 (26 January 1936), p. 18.

47. An ironic case in point is provided by the behavior of a big industrialist who was willing to engage in Aryanization relatively early, namely, Friedrich Flick. In early 1937 he backed away from his first attempt to acquire the Hochofenwerk Lübeck when he could not obtain a majority of its stock by normal commercial means after more than a year of effort. See Genschel, *Verdrängung*, pp. 221–223.

48. For one contemporary's view that November 1937 marked a turning point in the situation of his own substantial textile firm, see Benz, *Juden in Deutschland*, pp. 308–312.

49. See Schleunes, *Twisted Road to Auschwitz*, p. 218; Boelcke, *Deutsche Wirtschaft*, p. 211; Hayes, *Industry and Ideology*, pp. 170, 196; Adam, *Judenpolitik*, pp. 176–177.

50. Hitler, *Mein Kampf*, p. 679. Compare Genschel's often overlooked comment that the Nazis' renewed attention to Jewish economic influence resulted "not from the now considerably strengthened drive for autarky, but from the change of leadership in the economy and from the fact of acute preparation for war. If the Nazi image of Jewish defeatism in the First World War was taken seriously—which one has to assume for Hitler and many of his ideological followers—then the conclusion was inevitable that Jews had to be excluded from the German war economy"; *Verdrängung*, p. 141.

51. For a recent appreciation of this argument, see Herbert A. Strauss, "The Drive for War and the Pogroms of November 1938: Testing Explanatory Models," *Leo Baeck Institute Yearbook*, v. 35 (1990), pp. 267–278, especially the concluding section. I would emphasize, however, that the pogrom of 1938 was the dramatic culmination, not the beginning, of an interacting shift in policies that dated from November 1937. It is worth recalling in this connection that this month also saw the visit to Berlin of Lord Halifax, the British foreign secretary, whose outline of the concessions his government was prepared to make to Germany in Eastern Europe quite probably raised Hitler's estimate of what he could get away with.

52. See Hayes, *Industry and Ideology,* p. 170.

53. See Treue, *Das Schicksal des Bankhauses Sal. Oppenheim jr. & Cie,* esp. pp. 9–18; Michael Stürmer, Gabrielle Teichmann, and Wilhelm Treue, *Wägen und Wagen* (Munich: Piper, 1989), pp. 365–390; Rosenbaum and Sherman, *M. M. Warburg,* pp. 157–169; Fuchs, *Ein Konzern;* and Konrad Fuchs, "Zur Geschichte des Warenhaus-Konzerns I. Shocken Söhne unter besonderer Berücksichtigung der Jahre seit 1933," *Zeitschrift für Unternehmensgeschichte,* v. 33 (1988), pp. 232–252.

54. See Achinger, *Richard Merton;* Hayes, *Industry and Ideology,* pp. 201–202; and the articles collected in Stadtarchiv Frankfurt, Sig. S2/3223; "Wie Avieny Generaldirektor wurde," *Frankfurter Rundschau,* 11 August 1949, "Es war wie bei einem Kartenspiel," *Frankfurter Rundschau,* 13 August 1949, and "Die Kulissenvorgänge im Fall Avieny," *Neue Presse,* 13 August 1949.

55. However, neither Hjalmar Schacht, who was still the president of the Reichsbank, nor Finance Minister Schwerin von Krosigk ceased dissenting from the policy of rapid and forced Aryanization at knockdown prices, albeit on pragmatic political and economic grounds; see Genschel, *Verdrängung,* pp. 169–172.

56. See Gerhard Mollin, *Montankonzerne und "Drittes Reich"* (Göttingen: Vandenhoeck und Ruprecht, 1988), pp. 153, 184, 256; Hamburger Stiftung, *Dresdner Bank,* pp. xlii–xliv, 76–84; and Benz, *Juden in Deutschland,* pp. 554–560. Another financial incentive for the banks was the chance to acquire the continuing business of firms by providing loans to would-be Aryanizers. When the Deutsche Bank facilitated the takeover of the Norddeutsche Trikotwerke and its transformation into the Venus-Werke, its proceeds from that firm's business rose almost fivefold from 2,783 reichsmarks in the second half of 1938 to 12,364 in the first half of 1939; see SAD, Firmenbestand 222, Altbanken Chemnitz, A7/21/46-47, account reports of 1 March and 21 August 1939. Concerning the ways banks profited from takeovers, see Hilberg, *Destruction,* v. 1, p. 100.

57. Genschel, *Verdrängung,* pp. 146–147; and GLAK, Abt. 505-384, concerning the takeover of L. J. Ettlinger KG of Karlsruhe by the sales subsidiary of Gebr. Stumm GmbH.

58. Both of Flick's major takeovers, those of the Hochofenwerk Lübeck and of the Petschek brown coalfields, were urged on him in November 1937 by Göring's associates, then developed into excellent illustrations of the symbiotic relationship between his ambitions and those of the *Reichsmarshcall*. See United States National Archives (hereafter USNA), RG238/T301, NI-10123, Memo by Steinbrinck on conference with Hermann Göring, 16.XI.37, and NI-10124, Memo by Steinbrinck on conference with Wilhelm Keppler, 20.XI.37. It is also clear that Flick initially sought to retain the Jewish managers of Rawack & Grunfeld (NI-2627, Memo by Steinbrinck on conference with Oldewage, 21.XII.37), and to leave the Hahn family in possession of a minority of its shares in the Hochofen Lübeck (NI-1845, Agreement between Flick and Hahn representatives, 10.XII.37, and NI-4381, Memo by Steinbrinck on conference with Keppler, 10.II.38). Flick's *Arisierungspolitik* has yet to receive definitive treatment in the academic literature. Valuable but imperfect accounts are in Mollin, *Montankonzerne,* pp. 184–187, Hilberg, *Destruction,* v. 1, pp. 115–122, and Genschel, *Verdrängung,* pp. 216–236.

59. Hans Mommsen, "Zur Verschränkung traditioneller und faschistischer Führungsgruppen in Deutschland beim Übergang von der Bewegungs- zur Systemphase," in W. Schieder (ed.), *Faschismus als soziale Bewegung* (Hamburg: Hoffman und Campe, 1976), p. 176.

60. Genschel, *Verdrängung,* pp. 173–176. On the "Beutezug" in Austria during these months, see ibid., pp. 160–166, and Witek, "'Arisierungen,'" pp. 209–210.

61. Genschel, *Verdrängung,* pp. 188–189. The decree did not put an end to worries about legality, as indicated by Friedrich Flick's repeated efforts over the next few years to create the appearance of having been compelled to take over the, in effect, confiscated holdings of Ignaz Petschek.

62. On the procedural preconditions for the approval of an Aryanization, including the need for sanction from the local NSDAP and Deutsche Arbeiter Front (DAF), see Genschel, *Verdrängung,* pp. 152–160.

63. See Genschel, *Verdrängung,* pp. 197–198, as well as his comment that "whoever among the 'Aryans' dared execute the politically ordained solution under humane and tolerably fair conditions for the Jewish partner had to do so as inconspicuously as possible and be prepared to be upbraided by the Party or the press as a 'Jew lover' and treated accordingly"; p. 201. On the NSDAP's determination to prevent Aryanization from increasing concentration in the German economy or benefiting big business, see Fritz Nonnenbruch, "Die jüdische Geschaftsverkaufe," *Völkischer Beobachter,* no. 296 (20 October 1935), and "Die Ausschaltung der Juden," *Die deutsche Volkswirtschaft,* no. 33 (21 November 1938). On the prevailing parameters in setting prices, see note 44 above.

64. To be sure, largely because Göring's Four-Year Plan Office actually ended up with a profit in dollars on the transaction; see USNA, RG238/T301, NI-3306, Wohltat's summary of the J. Petschek deal, 16 December 1938. For another instance of official flexibility, see GLAK, Abt. 505/1489, on the takeover of the Rhenania Schiffahrts- und Spedition GmbH by the Haniel concern.

65. See YVA, R-4/32, Schlussbericht of Württemberg Industrie und Handels-, Beratungs- und Vermittlungszentrale GmbH, Stuttgart, 11 October 1938. For a similar instance, LBIA, AR6160, Collection Henry Ebert, Gauleitung Hessen-Nassau to Ludwig and Arthur Ebert, 3 August 1938.

66. Instructive in this connection is GLAK, Abt. 505/958, which documents the reluctant decision of Brown Boveri & Cie to take over the Kronstein Elektra-Lack GmbH, lest indispensable supplies be interrupted or terminated.

67. On the means by which the regime collected the proceeds and the total amounts thus confiscated, see Hilberg, *Destruction,* v. 1, pp. 132–138.

68. The best starting points for such a tally are two articles by Günter Keiser, "Der jüngste Konzentrationsprozess," and "Die Konzernbewegung 1936 bis 1939," *Die Wirtschaftskurve,* v. 19 (1939), pp. 136–156, 214–234. Better known, however, are the instances when ambitious young entrepreneurs exploited Aryanization to piece together the basis for new large firms out of many small ones, for example, the Horten department store chain and the Neckarmann catalog and travel business.

69. See USNA, RG242/T83 and T253.

70. On Degussa's role in processing precious metals taken from Jews, see YVA, R-4/26, Krüger of the Reich Economics Ministry to Kommunale Pfandleihanstalten, 24 August 1939; LBIA, AR6305, Ernst Wertheimer family file, two letters from the Stadt. Pfandleihanstalt Stuttgart AG to Hans Strauss, 1 June 1948; and Meyer to Degner, 2 April 1943, enclosing Lieferschein Nr. 116, and Guay to Oberbürgermeister, 1 April 1944, in *Dokumenty i materialy,* v. 3: *Getto Lodzkie* (Warsaw: Centralia Zydowska Komisja Historyczna, 1946), pp. 156–157, 163. See also Karl Heinz Roth, "Ein Spezialunternehmen für Verbrennungskreisläufe: Konzernskizze Degussa," *1999,* v. 3 (1988), pp. 27–30, 35–36.

71. For the figures that serve as the basis for this calculation, see Hayes, *Industry and Ideology*, p. 362.

72. See USNA, RG238/T301, NI-382, undated affidavit by Oswald Pohl, head of the SS Economic Administration Main Office. To date, the best point of access to the vexed question of which firms employed how many workers is the material collected for postwar restitution claims, YVA, M-32, Compensation Treuhandstelle, which includes tallies for such entities as Rheinmetall, Krupp, AEG-Telefunken, IG Farben, Siemens, Brabag, Heinkel, Mannesmann, Junkers, and Bochumer Verein, as well as individual documents referring to concentration camp laborers sent to such installations as Degussa's lampblack factory at Gleiwitz (v. 170). See also Bernard P. Bellon, *Mercedes in Peace and War* (New York: Columbia University Press, 1990); Zofka, "Allach-Sklaven für BMW," pp. 68–78; John Gillingham, *Business and Politics in the Third Reich* (New York: Columbia University Press, 1985), p. 125 (on the Ruhr coal industry); and Florian Freund, *Arbeitslager Zement* (Vienna: Verlag für Gesellschaftskritik, 1989). According to one estimate, some 700 German firms employed camp inmates at one time or another; see Barkai, "German Entrepreneurs and Jewish Policy," p. 146, note 44.

73. See Hayes, *Industry and Ideology*, pp. 359–360, on the death toll and the payment of 20 million marks in "wages" to the SS.

74. See Dietmar Petzina, *Die deutsche Wirtschaft in der Zwischenkriegszeit* (Wiesbaden: Steiner, 1976), p. 153; and Richard Overy, "'Blitzkriegwirtschaft'? Finanzpolitik, Lebensstandard und Arbeitseinsatz in Deutschland 1939–1941," *Vierteljahrshefte für zeitgeschichte*, v. 36 (1988), pp. 425–428.

75. Compare the argument in Sybil Milton, "The Context of the Holocaust," *German Studies Review*, v. 13 (1990), pp. 269–283, which follows that of much recent work emphasizing the eugenics policies that served as important precursors to the separation then murder of Jews, for example, Claudia Koonz, "Genocide and Eugenics: The Language of Power," in Peter Hayes (ed.), *Lessons and Legacies: The Meaning of the Holocaust in a Changing World* (Evanston, Ill.: Northwestern University Press, 1991), pp. 155–177.

76. See Barkai, "Unternehmer und Judenpolitik," pp. 246–247; Barkai, "Entrepreneurs and Jewish Policy," pp. 152–153.

77. See Peter Gay, *Freud, Jews, and Other Germans* (New York: Oxford University Press, 1978), pp. 13–14.

78. See Michael Marrus, "The Theory and Practice of Anti-Semitism," *Commentary*, vol. 72, no. 2 (August 1982), pp. 38–42.

79. Ian Kershaw, *Popular Opinion and Political Dissent in the Third Reich* (Oxford: Clarendon Press, 1983), p. 277.

4

Beyond Warsaw and Łódź: Perpetrating the Holocaust in Poland

Christopher R. Browning

In mid-March 1942 Nazi Germany stood at the threshold of a momentous assault on Polish Jewry. To fully understand the magnitude of what would transpire in the next eleven months, until mid-February 1943, I invite you to consider the following hypothetical scenarios. If the war had ended in June 1941, Nazi Germany would have been remembered above all for the systematic mass murder of 70,000 to 80,000 mentally ill in the gas chambers of the euthanasia institutes and for the reign of terror in Poland. Given the murder of Polish intelligentsia, the expulsion of hundreds of thousands of Poles eastward to "Germanize" the incorporated territories, and the shipment of hundreds of thousands of other Poles westward for forced labor in Germany, Jewish suffering—for all its deprivations, humiliations, and loss of life—would not have stood out as singular or exceptional from the fate of the Poles. Again hypothetically, if the war had ended in March 1942, despite the first sweep of the *Einsatzgruppen* and their half million Jewish victims,[1] even more prominent would have been the 2 million Russian POWs who perished in the first nine months of the Russian campaign and the nearly 1 million Russian civilians who starved in Leningrad, a fate that Hitler had decreed for them even if the city had surrendered. In spring 1942 the War of Destruction in Russia, not the Holocaust, was still the most infamous historical "achievement" of the Nazi regime.

By mid-March 1942 some 20 to 25 percent of all victims of the Holocaust had already perished. Outside of Russia and parts of Yugoslavia and Romania, however, European Jewry was still relatively intact. But in the next eleven months, over 50 percent of all Holocaust victims died. The Jewish communities of Germany, Austria, Czechoslovakia, and Yugoslavia were shattered; those of France, the Netherlands, and Belgium were gravely wounded.

Nowhere in Europe, however, was this terrible eleven-month Nazi blitzkrieg against the Jews more devastating than in Poland. In the eastern regions, occupied by the Soviet Union in 1939, killing had already begun when the German invasion swept through in summer 1941. Deportation to killing centers had commenced in the so-called incorporated territory of the Warthegau in December 1941, but in the two (and briefly three) gas vans at Chelmno, the killing pace was slow. The Warthegau Jewish communities were being bled to death gradually.

What started in mid-March 1942 with the assault on the ghetto of Lublin and ended in mid-February 1943 with the total destruction of Grodno and the decimation of Bialystok, therefore, went well beyond the earlier killing. In this eleven-month period, the German occupiers eliminated one Jewish community in Poland after another. Against their divided and isolated victims, the Germans continually chose the time and place to give unequal battle, concentrated their forces to gain sufficient local domination, and carried out their ghetto-clearing operations with unparalleled violence and brutality. When the onslaught had passed, most of the Jewish communities of Poland had been entirely destroyed. In greatly reduced remnant ghettos or in SS-controlled labor camps, about half a million Polish Jews[2] lived under a brief reprieve. Others clung to an increasingly precarious existence in hiding. But the vast bulk of Polish Jewry was dead.

Before the murder campaign began, less than one-fifth of Polish Jewry was already concentrated in the ghettos of Łódź and Warsaw. The rest, most though not all ghettoized, lived in more than 700 small cities and towns throughout Poland,[3] where they usually constituted at least 30 percent but in some towns were as much as 80 to 90 percent of the population. To carry out a massacre of the widespread Jewish populations beyond Warsaw and Łódź, the Nazi killers faced many problems: the coordination and timing of the murder campaign had to be organized; the logistical problems of transport, killing capacity, and body disposal had to be overcome; and sufficient manpower for the roundups had to be mobilized. How did the Nazis solve these problems of organization, logistics, and manpower?

First let us consider the interrelated problems of coordination, timing, and logistics. In the western portions of prewar Poland, the incorporated territories of the Warthegau and East Upper Silesia came under special jurisdiction. Their Jews were sent to the extermination camps at Chelmno and Auschwitz-Birkenau. In the east, prewar Polish territories also remained attached to the Reich commissariats for administering occupied Soviet territory, and their Jews—like those of the rest of German-occupied Russia—were for the most part murdered by firing squad on the spot.

Between these two border regions, nearly 2 million Polish Jews resided under German control in the five districts of the General Government and in the autonomous district of Bialystok.[4] The murder of these Jews—dubbed Operation Reinhard—had been entrusted by Heinrich Himmler to the SS and police leader of the district of Lublin, Odilo Globocnik.

Globocnik was only one of five SS and police leaders in the General Government, for one was assigned to each of the districts and charged with coordinating all activities involving mixed operations of SS units within his territory. Some of the SS and police leaders operated with no more than a skeletal staff of a dozen men and seemed genuinely puzzled about their specific duties and powers. When Globocnik's counterpart in Warsaw, Arpad Wigand, complained to his immediate superior in Kraków about his uncertain jurisdiction and role, the latter replied with Himmler's dictum "that a National Socialist makes out of his position what he himself is worth."[5] In the "totalitarian anarchy" and jungle war of internal Nazi politics, no one knew how to make more out of his position than Globocnik. By fall 1943 Globocnik had built himself a huge empire with a staff of 434 men. In addition to directing Operation Reinhard, Globocnik's staff was involved in his pet project of "Germanizing" the Zamość region in southeastern Poland and also managed a large array of SS economic enterprises and labor camps that had no parallel in other districts of the General Government.

Globocnik's jurisdiction clearly extended beyond the district of Lublin, as can be seen from his building of an extermination camp at Treblinka in the neighboring district of Warsaw. However, in the chaotic administrative world of the Nazis, nothing was uniform. The role that Globocnik and his Operation Reinhard staff played varied significantly from district to district, especially in terms of providing manpower and operational expertise, depending upon what the local SS and police leaders managed to do on their own. In one area his duties could not be divided or shared, however. Only his staff could coordinate the reception at the extermination camps of transports not only from the various regions of occupied Poland but from elsewhere in Europe as well. As ghetto-clearing and deportation operations proceeded in many areas of Poland and Europe simultaneously, this task of timing was exceedingly complex.[6]

The opening phase of Operation Reinhard began on March 16 and ended on April 14. During this period only a single extermination camp at Bełżec was as yet in operation. Transports arrived there from the two districts of Lublin and Galicia. Very quickly the camp's limited capacity was overtaxed. Body disposal was one problem. When Franz Stangl visited the Bełżec camp for the first time, he was greeted with the horrifying scene of a mass grave that had been overfilled. In the course of decomposition, fluids and even bodies had been pressed up and out, overflowing the surrounding area.[7] Gas chamber capacity was a second problem. A single wooden structure contained three small gas chambers, but they did not all function properly. Frequently, killing was carried out in only one or two at a time.[8] Thus, beginning in mid-April, the old wooden gas chamber structure was demolished, and for five weeks Bełżec received no transports while a new, larger stone building with six gas chambers was constructed on the same site.[9]

The deportation program therefore came to a complete halt until a second camp at Sobibor opened on May 3. It initially received deportations from the district of Lublin. When Bełżec opened once again in late May with enlarged facilities, it received the first transports from the district of Kraków. This wave of deportations ended on June 19 with a temporary ban on the use of scarce train capacity for all Jewish transports in the General Government.[10]

The transportation bottleneck was aggravated by several other factors. First, the railway line serving the Sobibor camp was in need of extensive repairs. The line was to be shut down, leaving Sobibor virtually inaccessible until October. Second, throughout these months the coordinators of Operation Reinhard in Lublin faced yet another complication. As they cleared the Lublin district, new trainloads of Jews poured in from Germany, Austria, the Protectorate, and Slovakia. These Jews from outside Poland were not sent directly to the extermination camps, whose reception capacity was so limited. Instead, they were at first sent to the recently vacated towns of the Lublin district before their turn came for the final trip to the gas chambers. Some of these towns, like Piaski, Izbica, and Miedzyrzec Podlaski, were appropriately designated "transit ghettos" and were in fact filled and cleared repeatedly.

At this point of crisis in early summer 1942, an obviously frustrated Himmler personally intervened, instructing his trusted aide Karl Wolff to telephone the state secretary of the Transportation Ministry, Albert Ganzenmüller, and relay the Reichsführer's urgent request for the "quickest possible elimination of these transportation stoppages."[11] He also turned up the heat on his men in Poland. On July 19 Himmler informed them that the "total purification" (*totale Bereinigung*) of the General Government was to be achieved by the end of the year.[12]

Operation Reinhard slowly resumed deportations in early July, when the transportation ban was partially lifted and twice-a-week death trains traveled from ghettos in Kraków to Bełżec. At the end of the month, trains from Galicia began arriving again in Bełżec as well. But it was above all the opening of Treblinka on July 23 that provided the killing capacity for the vastly intensified deportation pace that Himmler so urgently demanded.

Deportations from Warsaw began to arrive in Treblinka on July 23 and those from the district of Radom on August 2. Additional trains from the northern Lublin district began arriving on August 20. At this time, therefore, deportations from all five districts—Kraków and Galicia to Bełżec and Warsaw, Radom, and Lublin to Treblinka—were being undertaken simultaneously. By late August, on average some 10,500 Jews were arriving at the Treblinka camp each day.

Such a deluge of victims was simply beyond the camp's capacity. The trainloads of incoming Jews could not be gassed immediately upon arrival; waiting trains lined up and unburied bodies piled up. A livid Christian Wirth, initially the commandant at Bełżec but by now Globocnik's inspector for all three camps of Operation Reinhard, ordered Treblinka shut down for reorganization, and Franz Stangl was brought in from Sobibor as the new commandant. Unlike at Bełżec, where Wirth had torn down the old gas chamber building before constructing the new one, at Treblinka the first gas chambers remained operating while construction of a second, larger building of gas chambers was begun.[13] Thus, after one week of reorganization, Treblinka was ready to begin its killing operations once again, and deportations from Warsaw resumed. This time, however, transports from Radom and northern Lublin were accepted only when the Warsaw operation was winding down.

One by one the districts of the General Government were virtually cleared of Jews. With the exception of single transports in October and November, the deportation campaign in Kraków ended in mid-September. The Warsaw district was cleared by early October. In Lublin and Radom (again the latter with the exception of two trains in January 1943) deportations ended in mid-November. The trains from Galicia continued until mid-December. At this point Polish Jewry had been virtually destroyed except for two regions. In the incorporated territories in the west, reduced Jewish communities in Łódź and East Upper Silesia remained. In the northeast the province of Bialystok—part of prewar Poland but not attached to the General Government—the Jewish communities had suffered a wave of mass killing when the Germans passed through in summer 1941 but then were left strangely untouched by the ghetto-liquidation campaign until fall 1942.

The deportations from Bialystok constituted the final phase of the eleven-month onslaught against the Polish ghettos. In early November the inhabitants of the smaller ghettos were brought to collection centers and deported to Treblinka and Auschwitz. By mid-December only the ghettos of Grodno, Pruzana, and Bialystok and the remnants of a half dozen transit camps remained. At this point, nearly in sight of Himmler's proclaimed goal of eliminating Polish Jewry by the end of the year, the deportation program was halted by another train shortage. Himmler was informed by his higher SS and police leader in the General Government, Wilhelm Krüger, of an imminent one-month transportation ban on all nonmilitary trains beginning December 15. Krüger urged Himmler to intervene with the Armed Forces High Command (OKW) and Transportation Ministry in Berlin. Once again Himmler sent Wolff to see Ganzenmüller. This time, however, in the months before the final Stalingrad debacle and at the height of soldiers' traveling on winter leave, Wolff could achieve little. Only two more trains departed Bialystok before the end of the year; deportations then resumed after January 10.[14] Still unsatisfied, Himmler pleaded his case directly to Ganzenmüller: "If I am to settle this matter quickly, I must receive more trains. I know very well how tense the situation is for the railway and what demands are always placed on it. Nonetheless I must make this request of you: Help me and procure more trains."[15] Thereafter, Himmler got what he needed, and the Bialystok operation was complete by mid-February.

After compiling his data, Himmler's statistician, Richard Korherr, reported to the Reichsführer that in January 1943 only 300,000 Jews remained in the ghettos and work camps of the General Government, while 1,274,166 had been "dragged through" (*durchgeschleust*) the camps.[16] According to another source, between 150,000 and 170,000 Jews from the district of Bialystok had been killed between November 1942 and March 1943. Only about 35,000 to 40,000 Jews still remained alive in Bialystok.[17] Thus, the Nazi count in the General Government and Bialystok for this eleven-month period approached 1.5 million. With the ongoing killing in the incorporated territories as well, it is clear that more than half of prewar Polish Jewry had perished in this brief period.

In addition to overcoming problems of coordination and logistics to achieve this staggering death toll, Himmler and Globocnik faced problems of manpower. They were dependent upon countless local mobilizations of men and expertise to clear the ghettos, load the death trains, and track down the fleeing and hiding Jews. The personnel available for these tasks was limited. For the entire General Government, the Germans had available between 12,000 and 15,000 green-uniformed Order Police. These included small groups of metropolitan *Schutzpolizei* stationed in the major cities as well as scattered units of Gendarmerie in the countryside. In addition, each district was supposed to have a full regiment or three battalions (500 men each) of Order Police. In fact, not all districts were up to strength in this regard. The urban *Schutzpolizei* supervised an additional 12,000 to 14,000 blue-uniformed Polish police.[18] Moreover, there were 2,000 German Security Police, with 3,000 Polish employees. Finally, there was the 3,000-man *Sonderdienst* made up of alleged ethnic Germans, though apparently only 25 percent of them spoke German.[19] The *Sonderdienst* was divided into small units and attached to the head of the civilian administration in each county, or *Kreis*.

To supplement this scattered manpower pool, Globocnik created a training camp at Trawniki southeast of Lublin. There he trained Ukrainian and Baltic auxiliaries (so-called volunteers, or *Hiwis*) who had been recruited from the POW camps with the promise that they would not be used against the Red Army. Nearly 400 *Hiwis* were stationed as guards at the three death camps of Operation Reinhard. Other units were placed on guard duty in different parts of the General Government. But Globocnik also kept a standing force of two battalions or 1,000 *Hiwis* at Trawniki. From here they were dispatched as itinerant ghetto-clearers.

Globocnik and his fellow SS and police leaders cobbled together ad hoc ghetto-clearing armies in each district from the disparate manpower sources at hand. A brief look at three different ghetto-clearing actions within Operation Reinhard—Tarnow in the Kraków district, Czestochowa in the Radom district, and numerous small ghettos in the northern Lublin district—can provide a sense of how the system worked.

The SS and police leader in Kraków was Oberführer Julian Scherner. He initially operated with a minuscule staff of fewer than a dozen men, managed by his adjutant, Martin Fellenz. In preparation for his role in the Final Solution, however, Scherner doubled his staff by co-opting the Jewish desk of the Kraków Security Police. Scherner fulfilled his role quite methodically, summoning a planning conference of the district commanders of the various participating agencies in Kraków long before each projected action. After the respective responsibilities of the participants under his command—Security Police, Order Police, Waffen-SS units from the nearby Debica training base, and so on—had been fixed, the local authorities were mobilized as well. Finally, Scherner or Fellenz regularly arrived on the spot to conduct a last-minute briefing just before the action began.[20]

Tarnow, a city of some 70,000 people 60 miles east of the district capital, was in fact scheduled to be the site of the first provincial action after the initial deportations from Kraków itself in early June 1942. By this time some 40,000 Jews—many from the surrounding area—had been crowded into Tarnow and now constituted over half the total population of the city. There was no sealed ghetto, though most Jews had been forced into the northeast corner of town.[21] On hand the local authorities had limited manpower: a Security Police unit of twenty to thirty men, a *Schutzpolizei* unit of twenty, and a force of 100 Polish policemen. For the entire county of Tarnow, there was one company of Gendarmerie—about 150 additional police. The head of the civil administration also had at his disposal a unit of the ethnic German *Sonderdienst* and the local Polish labor service, or *Baudienst*.[22] To supplement this meager supply of manpower, Scherner brought in help from two outside sources: a company of Order Police from Police Battalion 307 and a company of Waffen-SS from the Debica training camp.[23] About 600 armed Germans, 100 Polish policemen, and an unknown number of Poles from the *Baudienst* faced 40,000 Jews.

Several days before the action was scheduled to begin, all Jews aspiring to a work certificate reported for a check of papers and a cursory physical examination. The check was conducted by the Tarnow Security Police and the Labor Office of the civil administration. The civil administration also put up placards around the city announcing the coming deportation and threatening with death any Poles who either helped Jews or helped themselves to Jewish property. Then on the morning of June 11, the Jews of Tarnow were assembled in the main square of town. Those with work stamps were allowed to remain. Those without stamps who could walk were marched to the train station. Those deemed too feeble for the march were put on trucks, driven to the forest, forced into a mass grave, and shot. For these shootings, the Germans in the district of Kraków invented one of the most macabre of Holocaust euphemisms: *örtliche Aussiedlung,* or "local resettlement."[24]

This procedure was repeated twice, on June 15 and 18. On these occasions, however, the ghetto-clearers dispensed with the long drive to the woods, and "local resettlement" occurred in the Jewish cemetery on the edge of town. The ban on Jewish transports temporarily brought the action to an end, though only after the Jewish population had been halved; about 10,000 Jews had been deported to Bełżec and perhaps another 10,000 shot on the spot.[25]

A now sealed ghetto held the remaining Jews of Tarnow until the Germans struck twice again in the fall. On September 12 one train took 4,000 Jews to Bełżec; on November 15 another 3,000 were taken. The remnant ghetto was renamed "forced labor camp" (ZAL) Tarnow. It survived until September 1943, when 2,000 Jews were fetched by the notorious Amon Göth for his work camp at Plaszow. The remaining 4,000 to 6,000 were destined for the gas chambers at Auschwitz, though the train cars were packed so tightly—150 people per car—that many suffocated before the train ever left the station. With six trains and three local shootings, carried out by no more than 600 armed Germans, the 40,000 Jews of Tarnow had ceased to exist.[26]

Czestochowa, a city of 130,000 on the western edge of the General Government, initially had a Jewish population of 30,000. As many Jews fled or were chased out of the neighboring incorporated territories, the Jewish population had grown to more than 50,000 by June 1942, making it the largest Jewish community in the district of Radom. The Czestochowa Jews had been ghettoized in April 1941, but the ghetto had never been sealed, since the main north-south street as well as the main commuter route to factories on the east side of town ran through its heart. However, police guarded the street exits and imposed a curfew every night.[27]

As did Scherner in Kraków, the SS and police leader in Radom, Herbert Böttcher, originally operated with a small staff. For carrying out the Final Solution, however, he co-opted men from the Radom Security Police and created a special commando—a miniature of Globocnik's Operation Reinhard staff in Lublin. He also received an itinerant ghetto-clearing unit of *Hiwis* that moved about Radom in the same way as Globocnik's battalions from Trawniki did further east.[28] Sometime in summer 1942, Böttcher and his staff visited Czestochowa, where Captain Paul Degenhardt commanded a *Schutzpolizei* unit of sixty German and 240 Polish policemen. Also stationed in Czestochowa were some 200 Order Police of Reserve Police Battalion 7. Böttcher placed Degenhardt in local command of the ghetto-clearing operation.[29]

On Yom Kippur, September 21, 1942, the *Hiwis*—already known to the local Jews as the *Judenvernichtungsbataillon* (Jew Extermination Battalion)—arrived in Czestochowa, bringing the number of German forces and Polish police to perhaps 1,000. That night the ghetto was surrounded, searchlights were set up at the ghetto's street exits, and a total curfew was imposed. The next morning clearing began in the northern section of the ghetto. All inhabitants of the designated area of the ghetto marched through the main square, where Degenhardt conducted the selection. Those with work permits were sent to one of several factories. All the rest, with no regard for keeping families together, were sent on to the railway station. From the beginning considerable force was applied, and horse-drawn carts followed the column of marching Jews to pick up the many bodies of those who had been shot along the way. A huge fifty-eight-car train was loaded and dispatched to Treblinka. It then shuttled back to Czestochowa for reloading, as the same pattern repeated itself seven or eight times. When the ghetto was empty, Degenhardt conducted a final selection on October 5 to weed out the so-called illegals from among the Jews incarcerated in the factories. In a mere two weeks, 40,000 to 45,000 Jews had been sent to Treblinka.[30]

Some 5,000 to 7,000 work Jews remained and were placed in a sealed ghetto. It, in turn, was cleared the following June, when many Jews were shot on the spot. Only some 1,000 to 2,000 Jews were still alive and working in the Czestochowa factories when they were liberated by the Red Army in January 1945.[31]

In the northern Lublin district in summer 1942, over 45,000 Jews still lived in many localities. The largest communities were in Miedzyrzec and Biala Podlaski, Łuków, Radzyń, Parczew, Końskowola, and Łomazy. Among the German occupation forces, there was a branch office of the Lublin Security Police in Radzyń with forty German police and "ethnic" helpers and an additional twenty *Hiwis*. This branch office also dispatched small units to supervise the three largest ghettos in Miedzyrzec, Łuków, and Radzyń. A platoon of forty to fifty Gendarmerie was scattered throughout the region, and a company of motorized Gendarmerie was based in nearby Puławy. The main German force in the region, however, was the newly arrived Reserve Police Battalion 101 of nearly 500 men.[32]

The assault in northern Lublin, interrupted by the June train stoppages, resumed in late summer. On August 17 one company of reserve policemen joined by forty *Hiwis* from Trawniki shot all 1,700 Jews in the village of Łomazy, which was located too far from any rail line to carry out a deportation. In two actions beginning on August 19, five platoons of reserve police (about 250 men) rounded up over 5,000 Jews in Parczew and put them on the train to Treblinka. On August 25 and 26, two companies of reserve police, the Radzyń Security Police, and a unit of *Hiwis*—some 350 to 400 men—descended upon Miedzyrzec Podlaski. In a ferocious action, over 10,000 Jews were packed onto the death trains. The Jewish Council was left to bury another 980 Jews killed during the two days of mayhem, an indication of the unfettered violence of the ghetto-clearers. These deportations from Parczew and Miedzyrzec were part of the vast influx of Jews that overwhelmed Treblinka at the end of August 1942, forcing it to close temporarily for reorganization.

Deportations did not resume from the region until October. Then in a brief six-week frenzy of activity, the task was done. Miedzyrzec and Łuków—with one company of reserve police operating at each—were turned into "transit ghettos." Repeatedly, they were stocked with Jews from the surrounding towns and villages. Repeatedly, the Jews interned there were deported to Treblinka, making way for others to take their place. Altogether, from late August to early November, more than 40,000 Jews had been dispatched to Treblinka. The one exception was Końskowola, where a minority of the Jews were selected for Globocnik's labor camps and the majority, about 1,500, were shot on the spot by one company of reserve police and the company of motorized Gendarmerie from Puławy.

Thereafter the Final Solution in the northern Lublin district entered another phase. As Treblinka was less than 100 miles to the north, word of the death camp had spread quickly. A number of Jews had fled into the forests, many hiding in well-concealed underground bunkers. These scattered survivors now had to be tracked down and killed. Frequent patrols—known simply as the *Judenjagden,* or Jew hunts—were sent out, usually on tips from a network of informers or simply from disgruntled peasants who did not want their crops raided by starving Jews. When the bunkers were found, the Jews were hauled out and shot in the neck at point-blank range. Their bodies were left to be buried by the closest Polish villagers. The Jew hunts lasted well into the winter, when snow tracks on the ground and concentrations of frozen feces made it increasingly difficult for the hunted Jews to remain undetected.

How significant a component of the Final Solution were the Jew hunts? We have no statistics from Reserve Police Battalion 101, but we do have the records of several units engaged in similar activities. Lieutenant Liebscher commanded an enlarged platoon of Gendarmerie—some 80 men—that patrolled the countryside outside Warsaw. Liebscher's daily reports from March 26 to September 21, 1943, have survived. They contain detailed descriptions of a variety of daily incidents. Initially, they always closed with the simple heading "Proceeded according to existing guidelines," followed by a date, place, and number of male and female Jews. In the end even the heading was dropped as superfluous, and only the date, place, and number of Jewish men and women were listed without further comment. The body count for this single platoon of police over a half-year period was 1,094—an average of nearly fourteen Jews killed for every policeman in the unit.[33]

We also have the records for one company of Reserve Police Battalion 133 stationed in Rawa Ruska in the neighboring district of Galicia to the east of Lublin. In six weekly reports for November 1 to December 12, 1942, this company recorded the execution of 481 Jews who had either evaded deportation through hiding or had been caught jumping from trains on the way to Bełżec.[34] Such reports hint at the desperation with which Jews sought to escape as well as the remorseless tenacity with which their killers tracked them down.

A number of conclusions can be drawn from this study. First, the destruction of the Polish ghettos and the murder of more than half of Polish Jewry in a brief eleven-month period was probably the greatest logistical achievement of the Nazis in perpetrating the Final Solution. Despite complex problems of coordination and timing, the constant shortage of rolling stock for transporting the victims, and the limited killing capacity of three primitive extermination camps, the staff of Operation Reinhard overcame every obstacle and just barely missed the end-of-year deadline that Heinrich Himmler had set in July 1942.

Second, the manpower available to the killers was quite limited. For each ghetto-clearing operation, the Nazis mobilized all the local police forces of the region—German and Polish—and then supplemented them with itinerant units of Order Police, Trawniki men, and, in the case of the Kraków district, trainees from the Waffen-SS camp at Debica. Usually fewer than 500 Germans faced ghettos of 5,000, 10,000, or even 20,000 Jews; fewer than 1,000 Germans faced ghettos of 30,000, 40,000, and 50,000 Jews.

Third, the German ghetto-clearers worked on a tight schedule. They had just a few days and a few trains to clear entire ghettos before the itinerant units were due elsewhere. One result was that, unlike in Łódź and Warsaw, where the ghetto-clearers worked through the Jewish Council and Jewish police to carry out the initial selections and roundups, in most other ghettos the Germans were too pressed for time to bother with an initial stage of leaving the dirty work to the Jewish ghetto authorities. The Jewish Council would be told to instruct the ghetto inhabitants to assemble, and Jewish police would go through the ghetto calling people into the streets, but almost immediately the Germans would lose patience and unleash their search squads to speed the process. On the very first afternoon in Tarnow, for instance, three members of the Jewish Council were shot because too few Jews had reported to the assembly area.[35]

Fourth, the Germans compensated for their compound problems of limited manpower and time pressures with a quick resort to extraordinary brutality in carrying out the ghetto-clearing operations. The victims did not merely march to the trains in passive compliance. They were driven by policemen and *Hiwis* who beat and fired on their victims at will. At Miedzyrzec Podlaski, for instance, when a ghetto-clearing squad of two police companies, a unit of *Hiwis*, and the local Security Police—about 350 or 400 men—cleared 11,000 Jews from the ghetto in two days, 980 were shot in the process.

Fifth, shooting was employed not just to drive the Jews onto the trains headed for the extermination camps. It was also employed on a massive scale for "local resettlement"—shooting on the spot when transportation was unavailable. When 20,000 Jews were taken from Tarnow in June 1942, half were taken directly to the shooting pits. In the Lublin district entire Jewish communities were destroyed by firing squad when rail lines were too distant or train cars too scarce. In short, mass execution by shooting was not unique to Soviet territory but was widely used in Poland as well.

Sixth, while at this stage the victims did not offer armed resistance in the ghettos, they did attempt to hide or flee in significant numbers. The emptied ghettos were routinely combed for Jews hiding in every conceivable spot that offered hope of concealment. For months afterward, German patrols engaged in a Jew hunt in the surrounding forests, tracking down Jews and eliminating the bunkers in which they had taken refuge. Without food and with scant help from the local population, the Jews continued to fall victim in the unequal struggle waged against them long after the last trains had departed.

Such conclusions raise another question. If the Germans were pressed for both time and manpower, and compensated for both shortcomings through immediate resort to extraordinary brutality, what kind of men were these "howling raiders" (to borrow a phrase from Raul Hilberg)[36] who descended upon the ghettos in such a bestial manner? To answer this question, let us look more closely at one unit we have already encountered in the district of Lublin—the nearly 500 men of Reserve Police Battalion 101.[37] The rank and file of this unit were for the most part middle-aged conscripts from the city of Hamburg, by reputation one of the least nazified cities in Germany. Averaging thirty-nine years of age, they had been drafted into the Order Police because the Wehrmacht considered them too old to be of use for frontline service. They were also old enough, therefore, to remember the values and norms of the pre-Nazi era. Over 60 percent were of working-class background—a social group noted far more for supporting the Socialists and

Communists than the Nazis before 1933. Dockworkers, truckdrivers, warehouse workers, seamen, waiters, construction workers, and machine operators were most prominent. About 35 percent were lower-middle-class white-collar workers, mostly lower-echelon office and sales personnel. Almost none of the rank and file had remained in school beyond the age of fourteen or fifteen. About 25 percent were Nazi Party members, most having joined since the reopening of the Party to new membership in 1937. Three-quarters of the men had no party affiliation at all.

The noncommissioned officers were men who had either sought a permanent career in the police or joined the police before 1939 to avoid military service. Their average age was younger—thirty-three and a half years old. Given the career goals of most of the NCOs, it is not surprising that about two-thirds were Party members. The battalion had seven reserve lieutenants. They were middle-aged conscripts who, because of their better education or middle-class background, had been sent to officer training. Five of the seven were Party members; none was in the SS. The youngest men in the battalion were two SS captains in their late twenties who had been shunted into a slow-track career in the Order Police. The battalion was commanded by Major Wilhelm Trapp, a fifty-three-year-old World War I veteran and recipient of the Iron Cross who had worked his way up through the ranks. Though despised by the two SS captains, he was beloved by his men, who called him "Papa Trapp."

Given the geographical origin, age, and social background of its men, Reserve Police Battalion 101 was anything but an elite unit specially selected for its potential to become hard-core Nazi killers. Furthermore, it was sent to Poland without the slightest warning of, much less training for, the primary task it was to perform. Indeed, Major Trapp did not learn of the battalion's first killing assignment until two days before the action; his officers were given one day's notice. Trapp did not inform his men until the very last moment, when they reached the village of Józefów in the southern Lublin district at daybreak on July 13, 1942. With tears running down his cheeks and his voice choking, Trapp visibly fought to control himself as he spoke. The battalion, he said plaintively, had a frightfully unpleasant task that was not to his liking, but the orders came from above. If it would make their task any easier, the men should remember that in Germany the bombs were falling on women and children, in America the Jews had instigated a boycott against Germany, and in Poland the Jews supported the partisans. He then explained what the men had to do. The battalion was to round up the Jews in Józefów. The male Jews of working age were to be separated and taken off to a work camp. The remaining Jews—the women and children, the frail and the elderly—were to be shot on the spot. He closed his speech with an extraordinary offer: If any of the older men among them did not feel up to the task that lay before them, they could step out.

After some hesitation, one man stepped out. His company commander, one of the two SS captains, began to berate the man as a coward and a disgrace to his unit. But the major intervened, silenced the SS captain, and took the man under his protection. Thereafter, some ten to twelve other men likewise stepped out. Some policemen who did not take up Trapp's offer before the assembled battalion at the beginning but later found themselves assigned to the firing squads also approached their NCOs and successfully asked for a different assignment. Only the other SS captain, in charge of the firing squads, refused such requests before the killing began. After the shooting started, many more of the reserve police quickly sickened of the task and asked to be released from the firing squads as well. They were all allowed out.

The shooting lasted all day. By nightfall 1,500 Jews had been shot in the woods near Józefów. With their uniforms saturated with blood and spattered with the brains and bone fragments of the victims they had shot at point-blank range, the men returned to their barracks. They ate little and drank a lot. Even those who had been able to kill all day were embittered, shaken, and angry about what they had been asked to do. One man expressed the feelings of many in the battalion when he complained to his first sergeant, "I'd go crazy if I had to do that again."[38]

Of course, this massacre was in fact just the beginning, as the battalion moved to the northern Lublin district and carried out many mass shootings and ghetto-clearing operations in the following months. The unwritten rule of the battalion established by Major Trapp that first day in Józefów, namely, that no one should be compelled to shoot who did not feel up to it, continued in effect. If virtually all the men in the battalion had been distressed by the initial killing at Józefów, under the impact of continuous actions and with a generous supply of alcohol, most of the reserve policemen simply became accustomed to their task; some even learned to enjoy it. In fact, the battalion roughly divided into three groups: one composed of enthusiastic killers who volunteered for the chance to shoot and even laughed and joked about it afterward; a second that did not volunteer for shootings but took part in all activities of the battalion when asked; and a third composed of men who did not shoot. One reserve policeman who had conspicuously evaded shooting the first day at Józefów explained his status within the battalion and his continuing immunity from the firing squads: "For these actions the officers took 'men' with them, and in their eyes I was no 'man.' Also other comrades who displayed my attitude and my behavior remained spared from such actions," he noted.[39] Such nonshooters were clearly the smallest of the three groups, however, constituting between 10 and 20 percent of the battalion.

The eleven-month assault on the Polish ghettos coincided with the most crucial stage of the war, from the beginning of Germany's second offensive in Russia to its disastrous defeat at Stalingrad. It should not surprise us to learn that during such a crucial period when Germany's military fate hung in the balance, Globocnik had been given the task of destroying Polish Jewry but no additional manpower to do the job. He had no elite units of specially selected, well-trained, highly indoctrinated, fanatically motivated Nazi killers. He had only the dregs of the manpower pool, and from these dregs he had to put together ad hoc armies of ghetto-clearers. Units like Reserve Police Battalion 101 were composed of ordinary men. Through a combination of many factors—wartime polarization, careerism, ingrained deference to authority, and conformity to peer pressure, to name a few—more than 80 percent of these men could be induced to commit the worst kinds of atrocities in the most bestial manner. They were transformed by what they did, and they became the vicious and cruel perpetrators of the Holocaust in Poland.

Notes

1. Raul Hilberg, *The Destruction of the European Jews*, rev. ed. (New York, 1985), 341.

2. According to the first Korherr Report for December 1942 (Nürnberg Document NO-5194), about 298,000 Jews remained under German custody in the General Government, 95,000 in the Warthegau, and 51,000 in East Upper Silesia. Probably an additional 40,000 Jews remained in Bialystok.

3. See p. 458 of Frank Golczewski, "Polen," *Dimension des Völkermords: Die Zahl der jüdischen Opfer des Nationalsozialismus*, ed. by Wolfgang Benz (Munich, 1991), 411–497.

4. Hilberg, *Destruction*, 484, estimates 1.6 million Jews in the General Government and 200,000 in Bialystok. Golczewski, "Polen," 448–457, estimates 1.77 million in the General Government and 193,000 in Bialystok.

5. Yad Vashem Archives (hereafter cited as YVA), TR-10/970; Staatsanswaltschaft (hereafter cited as StA) Hamburg, 147 Js 8/75, Indictment of Arpad Wigand, 35.

6. For dating the deportations within Poland organized according to the camp to which the Jews were sent, see the appendices of Yitzhak Arad, *Belzec, Sobibor, Treblinka: The Operation Reinhard Death Camps* (Bloomington, Indiana, 1987). For lists of deportations organized according to the counties (*Kreise*) and districts from which they originated, see the following articles in *Biuletyn Żydowskiego Instytutu Historycznego* (hereafter cited as BZIH): Szymon Datner, "Eksterminacja ludności żydowskiej w okregu bialostockim," BZIH, 60/1966, 3–50; Adam Rutkowski, "Martyrologia walka i zagłada Łudności żydowskiej w dystrykcie Radomskim Podczas Okupacji hitlerowskiej," BZIH 15–16/1955, 75–182; Tatiana Brustin-Berenstein, "Deportacje i zagłada skupisk żydowskiej w dystrykcie warszawskim," BZIH 3/1952, 82–125; E. Podhorizer-Sandel, "O zagładzie Żydów w dystrykcie krakowskim," BZIH 30/1959, 87–108; Tatiana Berenstein, "Eksterminacja ludności żydowskiej w dystrickcie galizja," BZIH 61/1967, 3–58; Tatiana Brustin-Berenstein, "Martyrologia, opór i zagłada ludności żydowskiej w distrykcie lubelskim," BZIH 21/1957, 21–91. I have also utilized various court records.

7. Gitta Sereny, *Into That Darkness* (London, 1974), 112.

8. Arad, *Belzec, Sobibor, Treblinka*, 71.

9. The entire Bełżec chronology, especially dating the construction of the second set of gas chambers, is a matter of some confusion. Adalbert Rückerl, *NS-Vernichtungslager im Spiegel deutscher Strafprozesse: Belzec, Sobibor, Treblinka, Chelmno* (Munich, 1977), and Arad, *Belzec, Sobibor, Treblinka*, 72–73, follow the conclusion of the Munich court judgment, explaining the temporary cessation of operations at Bełżec in mid-April by the sudden departure for Berlin of the camp commandant, Christian Wirth, and dating the construction of the new gas chambers to late June or early July. In doing so, they follow Oberhauser's 1962 testimony before the Munich court. Zentrale Stelle der

Landesjustizverwaltungen (hereafter cited as ZStL), 8 AR-Z 252/59 (hereafter cited as Bełżec trial), IX, 1683–1684 (Oberhauser, December 12, 1962). In my view his earlier testimony (Bełżec trial, IV, 656–660 [February 26, 1960] and 763–765 [April 20, 1960]) is more reliable. According to the earlier testimony, Wirth carried out experimental gassings in February, then left suddenly for Berlin and returned in mid-March to begin the Lublin action. The only period thereafter during which new construction could have taken place at Bełżec is the five-week interruption in deportations between mid-April and late May. The late June–early July interruption was due to transportation problems. In my view, in his 1962 testimony, Oberhauser was trying to give the false impression that until August 1942 (the period for which he was on trial) Bełżec only had the capacity to carry out small experimental gassings in a single gas chamber holding 100 people. In reality, between mid-March and August, despite the five-week interruption for constructing new gas chambers, over 100,000 Jews had been gassed at Bełżec.

10. Hans Frank, *Das Diensttagebuch des deutschen Generalgouverneurs,* ed. by Werner Präg and Wolfgang Jacobmeyer (Stuttgart, 1975), 511 (Polizeisitzung, June 18, 1942).

11. YVA, TR-10/385, StA Düsseldorf 8 Js 430/67, Indictment of Albert Ganzenmüller, 208 (Wolff testimony).

12. Nürnberg Document NO-5574; Himmler to Krüger, July 19, 1942.

13. Sereny, *Into That Darkness,* 156–164; Arad, *Belzec, Sobibor, Treblinka,* 89–96, 119–123.

14. For the Bialystok deportations, see ZStL, V 205 AR-Z 226/50 (Landgericht [hereafter cited as LG] Bielefeld, 5 Ks 1/65, Judgment against Altenloh), 47–106, 258–266.

15. YVA, TR-10/835: StA Düsseldorf 8 Js 430/67, Indictment of Albert Ganzenmüller, 217–223.

16. Korherr Report (NO-5194), printed facsimile in *The Holocaust: Selected Documents,* vol. 12, ed. by John Mendelsohn, 233, 235.

17. Datner, "Eksterminacja ludności żydowskiej w okregu bialostockim," 119.

18. The figure of 12,000 Order Police and 12,00 Polish police was given by the head of the Order Police in the General Government, Generalleutnant Becker, on November 21, 1942. Frank, *Diensttagebuch,* 574. Kurt Daluege, the head of the Order Police main office in Berlin, reported the figures of 15,186 Order Police and 14,297 Polish police in January 1943 (Nürnberg Document NO-2861).

19. Frank, *Diensttagebuch,* 574.

20. YVA, TR10/598: LG Kiel 2 Ks 6/63, Judgment against Martin Fellenz, 9–13.

21. YVA, TR-10/751: LG Bochum 16 Ks 2/70, Judgment against Walter Baach and Ernst Wunder, 19.

22. Ibid., 13, 16–19. YVA, TR-10/777: LG Bochum 16 Ks 1/68, Judgment against Karl Oppermann and Gerhard Gaa, 39, 42.

23. Fellenz Judgment, 29.

24. Ibid., 30.

25. Baach, Wunder Judgment, 25.

26. Ibid., 27, 42, 81–85, 99–101.

27. YVA, TR-10/85; LG Lüneburg, 2 a Ks 2/65, Judgment against Paul Degenhardt, 9–13; *Justiz und NS-Verbrechen. Sammlung Deutscher Strafurteile wegen Nationalsozialistischen Tötungsverbrechen 1945–1966* (hereafter cited as JNSV), vol. 12, no. 600a (LG Schweinfurt Ks 1/64), 326–328.

28. ZStL, II 206 AR-Z 16/65 (StA Hamburg, 147 Js 38/65, Indictment of Weinrich, Fuchs, and Kapke), 63–64, 77.

29. JNSV, vol. 12, no. 600b (LG Bamberg 2 Ks 4/60), 344; Degenhardt Judgment, 16, 19.

30. Degenhardt Judgment, 20–28; JNSV, vol. 12, no. 600a, 329–330.

31. Degenhardt Judgment, 32, 36.

32. The following is based on Christopher R. Browning, *Ordinary Men: Reserve Police Battalion 101 and the Final Solution in Poland* (New York: HarperCollins, 1992).

33. YVA, O-53/115/2–170 and 673–725.

34. ZStL, Ord. 410, 994–996, 498, 500–551 (weekly reports of Fifth Company, Reserve Police Battalion, 133).

35. Fellenz Judgment, 34.

36. Hilberg, *Destruction*, 495.

37. See note 32 above.

38. Browning, *Ordinary Men*, 76.

39. Ibid., 129–130.

5

Nazi-Jewish Negotiations

Yehuda Bauer

The very peculiar subject I have chosen obliges me to start with a piece of methodological apologetics; I would then like to put the cart firmly in front of my horse and present a general thesis on the subject at hand. Third, I give some of the historical sources on which the thesis is based. And fourth, I draw some tentative conclusions.

As a general rule, I think, historians deal with events that actually occurred and try to explain them. There is an injunction, often explicit, not to deal with events that might have happened, and any attempts to do so are immediately classified as nonscientific. Quite apart from the question whether history is a science—I personally am convinced it is not—this attitude, which I shared for many years, now seems to me to smack too much of determinism to be uncritically accepted. Events cannot be predicted on principle, because an infinite number of factors go into creating them, and infinite numbers are by definition unknowable. But surely the same applies to past events: They, too, were created by an infinite number of factors, and we try to establish which of these were more important than others. In the case of Nazi Germany, it is not difficult to show that things could have turned out differently than they actually did and that accidental and personal factors were involved. Our predilection is to assume that because things happened in a particular way, they had to happen that way, but this is obviously nonsense. We should break loose from our accustomed deterministic patterns of thinking and see history as it really is, namely, as a framework for an infinite number of causal chains, some of which led to recognizable events that we prefer to call historic events and some of which could have so developed but for a number of reasons did not. We are engaged here not with what should have been but with what might well have been and was prevented from being not by inexorable necessities but by other causal chains that turned from possibilities into actualities.

There were certain negotiations between Nazis and Jews that did not come to fruition, that were stopped at various times for different reasons. They took place within a certain general context that has to be unraveled in order to understand them. I believe that one can discern a pattern in these negotiations and that they were connected with significant developments in the history of Nazi Germany. The divergent aims both sides pursued at different times were never attained, and I think one can explain why. The point is to examine to what extent they could have been so attained, and in order to avoid specious speculation, one has to stick very carefully to the available evidence. What follows is, therefore, if you will, an exercise in the examination of possible developments that might have led somewhere but did not, and I would claim that they are significant for any analysis of the Nazi regime as such as well as for its Jewish policy.

What, then, is my thesis? Basic to it is the conviction that Nazi policy was centrally influenced by ideology but was tactically flexible enough to allow for zigzags and postponements of implementation of aims. The Nazis saw the Jews as a global, universal problem and as a force that ultimately stood behind all their enemies. There were two levels on which they considered the Jews: one was the practical level on which they dealt with the concrete German, later Austrian and Czech, and later still European Jews. The other level was the really important one, the imaginary world Jewish conspiracy, the abstraction called world Jewry, which was the real and ultimate enemy. Both had to be fought, and the pragmatic policy was to get rid of the Jews of Germany first, then the others. Until 1941 this was to be achieved by a policy of extrusion by increasingly brutal means, but always with the possibility of pursuing a less violent policy, depending on international circumstances—as long as the aim was kept in mind to get rid of that Satan.

When German arms triumphed in 1939–1941 and the policy of expulsion from German-held territory became progressively impractical, the quantum leap was made, with Hitler as the radicalizing factor, to mass and then to total annihilation. The policy of extrusion was not, however, abandoned on principle; it was abandoned because of new pragmatic considerations. When, at the end of 1942 at the latest, Himmler began to realize that there was a real danger that the war might end in a stalemate or that Germany might even lose, attempts began to be made, halfheartedly and in constant and increasing fear, to contact the West in order to achieve a breathing space, split the Allied front, and rescue National Socialist Germany while continuing the fight against the Soviets. A parallel attempt by elements of the conservative opposition to Hitler, for quite different reasons, is well documented in the historiography of World War II.

Himmler was aware in general terms of the conspiracy against Hitler and was aiming to achieve control of the conservatives' real and presumed contacts with the West. Within that framework, he was tentatively negotiating—both through intermediaries and directly—with Jews, whom he believed to be in control of the Western powers. He was most probably willing to pay for any success in that area by trading Jews for such advantages as he might get. He informed Hitler enough about these matters so that he could not be accused of acting contrary to the Führer's wishes, but he hid enough to be able to keep his options open. He was at first waiting to see how the conspiracy would fare, and after it failed he did his best to remove from the scene all those who knew of his contacts with the conspirators. His tentative attempts to contact the West, via the Jews as well as by other means, grew more frantic as the end approached.

At no time, I would maintain, did Himmler's policy regarding the option of negotiating a separate peace with the West and letting some Jews go within that framework contradict National Socialist ideology. Himmler returned to, or indeed had never abandoned, the combined policy of expulsion and violence that was inherent in Nazi ideology. The ultimate aim was and remained to remove the Jews, whether by extrusion or murder, and extrusion might in the end well mean murder. In order to achieve the continuation of National Socialist rule in Germany and the ultimate achievement of its aims, including those connected with the so-called Final Solution of the Jewish problem, a temporary retreat to the expulsion policy was perfectly justifiable. From the Jewish point of view, this would have meant the rescue of an indeterminate number of lives. It did not happen largely because the Jewish question, though one of the central problems in Nazi minds, played no role, or a negative role only, in Allied considerations. Even when Himmler offered Jews for sale—for money, goods, or political advantages—there were no buyers. I would therefore argue that from a Nazi perspective, the Final Solution was not final in an absolute sense. It depended on the vagaries of war and on the response from the opposing side. The possibility of returning to expulsion or extrusion was revived after 1942, and it did not contradict the policy of murder. But of course it did not happen. Thus far the thesis.

Now to the material. As a number of authors have shown,[1] Nazi policies toward the Jews had not been worked out when the Nazis came to power. Even without clear-cut guidelines, however, a consensus emerged, quickly and effortlessly, that the Jews should be encouraged to emigrate because they were an enemy race defiling Germany. The legal and other steps taken to discriminate against them, to remove them from a certain number of positions, and to turn them into second-class citizens, were in part the result of traditional anti-Semitic drives in the German population that the Nazis used and were in part a follow-up to their basic ideological premise that the Jews should be removed.

An element in the Jewish reaction to the Nazis' rise to power was the policy of individuals in Palestine, and then of the Zionist center there, to arrive at an arrangement with the Nazis that would enable propertied German Jews to emigrate to Palestine with at least some of their capital and without actually using non-German currency to do so. Negotiations with the German government were therefore initiated by a certain Palestinian Jew by the name of Sam Cohen, and these were then taken over by the Zionist leadership in Palestine. In summer 1933 the so-called Haavara (transfer) agreement was signed between the Jewish Agency and the German government, specifically its economic bodies. It provided for individuals to deposit their money in a special bank; that bank then paid German manufacturers, in marks, for mainly agricultural machinery to be shipped to buyers in Palestine (marginally also elsewhere in the Middle East), who paid the price into an account in the Anglo-Palestine Bank (owned by Zionist bodies), who then paid it out to the Jewish owners who emigrated to Palestine—with deductions, of course, to Zionist bodies as well as to the Germans. The actual process was more complicated than summarized here, and it involved the interests of German Templar settlers in Palestine and their banks in Palestine and Germany, but this brief outline will suffice for our purpose.

The questions we have to ask about this arrangement are quite significant: Why did the Germans desist from confiscating all Jewish capital even when, especially after 1935, they began pressing their Aryanization policy more and more energetically? Why did they agree to an export procedure that deprived them of income in foreign currency? How important to them were the partial economic advantages from this arrangement? Why did Haavara continue until the outbreak of war?[2]

First, contrary to much of accepted wisdom, foreign trade was a relatively small part of the German economic picture. It formed but 9.89 percent of the GNP in 1932 and 5.75 percent in 1936. Palestine's part of that foreign trade was small (2.96 percent in 1933, 4.27 percent in 1936). The point is that whatever advantages might have been gained from increased trade with Palestine, they were surely marginal. In contrast, the loss of hard currency was important: Whereas German foreign currency reserves were reasonably high in 1932, when they stood at RM 974.6 million (down from 2,405.4 million in 1928), they were quickly depleted in the following years and stood at only 75.2 million in 1936. That Jews were allowed to leave Germany and transfer their capital without any foreign currency accruing to the Germans therefore demands explanation. More than that: Up to 1936, Jewish capitalists were even permitted to convert their marks into scarce British pounds from the German reserves to pay the £1,000 needed to get an immigration certificate to Palestine.

As the years went on, the German economic ministries increasingly questioned the Haavara agreement, and in 1936–1937 the German Ministry of Economy, the Foreign Office section dealing with the problem, the Party Ausland Organization, the Templars in Palestine, and the section of the Reichsbank dealing with the issue all protested that the agreement was bad and that it should be canceled. When in mid-1937 Hitler himself, as well as the Foreign Office, expressed opposition to the plan of partitioning Palestine and establishing a Jewish state there, the Haavara to Palestine seemed doomed. And yet it went on until the war began. The reason was that Hitler himself intervened, seemingly a number of times, to state that emigration of Jews was more important than any economic considerations, apparently even more important than the opposition to a Jewish state, and that settled the matter: The Führer's wish was to have the Jews disappear from Germany, and Haavara was one of the means to achieve that aim.[3] I would argue that two policy lines emerged here: one of persecution and extrusion, and one of encouraging Jewish emigration by almost conventional means. They were in no contradiction to each other because they had the same aim: to get rid of the Jews. It also emerges, as some (including myself) have argued elsewhere,[4] that Hitler was directly and continuously involved in determining Jewish policies and that purely economic considerations took second place to ideological motives.

As a result of the Evian conference in July 1938, the newly formed Intergovernmental Committee on Refugees' representative in London, George Rublee, began negotiating with the German government about the emigration of Jews with some of their capital. These negotiations have been repeatedly described,[5] and they resulted in a preliminary agreement with Hjalmar Schacht, based on a prior proposal from German Jews, which followed the general scheme of the Haavara. German products that were to be bought by the emigrants would then be sold abroad and provide part of the resettlement funds, and the advantage that would accrue to the Germans would be the spread of German industrial production but no payment in foreign currency. All but some 200,000 German Jews (now including Austrian and Sudeten Jews as well) would ultimately emigrate, and only the old ones would be left. The Germans were prepared to commit themselves to let these people live out their lives without molestation, using up what would be left of Jewish property. Hitler gave his approval to this plan on January 2, 1939; at the end of that month he made the famous speech to the Reichstag in which he threatened the Jews with annihilation if another war broke out. The negotiations continued even though Schacht left the Reichsbank on January 20; the person conducting the negotiations, through intermediaries and in one case directly, was Göring, whom Hitler had nominated as the man responsible for solving the Jewish question, as Göring informed the participants at the well-known post-Kristallnacht meeting in his office, on November 12, 1938.[6]

There, Göring stated in very clear terms that the Führer had decided to solve the Jewish question through an international approach, that the solution to be offered to the other powers was emigration to Madagascar, and that the problem would be solved *so oder so*, one way or another. On January 24, 1939, another internal order by Göring, this time to Heydrich, established the Reich Central Office for Jewish Emigration, and the supervisory board included Helmut Wohlthat, Göring's representative in the Rublee negotiations.[7]

I would suggest that what emerges from an analysis of these developments is a picture of Nazi Jewish policy that in general terms leaves open two options: one of extrusion (presumably by force) to Madagascar, for instance, after an appropriate arrangement with the Western powers, and the other a more benign form of ordered emigration, if the illusionary international Jewry and the Western powers lent their hand to it. Such an alternate policy, of which Haavara was a part, found its expression in the Rublee-Schacht-Wohlthat agreement. In fact, President Roosevelt strongly pressured the American Jewish elite to agree to the Rublee-Wohlthat plan, and in early June 1939 the U.S. Jews even created a financial instrument, the Co-ordinating Foundation, whose task it would have been to raise large sums of money to parallel the sale of German goods by the emigrants and enable them to resettle. The war that erupted in September 1939 put an end to this project.

The question that arises is whether the Nazis meant what they were saying. The two Göring documents quoted, of November 1938 and January 1939, were of course internal, so no propaganda element can be attributed to them. It must be remembered that the war that actually broke out was not the war that Hitler had wanted. He had become convinced that Britain would not join in and that Poland might well stand completely isolated. He and his generals wanted to avoid a two-front war, and the idea of a compromise with Britain would not have precluded a settlement of the Jewish question, *so oder so*—on the contrary. I would therefore tend to assume that the Nazis did indeed mean to hold to a policy of forced emigration.

The purpose of these prewar contracts was, on the Jewish side, the pragmatic aim to get as many Jews as possible out of Nazi Germany with as much money as possible to facilitate their settlement elsewhere. The Nazis' policy of extrusion was based entirely on ideology, totally removed from any consideration of the reality of Jewish influence or presence in areas under their control, and it stood in contradiction to their economic interests as understood by their economic experts.

As we all know, by 1941 this policy had developed into a policy of massive, later total murder. I cannot here go into the questions of who decided on that policy and why;[8] what I wish to emphasize is that the impression in the historiography to date is that once they had decided on what they termed the Final Solution, they never looked back: That policy became *unwiderruflich* (unretractable), and the former policy of extrusion became redundant.

The problem becomes more complicated, however, when one examines the Byzantine byways of Nazi politics. On December 10, 1942, Himmler received Hitler's approval to allow the emigration of Jews who could deliver a significant amount of foreign currency. The permission did not state clearly whether individual Jews or groups of them were meant. In May 1943 a British proposal to evacuate up to 5,000 Jewish children from Poland was transmitted to the Germans by a member of the Swiss legation in Berlin, Feldscher, and approved by Himmler in principle. Eichmann made any agreement conditional on exchanging one Jewish child for four able-bodied German males. One thousand Jewish children from Bialystok were transported to Theresienstadt in August 1943, probably in response to these overtures, and kept there until October, when they were deported to the gas chambers of Auschwitz.[9] In Slovakia from November 1942 on, protracted contacts were maintained between a group of underground Jewish activists and Dieter Wisliceny, Eichmann's representative there. Was there then a possibility, at least from the Nazi side, of a break in the policy of the Final Solution?

Before we attempt to answer that question, let us remember that parallel to these tentative contacts, conservative circles opposed to the regime were trying to reach Western representatives as part of their conspiracy aiming to remove the dictator. One of the centers of this opposition was the foursome of top Abwehr (German military intelligence) operatives: Hans Oster, Hans von Dohnanyi, Dietrich Bonhöffer, and Josef Müller. As early as 1940 Müller had tried to contact the British through the Vatican but failed. In September 1942 the conspirators brought a group totaling seventeen Jews and their non-Jewish family members into Switzerland, supposedly to spy for the Abwehr. On the strength of that argument, Himmler himself approved the request of Wilhelm Canaris, head of the Abwehr, to let these people leave Germany. It is not very likely that Himmler was fooled into believing the Abwehr story—in any case, the release of Jews with $100,000 worth of foreign currency, the equivalent of which was paid in reichsmarks into the Abwehr coffers, ran counter to all Nazi policies.[10]

By 1942, too, the conspirators had established a trading company in Prague by the name of Monospol, run from Vienna and Munich, the purpose of which was to earn foreign currency for a black treasury that would finance antiregime operations. Some of the agents working there were Jews. The group was found out in September 1942 and investigated by Walter Huppenkothen of the Gestapo, who reported to Heinrich Müller. The investigation led to the arrest of Dohnanyi, Bonhöffer, and Josef Müller in April 1943 and the removal of Oster from his post. Field Marshal Wilhelm Keitel nominated Manfred Röder, a fanatical Nazi, to bring the conspirators to trial. It was obvious that Canaris, head of the Abwehr, had been in the know.

But when Himmler was approached to help—after all, the Gestapo had handled the affair—he retorted, *"Lasst mir doch den Canaris in Ruhe"* (Leave Canaris alone, for God's sake).[11] It was the SS that then maneuvered the overenthusiastic Röder out of his position and caused the nomination of another prosecutor, with whose help the three accused were sentenced to prison terms only (at that stage; Müller was eventually released, but the other two stayed in prison and were executed toward the end of the war). The indications are that Himmler was aware of a plot being prepared by the opposition, in this case the Abwehr. Heinz Höhne has made the point that he had been informed in some more detail in August 1943 by Johannes Popitz, one of the civilian conspirators. Neither Popitz nor Canaris nor anyone else was arrested, and as we have just seen, Abwehr operatives received a very peculiar type of protection from Himmler.[12]

I do not know what the SS knew of the contacts in Switzerland between Allen Dulles and Gero von Schulze-Gaevernitz of the OSS and Abwehr people. But it is quite clear that the conservatives were trying to persuade the Allies to support them in their struggle against Hitler. In return, they asked for help in stopping the Soviets from overrunning Eastern Europe. From all we know of Himmler's policies, it would seem that his immediate aims at least were not so dissimilar; his main worry was to stop the Soviets, and he was looking for ways, very hesitantly and cautiously, to contact the Western Allies to achieve that aim.

The conservatives' proposals were transmitted to the Americans via Dulles, who passed them on to Washington, where they were rejected, of course, because the Soviets had to be kept in the alliance and the conspirators were perceived as just another bunch of Prussian militarists. The Casablanca conference, moreover, had decided on unconditional surrender, and these people were talking about conditional surrender.

In spring 1943 and again in November, Helmut von Moltke, head of the Kreisau circle of the conservatives, supposedly a near pacifist uninvolved in the military conspiracy, appeared in Istanbul to contact his American friend Alexander Kirk, U.S. ambassador to Cairo, in the name of the generals. He, too, proposed stopping the Soviets on a line from Tilsit to Lwow and in return promised to topple Hitler and reinstate a conservative, Bismarck-like guided democracy. Kirk refused to meet with him, but Moltke's memorandum was transmitted to Washington, where it was, again, rejected. I do not know whether Himmler's SD was aware of these contacts at this stage, but they must have been aware at least of the general trend of the conservatives' efforts.[13]

In October 1943 Abraham S. Hewitt, an American lawyer and an acquaintance of Roosevelt's who was attached to the OSS, visited Stockholm, where he was treated for stomach pains by the ubiquitous Felix Kersten, Himmler's masseur. Kersten wrote to Himmler on October 24, asking him to send Walter Schellenberg, head of the SD, to Stockholm to negotiate with Hewitt. The basis for negotiations, Kersten wrote, would be complete German withdrawal from occupied territories, the removal of Hitler, the disbandment of the Nazi Party, a democratic constitution, and the trial of top Nazis for war crimes. Himmler sent Schellenberg, who met twice with Hewitt. Schellenberg's and Hewitt's accounts of these meetings, of course, differ very widely, but Hewitt's account exactly repeats Kersten's points. Hewitt may have seen Kersten's letter in 1943; nevertheless, his account seems credible enough. According to Kersten's memoirs, Himmler could not accept the idea of a trial of top Nazis but was prepared to continue the negotiations. However, when Schellenberg returned to Stockholm after reporting to Himmler, Hewitt had already left. The Americans rejected these contacts, but the interesting point is that Himmler was prepared to send his man to negotiate despite the very harsh preconditions that Kersten had set down. The originals of the Kersten letter, Hewitt's report, and Schellenberg's postwar testimony can be found in recently released OSS materials in the National Archives.[14]

What emerges is a pattern of halfhearted attempts by a hesitant Himmler, who recognized the increasing danger to which Nazi Germany was exposed, to try to get in touch with the Western Allies and to follow what the conservatives were doing in the expectation that if they succeeded, he might pick up where they had left off. It would seem that while he had no stomach for anti-Hitlerian conspiracies himself, he was going to wait and see whether the opposition managed to get rid of his revered Führer. If it did, one may surmise, he thought *he* would gain power rather than the weak and politically naive conservatives. In that eventuality he would try to make the separate peace he became increasingly convinced was necessary to save national socialism and Germany.

It is within this context that one should, I think, see the SS contacts with and about the Jews. Chronologically, the Slovak contacts came first. They were started in November 1942 after the group of Jewish underground leaders there became convinced—wrongly, as it turns out—that by bribing Wisliceny they had managed to stop the deportations of Slovak Jews to Auschwitz, which had been going on since March 26. They now approached the Nazi officer with an offer to pay ransom in foreign currency if the Nazis stopped deportations to Poland from western and southeastern parts of Europe (the latter regions were not yet under direct Nazi control, but the Jewish leaders thought they soon would be). Wisliceny, according to the sources at our disposal, asked Himmler whether he should negotiate. But the sources are problematic: They consist of contemporary letters of the Jewish negotiators and their postwar testimonies, postwar testimonies of Wisliceny, and some hints extracted from Eichmann in Jerusalem.

It seems Wisliceny never met with Himmler on this question but received his approval to negotiate from one of Himmler's secretaries, Suchaneck, and from an apparently reluctant Eichmann. It is clear, though, that without Himmler's approval Wisliceny would not have stuck his neck out to negotiate with Jews. He led the Jewish negotiators by their noses, promising them all kinds of cancellations of deportations in return for sums of money (the details need not concern us here, but they are now increasingly available, though not in English). The negotiations started in November 1942 and terminated in August and September 1943. The down payment Wisliceny demanded did not become available until August because the Jewish organizations thought that this was nothing but an extortionist trick; also, as far as the American Jewish Joint Distribution Committee (JDC) was concerned, that organization simply had no way of transferring dollars to Switzerland in 1942 because the Swiss refused to accept philanthropic dollars—they could not buy any American goods with them because of the blockade restrictions. In the end, most of the money required as a down payment ($200,000) was sent to Slovakia in the summer, but by then Himmler had intervened again, this time to tell Wisliceny to stop negotiating. We do not know why, but Wisliceny at the time hinted that high-ups in the Party had got wind of these contacts and Himmler feared that they would be asking questions.[15]

I think we should remember that these contacts took place at the same time as the Feldscher negotiations; Wisliceny was talking to the Slovak Jews about children and said that the Bialystok children were proof of the Nazis' seriousness. Those children were therefore used not only as a backup for the Feldscher plan but possibly also for the Slovak contacts. As the Feldscher contacts were official, involving the German Foreign Office, they were probably thought to be preferable to the Slovak ones, which had not led to any material results. This very concept of material results, however, does not mean only money. The $200,000 down payment and the $3 million or so bandied about by Wisliceny as the price for the stoppage of deportations from the west and the south to Poland were in themselves interesting because they were relatively puny amounts. The property and money of Jews anywhere came to much larger sums than that, and it is perhaps permissible to conjecture that these amounts were not what the SS was after. Wisliceny insisted on seeing proof that the money was being sent from abroad and wanted to be in touch with "international Jewry." If, as one of the Jewish negotiators, Rabbi Weissmandel, said, his purpose was other than just pecuniary, then that would fit in with the Feldscher and Schellenberg episodes.[16]

What emerges are options Himmler very carefully prepared. Had they succeeded more than they did, might they have led to a temporary halt in some of the deportations from the west, without thereby putting a stop to the mass murder in the east? Might not Himmler, in accordance with his nature, have then adopted a wait-and-see attitude regarding the conservative plot, or might he not have gone to the Führer to suggest negotiations with the West to attain a breathing space? In summer and early fall 1943, he appears to have had several irons in this particular fire: He was about to send Schellenberg to see what the Americans were saying; via the German Foreign Office through the Swiss, he was negotiating on evacuation of Jews; and he was in contact (or so he thought) with world Jewry through Slovakia. At the same time he knew that the generals and the Abwehr were preparing a conspiracy against Hitler, and he was apparently determined to sit that one out. If they failed, he would pounce on them; he had sufficient knowledge of their group to be able to do so. If they succeeded, he would become the top Nazi, perhaps along with Göring, and save National Socialist Germany by negotiating a separate peace with the West, something he must have suspected the generals were doing, or at least wanted to do.

The mission of Joel Brand and Bandi (Antal) Grosz was, as I have pointed out elsewhere[17] a direct continuation of the Slovak affair and was initially conducted by Wisliceny on the basis of a letter Weissmandel wrote to Hungarian Jews he thought capable of negotiating with the Nazis on the basis of ransom. But Eichmann soon removed Wisliceny from these talks. Here our sources are much more solid and quite detailed. Crucial to our understanding are the very thorough interrogations that the British MI9 (called SIME in Cairo) conducted, in June–July 1944, of the two emissaries from Hungary, Brand and Grosz. This comes on top of contemporary testimonies and other statements by Brand and a postwar statement by Grosz as well as reports by British and American intelligence agencies and by Ira Hirschmann of Roosevelt's War Refugee Board. The overall picture that emerges is that there were two parallel German initiatives: One was the famous Eichmann offer of 1 million Jews for 10,000 trucks and various amounts of luxury foodstuffs. The other was the offer brought by Grosz to conduct negotiations, preferably in Switzerland, between high SS officers and American intelligence people to examine the possibilities of a separate peace. According to Grosz in his interrogation, he was charged with the task of bringing this proposal by Obersturmbannführer Otto Clages, head of the SD detachment in Hungary, a man of equal rank with Eichmann, who told Grosz that he had direct contact with Himmler. Grosz also said that the other man who participated in the preparation of his mission with Clages was Ferdinand Laufer, who he thought was a high SS officer. We now know that he was Frantisek Laufer, a Jewish ex-waiter from Prague. This man, who was wearing an SD uniform in Budapest, had been an Abwehr agent before, and in 1943 and again in spring 1944 he had brought much the same offer directly to the OSS in Istanbul, to Alfred Schwarz (alias Dogwood), the organizer of one of the more important American information rings in Central Europe. This at least is what Schwarz tells us. From a comparison between our sources, I would draw the conclusion that Eichmann was forced to accept Grosz at the insistence of the SD, whose head of course was Schellenberg. The Brand mission offered what was obviously a preposterous proposal that Eichmann must have hoped would be rejected and that was indeed designed, among other purposes, to cause a rift among the Allies. In addition, it may well have been a teaser to see what counteroffer the Jewish masters of Germany's enemies would make. Eichmann stated that he had received the order to make this offer from Himmler, and it is unimaginable that it could have originated from any other source. It is equally certain that Himmler was the source of the second proposal, namely, Grosz's message that the SS was seeking negotiations with the Americans.

Given the Nazi belief in the rule of the Jews over their enemies and from what we know of Himmler's shifting views in spring and summer 1944, the two proposals were not necessarily different, certainly not contradictory. The trucks proposal could lead to the same type of negotiations that were offered through Grosz. Nevertheless, I would stick by my argument[18] that the Grosz mission of the SD was the central one and that Brand's served, in a sense, as a cover to it.

That these proposals were taken very seriously indeed by the Western Allies emerges from an examination of both the British and American materials. The results of the Grosz interrogation in Cairo reached London on July 13, 1944, and were brought to Churchill's attention the same day. The British had known of the Brand proposals for more than six weeks and were prepared not to reject them out of hand in order, if possible, to save Jewish lives. But now, when they realized that what was behind them was a German peace offer, they decided immediately to break off all contacts. Not so the Americans, who, as far as I can tell, may never have received from their British Allies the full Grosz interrogation report. The United States was prepared for neutrals of some sort to enter into holding negotiations with the Nazis in order to save lives, provided no ransom was paid in goods or money.

The dates of this mission should be remembered: Brand and Grosz came to Istanbul in May 1944, which was three and a half months after another little scandal, also in Istanbul, had caused Hitler finally to break with Canaris and abolish the Abwehr, which was then absorbed by the SD. Himmler's people now had the lines of contact with the West in their hands, but they found out very quickly that they could not rely on the Abwehr operatives, who were basically antiregime. The whole Istanbul operation of the Abwehr had collapsed, and Jews would be a welcome medium to get in touch with the West. An individual like Grosz, who was a petty criminal and a low-grade, multiple-double-crossing agent, was an ideal conduit for an SS offer. He could always be disavowed, but if the Allies were to check on his information, they would find it to be true.

Even more important to remember is that the Istanbul mission took place two months before the attempt on Hitler's life. It is, in my view, more than just likely that as the indications of a conspiracy thickened, Himmler was preparing for one of two possible outcomes: In case of the removal of Hitler, contacts would have to be prepared for dealing with the West; in case of failure, the Führer might wish to utilize such preparations to re-form his political and military defense lines in order to ensure the survival of the Nazi Reich.

The SS attempts to reach the Allies were exposed by one of Himmler's enemies in the Reich, Ribbentrop, and this became obvious when the British published the Brand offer in July 1944. On July 20, however, the attempt on Hitler's life and Himmler's indispensability to the preservation of Nazi rule pushed this little scandal into the background. The opposition leaders were speedily eliminated, and at the same time further attempts were initiated to reach the Western Allies, despite Casablanca and despite rebuffs that Himmler had experienced. The Jewish line was tried yet again, in continuation of the failed Brand-Grosz mission.

It is at this point that the figure of Kurt A. Becher appeared on the scene. Becher was the administration officer and for a while the operations officer of the First SS Cavalry Regiment during the Pripjet operation in Russia in summer 1941, when his unit murdered at least 15,000 Jews. After the war, poor Obersturmbannführer Becher unfortunately suffered selective amnesia regarding his Russian activities. Today, multimillionaire Kurt Becher of Bremen remembers even less. After having been successfully treated for venereal disease and after a stint of duty at the SS Führungshauptamt in Berlin, Becher, an expert in horses, was sent to Budapest in March 1944 to get horses for the SS. Some of the "horses" were unique indeed: He managed, on behalf of the SS, to lay hands on the greatest industrial empire in Central Europe, the Manfred Weiss combine of heavy and other industries. The Weiss and Kornfeld families—originally Jewish but by that time only partly so—and their non-Jewish relatives were arrested and forced into signing an agreement that left the combine in the hands of the SS as *Treuhänder* (trustees; literally, honest hands). The Reichsführer's most obedient Becher became a member of the supervisory board. Most of the Weiss-Kornfeld family was flown to Portugal and Switzerland, with a few remaining as hostages in Vienna. It is clear that this was done in accordance with the permission Hitler granted in December 1942 to release Jews for considerable sums of money.

Under Himmler's direction, Becher then turned his attention to the Eichmann-Brand negotiations. When Brand and Grosz failed to return from Istanbul—they had, it will be remembered, been arrested by the British and were held in Cairo—Becher entered into contact with Reszoe Kastner, head of the small underground Zionist Rescue and Aid Committee, of which Brand was a member. For Kastner, who was trying to save Jewish lives by negotiating with the Nazis, the appearance of Becher was a godsend. Becher was equal in rank to both Clages and Eichmann and had a direct line to Himmler. In June 1944 Eichmann and Becher agreed, obviously with Himmler's consent or at Himmler's initiative, to send a trainload of 1,684 Jews out of Hungary. It is obvious from the way the train was sent out that there were disagreements among the SS commanders where the train should go. In the end it landed in Bergen-Belsen, which was an *Austauschlager,* an exchange camp, for Jews who could be used for exchanges of civilian prisoners.[19]

Through Kastner's intercession, Becher was able to start negotiations on the Swiss border with yet another representative of so-called international Jewry, Saly Mayer, the JDC representative in Switzerland. I have detailed these negotiations elsewhere,[20] and all that is needed here is to put them into context: As a result of the start of these negotiations, a part of the Kastner train reached the safety of Switzerland, and (more importantly, perhaps) Himmler gave an order not to deport the Jews of Budapest to Auschwitz. The Swiss negotiations were about the supply of goods to the Nazis in return for either assuring the safety of Jews still under Nazi rule and/or the release of some of them. The problem was that Mayer was not empowered by the Americans who controlled him—or so they thought—to offer either money or goods. He managed to continue to negotiate and not break off the contacts, and it soon emerged what Becher, in Himmler's name, was really after: direct contact with the Americans, obviously not about Jews. Mayer actually engineered a meeting between Becher and Roswell D. McClelland, the War Refugee Board representative in Switzerland, on November 5, 1944, though of course the meeting ended without agreement on anything substantial.

We know now, from a variety of sources, that Himmler masked his negotiations with the argument that all he was doing was trying to procure badly needed war material from Switzerland. He did not, however, limit himself to the Becher-Mayer line only. In October–November 1944 he began negotiating, through Schellenberg and then personally, with Jean-Marie Musy, a pro-Nazi Swiss politician who wanted to restore his good name by saving some Jewish lives. Musy acted in the name of yet another of the mutually hostile Jewish organizations, the Vaad Hatzala Rescue Committee of American Orthodox Rabbis, who were offering what Mayer was talking about, too, but were equally unable to deliver because McClelland and the Americans prevented them from doing so. Other SS figures made minor efforts along parallel lines via Switzerland at the same time.

In January 1945 an exasperated Himmler wrote his note asking who had the contacts to the Americans—Was it the "Joint" (JDC) or the rabbinical Jews?[21] By that time his quest for contacts with the Americans via the Jews was obvious. By that time, too, it was too late. But, it must be said, these efforts that continued until the end of the war probably did save the lives of tens of thousands of Jews; the camp of Bergen-Belsen, for instance, was handed over to the British without a fight after the intervention of Becher and Kastner. I will not deal with these last months because they add nothing to our theme except for a harrowing tale of the most terrible suffering imaginable of hundreds of thousands of camp prisoners who were forced on death marches criss-cross through the dying Thousand-Year Reich.

A crucial problem is whether these half-baked moves to use Jewish intermediaries to contact the West in search of a separate peace stood in contradiction to the murder policy of the Final Solution. I would suggest that this is not the case. I would argue that Himmler remained true to his convictions as expressed in a famous memorandum that he presented to Hitler on May 25, 1940,[22] in which he argued for the expulsion of the Jews to Madagascar a year before the policy of murder was initiated. Of course, when his beloved Führer gave the instruction to kill, he executed it as best he could. But he returned to the idea of expulsion even in his talk with Norman Mazur of the World Jewish Congress on April 21, 1945. You could solve the Jewish question *so oder so,* as long as there were no Jews around when you were through with it. If one could save the great ideas of the Führer by a cessation of the murder, perhaps only in part, perhaps only temporarily, this was justified. More than that, if the Führer himself was in the way of realizing his own ideas and provided somebody else did it, then perhaps the Führer— perish the thought—might have to go. Then he, the loyal Heinrich, would realize Hitler's dream. At a recent historians' conference in Chicago, my friend and colleague Saul Friedlander suggested that the phenomenon of Himmler defies final understanding because we cannot put ourselves in Himmler's shoes, we cannot identify with him as we can with other historic personalities. If that were true, it would prevent us from understanding a host of historical figures other than Himmler as well. I believe the analysis presented here may provide a way pragmatically to achieve a measure of such understanding. One of the peculiarities of Nazi thought and action is the destruction of the bridge between the planning for life and the planning for death, the breakdown of all barriers to total human engineering in the service of the specific Nazi brand of a universalist idea. I hope that this is peculiar to Nazism, though I am not sure at all that that is indeed the case. In any event, I am afraid we do understand it. When we say we don't, we may be protesting too loudly.

Notes

1. See Uwe D. Adam, *Judenpolitik im Dritten Reich* (Düsseldorf: Droste, 1972); Karl A. Schleunes, *The Twisted Road to Auschwitz* (Chicago: University of Illinois Press, 1990).

2. Avraham Barkai, *Vom Boykott zur "Entjudung"* (Frankfurt: Fischer, 1988); Avraham Barkai, "Haavara," unpublished manuscript.

3. See, for instance, *Documents on German Foreign Policy, 1919–1945,* series D, vol. 5 (Washington: U.S. State Department, 1953), doc. no. 579, pp. 783 ff., 1/27/38, Memorandum by Clodius, deputy director of Economic Policy Department:

The Führer's general directive to facilitate Jewish emigration from Germany by all available means cannot be fulfilled if Palestine is excluded in this connection. ... According to the Aussenpolitisches Amt, the Führer has recently decided again, after another report by Reichsleiter Rosenberg, that Jewish emigration from Germany shall continue to be promoted by all available means. Any question that might have existed up to now as to whether in the Führer's opinion such emigration is to be directed primarily to Palestine has thereby been answered in the affirmative.

4. See Yehuda Bauer, "Who Was Responsible and When," *Holocaust and Genocide Studies,* vol. 6, no. 2, 1991.

5. Yehuda Bauer, *My Brother's Keeper* (Philadelphia: JPS, 1974), pp. 274–285; Adam, *Judenpolitik,* pp. 226–227. For a different interpretation, see Schleunes, *Twisted Road,* pp. 232–234.

6. Nürnburg Trial Documents (NTD), PS-1816.

7. NTD, NG-254586-A.

8. See above, note 4.

9. Himmler's *Vermerk,* 12/10/42, in Bundesarchiv Koblenz, Bestand Alg. Schumacher 240 I; the Feldscher correspondence with the German Foreign Office in National Archives, Washington, Microfilm T120/4202, esp. E422447–E422448, E422480, K207714–K207715.

10. Yad Vashem, Department for Righteous Gentiles, Dietrich Bonhöffer File; also Eberhard Bethge, *Dietrich Bonhöffer* (Munich: Kaiser, 1967), pp. 838–841.

11. Heinz Höhne, *Canaris* (New York: Doubleday, 1979), p. 508.

12. Institut für Zeitgeschichte (IFZ), Munich, Trial of Manfred Röder, Lüneburg, 1947; Yad Vashem, Nuremberg pretrial microfilms, Walter Huppenkothen interrogation, 2/9/47, 2/12/47, 1/29/48; Heinz Höhne, *The Order of the Death's Head* (London: Secker and Warburg, 1969), pp. 525–527.

13. Ibid.

14. IFZ, F44/4, Kersten; OSS-Schellenberg, "Final Report," 9/30/46.

15. IFZ, Fa 164, Wisliceny; Eichmann Trial Documents, 06-856, pp. 1 ff.; Andrej Steiner testimony, JDC-Givat Joint, Geneva Records, box 14 B/C-36.038; Yad Vashem, Bratislava Trials of Slovak War Criminal Onl'ud 17/46, p. 146.

16. Michael Dov-Ber Weissmandel, *Min Hametzar* (New York: Emunah, 1960), p. 45.

17. Yehuda Bauer, *The Holocaust in Historical Perspective* (Seattle: University of Washington Press, 1978), pp. 94–155.

18. Ibid., pp. 147–149.

19. Kurt Emmenegger, "Reichsführer's Gehorsamster Becher," *Sie Er,* December 1962–April 1963.

20. Yehuda Bauer, *American Jewry and the Holocaust* (Detroit: Wayne State University Press, 1981), pp. 408–459.

21. Yad Vashem, 0-51/DN-39/2119.

22. NTD, NO-1880.

PART TWO

Philosophical and Literary Analyses of the Holocaust

6

Through a Glass Darkly

George Steiner

Almost wholly unexplored, in some Freudian sense perhaps suppressed, is the historical moment that determined the tragic destiny of the Jew over these past 2,000 years. It is the moment in which the core of Judaism rejects the messianic claims and promises put forward by Jesus of Nazareth and his immediate adherents.

We have modern histories of the early and intricate relations between first-century Judaism and the nascent Christian communities, between the complexly divided Jewish traditions and usages in the eastern Mediterranean world on the one hand (with their rich variety of Pharisaic, Zealot, and Hellenizing branches) and the new churches (Judeo-Christian, Pauline, pre-Gnostic) on the other. But the key motion of spirit, that whereby Jews refused the "good news" brought by Jesus and affirmed by his resurrection, eludes us. When did the crucial repudiation by Jews occur? The first century was one of the most somber hours in Jewish history—a time of the murderous suppression of national insurgence and consequent destruction of the Temple, a time when the Jews would not acknowledge or accept the concordat of human rebirth and divine pardon offered by the Galilean god-man and his apostles.

We have no documents—so the scholars tell us. Neither Josephus nor Tacitus considers the radically challenging (in the full sense of that word) act of Jewish repudiation of the Son of man. The versions given in the Gospels, Acts, and Epistles are, by very definition, polemical and prejudicial. Rabbinic voices, so far as they have come down to us, speak only later, when Christianity, though still splintered, is dynamically ascendant. And even then, they say very little. This hiatus is itself perplexing in the extreme. It constitutes a black hole near the actual center of Jewish history and fate. I resort to this image precisely because black holes are thought to be charged with almost incommensurable energies, both implosive and explosive; because they are believed to draw matter into their unlit compaction but also, under other conditions, to eject formidable radiation. Both the in-gathering and the fierce scattering have their obvious counterpart in the experience of Judaism after Jesus. And their source is that hour, somewhere in the mid-decades of the century of Jesus's ministry and death, about which we seem to know so very little.

Why did the Jews—or, more exactly, why did Judaism so far as it can be defined in relation to Torah and Talmud, to nationhood, and to exile—say no to the kerygmatic revelation when compelling elements from within Torah and prophecy had prepared that very revelation?

Here we are on well-trodden ground. Not only the general circuit of Christ's life, ministry, and Passion are foretold in the Old Testament, most notably in the Psalms of the Suffering Servant and in Deutero-Isaiah, but numerous specific traits are also announced. The just man of suffering is to be mocked, scourged, and hung upon the tree of death. A virgin birth—though Hebraists insist that there is at this point a forced, overdetermined reading of a phrase signifying rather "a young woman"—has often been held to be adumbrated. The garments of the martyred Servant are to be divided by lot. In Amos, the most ancient of prophetic texts, we learn of sale and betrayal for a handful of silver.

Modern narratology and structuralism invert the relation between these numerous predictions and the event. They ascribe to the writers of the Gospels a deliberate appropriation of these prophecies so as to compose fictions of prefiguration, thus validating their claims for the crucified and risen Christ. It is difficult to conceive of such a device as transparent to first-century Jews or Judeo-Christians. To them, the accomplished enactment of the precisely foretold entailed a natural logic. Why—indeed, how—could the Jews deny that which their own revealed books and prophetic visions had so concretely anticipated?

The issue is a more general one. Recent historical inquiry has made palpable the climate of apocalyptic impatience and expectation that prevailed at the relevant time. Messianic claimants were recurrent. Millenarian ascetics, perfectionists of daily practice in literal awaiting of the apocalyptic end of Jewish history, gathered in the desert and cliff caves around the Dead Sea. In a complicated mesh of visionary hallucination and nationalist politics, Zealots of various nuances called for Armageddon and programmed the coming of the heavenly host. There burnt a fever in time itself. Jesus's assertion of the imminence of God's kingdom, his summons to humankind to cleanse its ways and its spirit in the face, at once terrible and transfiguring, of the nearing Last Judgment, accorded seamlessly with contemporary symbolism, textual interpretations, and sensibility in Judaism (most emphatically, we learn, in Galilee and in the thronged Jerusalem around Passover). Even the seemingly blasphemous dictum that he, Jesus of Nazareth, would lay waste the Temple, has been shown to be in perfect congruence with prophetic and mystical perceptions of the antinomian, violent acts that must precede and bring on the eschatological coming of the messianic hour. There was in Jesus's career a most brilliant opportunism of the eternal.

At the heart of that career lie the teachings embedded in the parables and in the Sermon on the Mount. As had been amply demonstrated, these teachings and the specific language in which they are put correspond very nearly point for point with cardinal tenets of the Torah and with the ethics, unsurpassed, of the Prophets, most especially Isaiah. Where there are departures from the canonic norm, in respect, for example, of the need to keep company with the publicans and the sinful or in regard to the primacy of healing and salvational acts even over the sanctity of the Sabbath, such dissents do not go signally beyond queries and challenges to Pharisaic observance as we find them among other Jewish "liberals" or apocalyptics at the time. On the contrary, it could well be argued that an acceptance of the moral prescriptions and exemplary deeds of the man Jesus meant an acceptance of a purified, humanely resourceful, and compassionate Judaism, preparing, strengthening itself at the advent of a possibly terminal crisis (the destruction of the nation, the dispersal of its people as these had been graphically prophesied in Jeremiah, Amos, Ezekiel, and countless apocalyptic texts).

In short, at essential points, on several levels—textual, symbolic, figurative, eschatological, and, first and foremost, ethical—the phenomenon and phenomenology of the coming and Passion of Jesus matched perfectly the expectations, the needs, the hopes of Jews in those decisive decades of the first and second century. Yet he was denied. Jews—we do not know just how many; we do not know the pertinent proportions out of the total—in manifestly significant numbers chose to remain Jews. For them, for us, the Messiah had not come and the titles bestowed upon Jesus, even if he had in some actual or ritualized way sprung from the house of David, were spurious.

Again, one asks why, knowing both that the evidence is so opaque as to be unrecapturable and that this question, so rarely pressed, defines our history and, indeed, present estate. It is in this perplexity, authentically dialectical, that one ventures to speculate.

* * *

There had been too many soothsayers, magicians, roadside preachers, epileptic *illuminati,* heralds of one greater to come and of time's foreclosure, plotters against Herod or Rome, ascetic fundamentalists out of Galilee or the desert. There had been too many so like him, roaming the backlands and the wilderness with a fistful of more or less fanatical loyalists, speaking in riddles in a grammar of imminent finality—figures such as that of the baptist of the successive Zealot-healers and prophets crucified after they had sparked local, risibly doomed rebellions. He ran too true to form. Even the miracles his followers bruited and embroidered upon were distinctly a part of the known scenario (with the possible, profoundly problematic exception of the resurrection of Lazarus). Thus, paradoxically, numerous Jews may scarcely have noticed Jesus's passage among them in those turbulent, clamorous days. This, assuredly, is borne out by the terse, almost casual allusion in Tacitus. But even this hypothesis is obscure, if only because we lack even tentative insight into the status of the miraculous in contemporary popular or educated perceptions. Were the transmutations of water into wine, the casting out of devils, the healing of the blind and of the lame thought to be magical turns, a faith healer's or sage's traditional skills or suspect bits of jugglery and of motivated rumor? Were they believed at all? We have no answers to these crucial queries.

But let us allow that some considerable portion of Jesus of Nazareth's sayings and teachings *did* reach Jews outside his immediate circle. It could then be that there were, among so many orthodox and edifying examples, precepts, inferences grievously outrageous to current Judaic perceptions. Is there, for a Jew, any duty greater than that of bestowing burial on his parents, of saying *kaddish* for them aloud and under his remembering breath? But Jesus had bidden "the dead bury their dead" and had commanded his would-be disciple to forgo his father's burial in order to follow him at once. And what of the claim, at moments ambiguous and resistant to paraphrase in the Gospels, to "sit on right of the Father," to be his Son in a sense more singular, more directly filial, than is that allowed all human beings who may seek to image themselves as children of the Almighty? Might these have been the node of outrage and the imperative of rebuttal? Again, we can only reflect on suppositions, observing the evasiveness with which not only Gospel dicta but early Christian heresies, Arianism above all, circle around the exact tenor of Jesus's divinity. Here, undoubtedly, the incitement of doubt or frank denial was sharp.

If we read between the sparse lines accorded our theme in rabbinic exegesis (lines, unless I am mistaken, from the medieval period rather than antiquity) and if we attend to modern religious historians and cultural anthropologists, a further motif surfaces. It is that of Jewish revulsion (the word is not too strong) at the mere notion and image of a crucified god, of a messiah done shamefully to death. From the outset, we are told, this revulsion, unattenuated by the wholly implausible epilogue of the ascent from the empty tomb, an epilogue of which even Mark seems to have been darkly uncertain, made impossible acquiescence in Jesus and in the claims of messianic divinity urged for him. Yet, again, there are problems. Judaism knows exemption from death for Enoch, the miraculous effacement of any known burial for Moses, a translation into heaven for Elijah. The proposition that some mode of *kenosis,* of divine self-bestowal in human form, was too anthropomorphic to pass muster in Jewish beliefs is contradicted by the strong vestiges of the anthropomorphic, of the divine "physicality" in the Torah, notably in God's direct, carnal encounter with Moses. Insofar, moreover, as it was the chastisement passed by Rome upon rebels, including those who led nationalist-fundamentalist insurrections in Judea, crucifixion need not have carried, of itself, any stigma of abasement.

A fourth ground for negation would be pragmatic. The coming and the going of the wonder-worker from Nazareth had changed nothing. The world was as cruel and corrupt and chaotic as before. The messianic must comport an eschatological transformation. The promise of the new kingdom had not been fulfilled at the time of Jesus's death and was now being either adjourned or metamorphosed by the preachings of the early churches. (Inevitably, one recalls Gershom Scholem's cunning *boutade* whereby the Messiah has either already passed among us or is about to do so, but that the changes he has brought are so slight that we do not even notice them or his passage.)

Clearly, there is force in this ascription of a Jewish refusal to watchful common sense. There is, in turn, a suspect circularity to the Christian apologetic argument that the mutation caused by Christ was intended to be, is, an inward one and that the man or woman who has espoused Christianity is indeed a being reborn and of a new world. More resistant to refutation is the undoubted fact that Judaism has, at critical junctures in its troubled affairs, welcomed and invested fanatical credence in messianic claimants such as Sabbatai Sevi, figures whose a priori pretentions and whose subsequent acts were assuredly less poignant than those of the Son of man.

Once more we ask, Why *il gran rifiutto?*

A school of recent German theologians who have made of the relations between Christ's agony and the Shoah the fulcrum of their reflections has offered a witty intimation (where wit in no manner excludes insightful gravity). Thinkers such as Markus Barth have asked whether the entire constellation of Judaic messianic tenets is not inherently ambivalent. The Old Testament and the Talmud, rabbinic teachings and Jewish historicism are unquestionably brimful of the messianic promise and of the awaiting of the Messiah in moods both anguished and exultant. Does the Jew in psychological and historical fact truly believe in that coming? More searchingly, does he truly thirst for it? Or is it, was it perhaps from the very first, what logicians or grammatologists might designate as a "counterfactual optative," a category of meaning never to be realized? One of the images used by these theologians—it has its provenance in a celebrated phrase of Hegel's—is that of an ontological addiction to the morning paper. Given the choice, the Jew prefers tomorrow's news, however grim, to the arrival of the Messiah. We are a people unquenchably avid of history, of knowledge in motion. We are the children of Eve, whose primal curiosity has modulated into that of the philosophic and natural sciences. In his heart of hearts, the Jew cannot accept the messianic end-stopping of history, the closure of the unknown, the everlasting stasis and ennui of salvation. In denying the messianic status of Jesus, in subverting early Christian beliefs in the proximity of the eschatological, the Jew gave expression to the genius of restlessness central to his psyche. We were, we remain nomads across time.

Strikingly, this reading does accord with a dialectical tension undeniable in Jewish thought and feeling. One need cite only Maimonides's insistence on a purely figurative, allegoric sense of the expectation of the Messiah or Franz Rosenzweig's strenuous deconstruction of the concept of a messianic actuality. Much in philosophic-historicist Judaism has indeed argued a perennial adjournment of the Messiah. Contrary strains of credence have been no less intense. Time and again more orthodox or charismatic authority has insisted on the concrete verity of the messianic, has declared that Jewish suffering and survival would be tragic non-sense unless the Messiah were to come, although the temporalities and modes of that coming are privy to God alone. The debate, the difference in sensibilities persists. It affects deeply the degrees of Jewish recognition of the State of Israel both inside the nation, whose legitimacy is denied by those in ritual attendance on a literal arrival of the Messiah, and within the relations between Israel and the Diaspora. Or to insert this debate in the context of these remarks: In what measure, at what level of consciousness, was the Jewish refusal of Jesus, at the time and thereafter, a symptom of radical psychic commitments to historical freedom, to the creative daimon of existential destiny on a changing earth?

Each of these five orders of causality and the undecidable complication of interplay between them may or may not serve to account for the abstention of the Jew from the Nazarene and his new synagogue, from the revelations and promise that he brought and incarnated. We do not know. But what we do know is this: However motivated, this abstention, this tenacious dissent has marked, to their very depths, the histories of Judaism and of Christianity. The identifying destiny of the Jew, but also in a more oblique sense, that of the Christian, is that of the ineradicable scars left by that hour of denial, by the veto of the Jew.

* * *

The imperceptions, the blank ignorance Jewish self-examination and consciousness so often exhibit in respect of Christology, of Pauline doctrine, of the soteriology developed by Paul and the church fathers, has psychologically legitimate and transparent sources. There is also a more central awkwardness. The concept of theology per se is largely foreign to Judaism. The revealed history that identifies the Jew, the Talmudic and Midrashic readings of that history, are teleological, not theological in any philosophic metaphysical sense. Judaism produces eminent moralists, visionaries, exegitists, but very few theologians of mark. So-called post-Holocaust theology articulates condign pathos, some arresting images and metaphors. It is not a rigorous theological revaluation in any intellectual-analytic sense, and it has signally failed to set the matter of final inhumanity, of the systematic bestialization of the human species, at the pivot of current philosophic inquiry, where it belongs.

Whatever the reasons, Judaic inattention to the New Testament, to Patristic literature, to Augustan and Aquinian propositions, comports a consequential void. For it is in these writings that the record of Jewish suffering among the Gentiles and of the Shoah is, as "through a glass darkly," writ large. Let me be absolutely clear on this. Positivist examinations of the roots of the Shoah and of modern anti-Semitism are of self-evident weight. Political history; sociology; the history of economic and class conflicts; the study, rudimentary as it is, of mass behavior and collective fantasies have contributed much. But the sum of empirical understanding falls drastically short of any fundamental insight. We will not, we cannot, of this I am persuaded, be capable of "thinking the Shoah," albeit inadequately, if we divorce its genesis and its radical enormity from theological origins. More specifically, we will not achieve penetration into the persistent psychosis of Christianity, which is that of Jew hatred (even where there are no or hardly any Jews left), unless we come to discern in this dynamic pathology the unhealed scars left by the Jew's "no" to the crucified Messiah. It is to these unhealing scars or stigmata that we may apply, in a dread sense, Kierkegaard's injunction that the "wounds of possibility" must be kept open.

How readily we forget that not only Jesus but the authors of the Gospels and Acts, all his first followers, were Jews. The beginnings of the macabre history of Jewish self-hatred are inextricably interwoven with those of Christianity. Although, so far as I know, hitherto unexamined, the thought presses on one that Christianity is at fundamental points a product and externalization of just this Jewish self-hatred. This is palpable in Luke. We can, moreover, read his detestation of his fellow Jews, his resolve to brand them with deicide, with corruption, with outrage and betrayal in the face of God, as partly encoded. To hand over Christ the Messiah for shameful execution is grievous enough; worse is the recalcitrance of the Jew before Christ's divinity, his refusal of the identity and epiphany of the Savior. Betrayal and judicial murder can be repaired by a belief in Christ's Resurrection and a conversion to his promise. The obdurate abstinence of the Jew from such conversion amounts to deicide persistently renewed. The mere existence of Jews is a repetition of Christ's suffering. It underwrites Pascal's awesome finding that no one has a right to sleep because Jesus remains in agony till the end of time.

Paul (whom the twelfth Benediction of the Eighteen Petition Prayers declares an apostate) is among a handful of supreme thinkers and writers whose almost every sentence is not only prodigal of tensed eventualities of meaning and interpretation, but the brimming density of whose persona may, crucially, have been opaque to itself. Much of Western history can be said to spring from uncertainties in the Pauline Epistles, and it is in Romans 9–11, Ephesians 2, and 1 Thessalonians that the victimization of the Jew and the necessity of this victimization for the Christian churches are made fatal. Yet such is the rhetorical depth and psychological involution of Pauline pronouncements that much in these doomsday texts allows only arguable, intuitive decipherment. Jesus's Jewishness and the biologically elect, privileged status of the "people of God" are evident to Paul, as is the absolute implication of Christianity in Jewish prophecy and in the critical situation of the house of Israel on the verge of national ruin. The man from Tarsus is obsessed by the virulence of his past and present Judaism—present in its miraculously informed and hallowed guise, in the covenant of rebirth in Christ, the Jew whom God's unfathomable love has made Son and flesh. At moments, Paul urges loving compassion for the Jewish "remnant" and a watchful expectation of the entry of the Jews into the greater *communitas* of the *ecclesia*. There is, he adverts, to be no triumphalism on the part of Christian Jews and of the uncircumcised now admitted to the Lord's table.

But at other moments far blacker impulses and spurts of menace are unmistakable. No volume, and it is never-ending, of commentary of hermeneutic "gentling," however subtle, can blunt the terrible edge of degradation in Romans 10–11 or Thessalonians. Now that the Son and Deliverer has come, "ungodliness is taken away from Jacob" and Israel is redeemed only insofar and exactly insofar as it ceases to be itself. Any willful self-exclusion from the new dispensation shall make of it an "un-people," a vestigial absurdity and lamentable remnant. But why should the existence, so obviously marginal and pitiful, of this obdurate remnant so trouble the Apostle? Why should it be a vexation to a Christendom already on the way to its Constantine triumph?

This, I believe, is where Pauline intimations are the most acute and consequential. The Jew holds hostage Christianity and, indeed, mankind inasmuch as it is the object of Christ's sacrificial, redemptive love. By refusing to accept Jesus Christ, the Jewish "remnant" has condemned humanity to the treadmill of history. Had the Jews acknowledged Jesus as the Son of God, had they received his concordat of grace, that filiality, that salvation, would have been proved. The New would then have been shown to be beyond cavil the fulfillment of the Old Testament. The cross would have canceled the fatal tree in Eden. The Jewish rebuke to Christ prevents the coming of the messianic realm. It pries and forces open the ravenous jaws of history. It holds time to ransom. In the theology of Maritain, this capital charge is plainly voiced. In that of Karl Barth (who wrestled lifelong with the enigma of "the remnant according to the election of grace"), it is an agonizing undecidability. It yields Barth's overwhelming, scarcely translatable utterance that the Jew and the Jewish people are "God-sick," "sickened by" their intimacy with a God whose supreme act of love and self-donation to their election they have chosen to refuse or leave in abeyance.

In the wake of the Shoah, Christian theologians (notably, as I have mentioned, in Germany) have distinctly echoed Karl Barth's ambiguities, laboring to redefine the reciprocities between synagogue and church, between Jewish survivance and Christianity. The principal strategies of argument are familiar.

The church has "replaced" Judaism. It is now the Christian, fully cognizant of his Jewish origins and of his debt to the Torah and the Prophets, fully cleansed of the great Marcionite heresy whereby there is an absolute discontinuity between the old and the new Scriptures, who is now the true chosen of God, the true Israel. The promised heritage of Abraham is that of worldwide Christianity. A second stance is that which concedes to the Jewish remnant a peculiar and privileged role in the continued development of Christianity. There is a "spiritual heritage" that Christians can derive only from the tree of Jesse, an unbroken validation of the message and meaning of Jesus forthcoming from the election of Abraham and of Moses. Almost opportunely, the very slow conversion of Jews to Christianity (and it does, after all, occur) and the stubbornness of the as yet dissenting Jews demonstrate that Christ's ministry is not yet accomplished, that there is further love on offer. More self-critical is a third valuation, that of a scandalous schism in the house of the one God. An eloquent, philo-Semitic theologian such as Moltmann insists that both Judaism and Christianity are, by virtue of their division, thorns in each other's sides. Judaism poses to Christianity questions, most sharply that of the unchanging tragedy of the historical after the alleged coming of the true Messiah, that Christianity has, until now, failed to answer adequately. In ways as yet impenetrable to satisfactory understanding or therapeutic action, Judaism and Christianity demand each other's separate and even conflictual incompletions if God's choice of his people is to be made visible. Fourth, and here the demarcations are necessarily fluid, synagogue and church can be held to be complementary. Israel remains the matrix of Jesus's life and teachings; the mission of Christianity is one of ecumenical and global propagation. The Messiah awaited by Jews is the same Messiah whose *re*appearance is awaited by Christians. Coexistence is *pro*-existence in a formulation by Markus Barth that closely reflects similar suggestions in Rosenzweig, Baeck, and Buber.

Each of these positions and their overlap have their theological entailments and behavioral consequences. Each testifies to an unresolved crux—truly that of the "cross"—explicit in historical and contemporary Christianity and, unless I am in error, subconsciously present in the condition of Judaism. But none of these models, forceful as they are, seems to me to plumb the depths.

Even metaphorized (and metaphors can turn murderous), Paul's construal of mankind as in some sense hostage to the Jews' "no" to Christ is pregnant with catastrophe.

Throughout my work, I have argued that the Judaic initiation of monotheism, whether by virtue of divine revelation or by virtue of anthropomorphic invention, has exercised an intolerable psychic pressure on Western consciousness. Made inaccessibly abstract yet punitively close by Mosaic and Prophetic formulation, the God of Israel sought to eradicate the sensuous pluralities, the neighborly liberalities of pagan polytheism. What fallible man or woman can be adequate to the demands of the God of Sinai or find any mirroring of his or her profane, imperfect nature in the tautology of the Burning Bush, blank and consuming as is the desert? By definition, mankind is always in the wrong in the face of the Mosaic deity and of its imperatives of perfection. The answer to Job is, famously, one of literally inhuman enormity. Ordinary humankind knows that under the weight of the love of this God and of his commandments of reciprocity in love, the soul breaks. What thinking, feeling Jew has not, at some hours, shared Pompey's horror when that Roman intruded by the Holy of Holies in the captured temple and found it empty?

Twice more, Judaism presented to the West the graphic claims of the ideal. Jesus the Jew renewed and stressed the exigence of perfect altruism, of self-denial, of sacrificial humility even unto death, set out in Mosaic monotheism and in the Law. He asked of man fraternal love, unworldliness, abstentions from pride and benefit formidably beyond the reach of any but saints and martyrs. The trinitarian construct, the suspension of the Law in the name of love abounding, the development of explicit scenarios of celestial compensation by Christianity and its churches, enact specific attempts to paganize an underlying Judaic monotheistic heritage. They constitute tactics of attenuation and dissipation aimed at making bearable that God of Abraham, Isaac, and Jacob whom a Pascal still invokes with an apprehension of his original and authentic terror. The Gnostic-Hellenistic hybrid with Judaism that is Christianity, the pantheon of its saints, palpable relics, indulgences, confessional absolutions, and neon-lit paradise, proved magnificently marketable. But at its militant and triumphant center, the pressure of Mosaic and Nazarene demands, the summons to perfection, remained. Time and again, be it in desert monasticism or Savonarola, be it in Kierkegaard's "fear and trembling" or in Karl Barth's stress on the abyss separating God from man, Christianity has been drawn, perhaps unwillingly, toward the Judaism within itself.

The third of the principal motions of spirit whereby Judaism visits on our civilization the blackmail of utopia is that of the diverse shades of messianic socialism and Marxism. Marxism is, in essence, Judaism grown impatient. The Messiah has been too long in coming or, more precisely, in not coming. The kingdom of justice must be established by man himself, on this earth, here and now. Love must be exchanged for love, justice for justice, preaches Karl Marx in his 1844 manuscripts, echoing transparently the phraseology of the Psalms and the Prophets. There is in the egalitarian program of communism, in the economics of finality as outlined by Marxist-Leninist doctrine, little that is not called for, implacably, by Amos when he announces God's anathema on the rich and God's loathing of property. Where Marxism prevailed, even or especially in its more brutal modes, it fulfilled that vengeance of the desert on the city so strident in Amos and other prophetic-apocalyptic texts of social retribution. (It need hardly be said that the current crisis and conceivable collapse of Marxist messianic immanence will reach deep into the affairs and future of Judaism.)

Three times, therefore, the Jew has been the summoner to individual and to social perfection, the night watchman who does not ensure repose but, on the contrary, wakes us from the sleep of common comforts and self-regard. (Freud even woke us from the innocence of dreaming.) This triple exaction has, I believe, bred in the Western psyche deep-lying detestations. It is not the God-killer whom Christianity has hounded to the rim of extinction in Europe since the Middle Ages, it is the "God-maker" or mouthpiece who has reminded mankind of what it *could* be, of what it must become if man is indeed to be man, if a being of Jesus of Nazareth's ethical radiance can legitimately be called a Son of man. Is there anyone we hate more than he or she who asks of us a sacrifice, a self-denial, a compassion, a disinterested love that we feel ourselves incapable of providing but whose validity we nevertheless acknowledge and experience in our inmost? Is there anyone we would rather annihilate from our presence than the one who insists on holding up to us the unrealizable potentialities of transcendence?

Thus there has been in every pogrom and in the Shoah a central strain of Christian self-mutilation, a desperate endeavor by Christianity and by its pagan-parodistic offshoots such as Nazism to silence once and for all the curse of the ideal inherent in the Mosaic covenant with God, in the more-than-human humaneness of Isaiah, in the teachings of Jesus the Jew. Eradicate the Jew and you will have eradicated from within the Christian West an unendurable remembrance of moral and social failure. There is, in consequence, an awful symmetry in the fact that by instituting and allowing the world of the death camps, European gentile civilization has striven to make it unbearable for Jews *to remember.* For it is in Judaism that there has been the obsessive, maddening remembrance that Christianity worked furiously to stifle inside itself.

But in the perspective of Paul's lineaments of mankind held to ransom by the denying remnant of Judaism, by the simple survival of this inexplicable vestige, we can consider even further the twists of menace. We can follow the logic even of Luther's call for the murder of the Jews once they had renewed their original refusal of Christ by rejecting the Reformation and its ardent, sincere proffer of Zion regained and renewed.

Where religious imaginings and their kindred perversion touch on the pulse of the subconscious, the monstrous is not far off. Yet we must try to perceive clearly. Men have massacred men, there has been what is sometimes loosely called genocide, from the Book of Joshua to Pol Pot. If we sense in the Shoah a singularity, a quantum jump in our long chronicles of inhumanity, it is because mass slaughter and planned elimination, both of which have manifold precedent, were accompanied by, were explicitly designed as, the dehumanization of the victim. He was to be recognized as a being less than human. Torture and fear were to reduce him to subhuman status. In the fantastications of Nazism, those starved, beaten, gassed to extinction were not men and women and children but vermin, members of a species other than that of humans. Now observe the symbolic symmetry. In the eye of the believer, God had, through the incarnation of Christ, through the descent of the divine into human form, affirmed, attested to the literal godliness of man. Man had, in Christ, been of the nature of God. This modulation had been scorned by the Jew. Was it not inevitable that the Jew, who had refused transcendence for man, should bear the final, logical consequence, which is to be made less than man? The Shoah, the death camps have lowered the fragile threshold of humaneness. If the victims were "unmanned," so were the butchers whose intent and acts diminished them to bestiality. The Jew on his way to the gas chambers was more than scapegoat. He was, in a sickness unto death of logic, of reciprocity, the provocation to, the occasion of, his persecutors' descent into animality. In both his agony and in the sadistic beastliness that brought on that agony—the two being rigorously inseparable—it was the Jew who put in question the belief that our kind, that *Homo sapiens* has, in some manner, been created in God's image. Without the Jew, there would not, there could not have been the cancellation of man that is Auschwitz—a cancellation so symmetrical with that embodied in

Judaism, the remembrance of the rejection of the claims to the divine in Jesus. Erasure for erasure: the eclipse of light over Golgotha and the black hole in history of the Shoah, darkness calling to darkness and the Jew centrally implicated in both.

* * *

What follows (however tentatively)?

It is my instinct that ecumenical programs, in respect of reconciliation between Jew and Christian, may be of some social, political use. But I cannot see that they have any foundation in theological fact. "With the complete physical extinction of all Jews from the face of the earth the demonstration and proof of God's existence would collapse and the church would lose its *raison d'être:* the church would fall. The future of the church lies in the salvation of all Israel" (M. Barth). One values the penitential generosity of such sentiments. But neither Rome nor Geneva would, when being true to themselves, need to accept them. The survivance of the Jew has nothing whatever to do with any ontological proof of God's existence such as we find in Anselm, Aquinas, or, in a different but related tenor, Calvin and Karl Barth. We have seen that this survivance is, from the point of view of Pauline and Augustinian historicism and teleology, a scandal, at best ambiguously recalcitrant to interpretation, at worst to be eradicated so that Christ may return in salvation and in glory.

For his part, the Jew cannot negotiate his rejection of a messianic Jesus. He cannot, in however metaphoric a translation, accept the "God-entrance" into the Galilean sayer of parables and the latter's Resurrection and ascent to shared divinity. Precisely to the extent that Jews remain Jews, these denials must stand and must, by the existential fact of continued Jewish life and history, be constantly reaffirmed. So what is there "really," taking reality to be of the essence, to be talked about? (A theocratic and prophetic "primitive" such as Solzhenitsyn has seen this plainly and made no cant of his christological distaste for the Jew.)

Second, one conjectures, but I speak as an outsider, that Christianity itself is sick at heart, that it is lamed, possibly terminally, by the paradox of revelation and of doctrine that generated not only the Shoah but the millennia of anti-Jewish violence, humiliation, and quarantine that are its obvious background. It stands, or should stand appalled by its own image, by its fundamental failings, whether by omission or commission, in the season of barbarism, increasingly conscious that the death camps were modeled on the long habituation of Christian Europe to blueprints of hell (a concept antithetical to Judaism); Catholicism and Protestantism hardly know themselves. We do hear sincere calls to self-examination, to a rethinking of a profoundly flawed history. There are poignant attempts to reemphasize and make consequential the Judaic substance in Christianity. But these cannot be pressed too far, if Christianity is not to efface or trivialize the basic tenets of its revelation. How can there be authentic truth and salvation outside Christ? How can the Jew's veto, be it that of an impotent, despised minority, of a fossilized vestige—an image perennial in Christian apologetics and polemics—be accepted, let alone be made concordant with the Christian creed and the life of the churches? Charles Péguy devises the harrowing conceit whereby the actual physical agony of the crucified Jesus only begins at the exact moment in which Jesus realizes that his infinite powers of love cannot obtain pardon for Judas. I do not doubt that agony, nor can I doubt the impossibility of that pardon.

Seriously questioned, the current condition of Judaism is scarcely more consoling than is that of its most successful and ungrateful heresy. The notion of "coming to terms" with the Holocaust is a vulgar and profound indecency. Man cannot, he must not ever "come to terms," historicize pragmatically, or incorporate into the comforts of reason his derogation from the human within himself. He must not blur the possibility that the death camps and the world's indifference to them marked the failure of a crucial experiment: man's effort to become fully human. After Auschwitz Jew and Gentile go lamed, as if the wrestling bout of Jacob had been well and truly lost.

As I have noted, this laming has on the Jewish side generated no theological-philosophical renewal (perhaps it could not do so). Jewish orthodoxy continues in its often jejune formalism, in its feverish atrophy in ritualistic minutiae. Worse: In Israel it has fueled state savagery and corruption—for let us never forget that each time a Jew humiliates, tortures, or makes homeless another human being, there is a posthumous victory for Hitler. In liberal Judaism, in Judaism at large, the winds of spiritual development, of metaphysical exploration, blow faint. Where, now, is there "a guide for the perplexed" or a voice out of the register that produced a Spinoza, a Bergson, or a Wittgenstein? With the breakdown of messianic radicalism throughout the Marxist domain, the fertile stress of critical questioning, of utopian immanence, withers away. How Jewish was Paul when he spoke in bitter contempt of those who "blow neither hot nor cold."

There cannot, I suggest, be any advance inward in Judaism's sense of its purpose, in its grasp of the mystery of its survival and of the obligations this mystery entails, unless the Jews grapple with the notion that Christianity originated *from the heart of Judaism*. We must strive to gain insight not only into the logic, into the psychological and historical validity of this genesis of the Christian out of the Jew; we must also seek clarity in regard to the tragic, possibly mutually destructive bonds that have since tied Jew to Christian, Christian to Jew, or, to put it nakedly, victim to butcher. Jews are compelled to envisage, if not to allow, if not to rationalize, the hideous paradox of their innocent guilt, of the fact that it is they who have, in Western history, been the occasion, the recurrent opportunity for the Gentile to become less than man.

The challenge to be faced is that put to us by Sidney Hook in a posthumously published interview. Hook asked whether "it had really been worth it," whether Jewish survival from persecution to persecution, in pariahdom and across the abyss of the Holocaust, could be assessed positively. Had there not been too much pain, too much horror? Would it not have been preferable, asked Hook, if the Jewish remnant after Christ had melted into the commonwealth of Hellenistic and Roman Christendom, if it had more or less "normally" lost its identity and apartheid as did other peoples no less gifted, such as the ancient Egyptians or the classical Greeks? To which absolutely unavoidable question the coda could well be: Does the unexamined axiom of national survival justify the necessary policies of the state of Israel at its borders and, what is far graver, inside them? To what end the unquenchable constancy of Jew hatred, to what end Auschwitz and the everlasting brand it has put on Jewish memory, on any responsible use by a Jew of the past tense?

I have ventured to propose that Hook's inquiry concerns not only the Jews to whom it is addressed but the Christian who has established its somber context. For after such remembrance, what forgiveness, what self-forgiveness?

All too plainly, the issues defy the ordering of common sense. They seem to lie just on the other side of reason. They are extraterritorial to analytic debate. They take substance from the question of God, from the question of his existence or nonexistence. We can define modernism as the sum of impulses and psychological-intellectual configurations in which the enormity of that question is experienced only fitfully or in metaphors grown pale. One is very nearly tempted to hope for a moratorium on future discourse. We Jews have said no to the claims made for and, in certain opaque moments by, the man Jesus. He remains for us a spurious messiah. The true one has not come in his stead. Today, who but a fundamentalist handful awaits his coming in any but a formulaic, allegoric sense, a sense bitterly irrelevant to the continuing desolation and cruelty of the human situation? In turn, 1 Thessalonians 2:15 proclaims the Jew to be a deicide, a slayer of his own prophets and therefore one "contrary" or "enemy to all men." Vatican II sought to attenuate or even cancel this sentence of death in the troubled light of modern squeamishness and the Holocaust, in view of the "final solution" that this Pauline verdict determines. But the text is no accident: It lay, it continues to lie, at the historical and symbolic roots of Christendom.

On both sides, might it not be salutary if words now failed us?

We must learn to persist in some dispensation of twilight with what dignity and minor virtues we can muster. If we are able to do so, we ought to apprehend our own location in a biologically brief history as that of a prologue to the coming into being of a more humane humanity. The most darkly inspired of all twentieth-century imaginers of God, Franz Kafka, reportedly said, "There is abundant hope, but there is none for us." What we may do is to attempt to hear from within this abdication from the messianic, be it Jewish or be it Christian, the promise of an eerie freedom.

7

Primo Levi:
The Survivor as Victim

Alvin H. Rosenfeld

News of the death of Primo Levi in April 1987 brought with it a sense of loss, painful at the time, that has not entirely receded to this day. Levi's death was reported to be self-inflicted, reason enough to feel more than just saddened by the passing of an exceptionally fine writer. Such an end was altogether unexpected and was therefore accompanied by an almost paralyzing sense of shock and perplexity. Inevitably, and almost against one's will, the names of others came to mind: Paul Celan, Tadeusz Borowski, Piotr Rawicz, Jean Améry. As a writer who reflected continually and with increasingly refined insight on the crimes of the Third Reich, Levi naturally belonged in the company of these writers, but one was reluctant to place him among them as a fellow suicide. How could he—whose books were distinguished by such measured temperament, emotional balance, and rational control—how could *he* of all writers take his own life? Did he in fact kill himself, or, as some have claimed, did he experience a momentary blackout and fall accidentally to his death? However one viewed it, Levi's death was recognized as tragically premature and, as such, had to be mourned as an enormous loss to the world of letters. Beyond that, though, if his was indeed a death by suicide, the implications were all the more troubling, for Levi's violent end would necessarily raise once again the awful possibility that the Nazi crimes could continue to claim victims decades after Nazism itself had been defeated. The question that then came to the fore transcended the personal and, in the most disturbing way, became deeply psychological and broadly cultural in its implications: Was there latent within the memory of these crimes a peril that, years later, might overwhelm those who seemingly had managed to escape them—and not just escape them but, as in Primo Levi's case, prevail over them?

Levi, we thought, had triumphed through an act of mind that could record the worst of human experience and simultaneously contain it in a language whose fundamental clarity, sobriety, and formal elegance seemed to be safeguards against any lingering threats from the past. Among all those who had survived the death camps and gone on to write about them, he seemed to be one of the few who had achieved some permanent measure of artistic control over his experience. His writings never shrank from a direct confrontation with the horrors of Nazism, but at the same time they were conspicuously free of outrage or self-pity, of overt expressions of bitterness, emotional fury, or uncontained rage. "My personal temperament is not inclined to hatred," he wrote. "I regard it as bestial, crude, and prefer on the contrary that my actions and thoughts, as far as possible, should be the product of reason."[1] Following his temperamental inclinations, Levi typically wrote in a prose style that suppressed whatever impulses he might have had to express reproach or resentment, and he denied altogether whatever temptations he might have felt for revenge. Hatred and vengeance are passions that simply do not appear in his writings, and even common anger is rare.

Although he had plenty to be angry about, Levi had reached an unusual level of intellectual and moral poise in his books and, so it appeared, had achieved a degree of inner peace that might almost be taken as a form of serenity. In short, it seemed that he had come through his ordeal and, in his person as well as in his writings, showed that it was possible for the civilized values of intelligence and humane feeling to survive the Nazi assault against them. This sense of Levi was badly shaken by the news of his death. To be sure, it was not the case that his writings were suddenly invalidated or meant less than they had before but that in the end they were not strong enough to shield the author from the lacerating memories of personal and historical extremity that they recorded. Worse still was the real possibility that by keeping these memories alive and by returning to them in book after book, Levi may have prolonged and even intensified the trauma that had so cruelly marked his earlier years and that retained the power, it now appeared, to suddenly overwhelm him and put an abrupt end to his life. He was a survivor but, by right of his intense absorption in the past, was he not also increasingly a victim? Simply put, the question that has to be asked is this: In what ways might writing itself be implicated in Primo Levi's death? His books are both testimony and reflection, a vivid evocation of the past and a continuing meditation on it by a survivor-witness. Is it necessary for us now to regard that status, that self-chosen vocation, as ultimately a vocation of doom?

These are the kinds of questions that I wish to raise in this essay. In a search for answers, I look to Levi's published writings as well as to unpublished correspondence with him that I accumulated over the past decade. It was my privilege to be a friend of Primo Levi's in his later years. We spent time together in Italy in March 1981 and then again in Bloomington, Indiana, in April 1985. In addition, we exchanged numerous letters, mostly about his writings, from 1980 until just days before his death in April 1987. Some of these letters are pertinent to the issues before us, and I cite them at the end of my essay. I do not pretend to be in a position to offer conclusive answers to the questions arising from Primo Levi's death, but I attempt to clarify some of the factors that I believe may have contributed to it as well as some of the implications that remain with us in its aftermath.

Survivor as Writer, Survivor as Victim

The idea that survivors are also victims is not new, although we are still far from understanding the complex and troubled nature of survivorship and the kinds of torment that former camp inmates can continue to experience for years after their liberation. There is by now a sizable literature on this subject, as there is on most other aspects of the Holocaust. It deals, from a psychological and often from a psychoanalytic point of view, with such issues as Holocaust-induced pathology, the effects of massive traumatization on the psychic structures of former camp inmates, on the possible transmission of such trauma to the children of Holocaust survivors, and so on. There are obvious insights to be gained from reading in this literature, but for present purposes I prefer to look elsewhere, to the writings of survivor-authors themselves.

Levi understood himself as a writer-witness and wrote from a point of view that he shared with others who had undergone analogous experience. Although it is true, as he acknowledged, that no two survivors share a common understanding of their time in the camps, it is also true that those who had been in those places and managed to survive them and tell about them almost certainly have more in common with one another than they do with those who had not been forced to undergo such suffering. What they share, in fact, is not only a personal connection to unimaginably harrowing experiences but the memory-wounds from such experiences, which remain with them seemingly for the rest of their lives and can erupt without warning, often explosively, at any time.

One of these writers was Jean Améry, who had been incarcerated in Auschwitz-Monowitz at the same time as Primo Levi and, for a short period, had even shared a barracks with him in that camp. In the title essay of *At the Mind's Limits: Contemplations by a Survivor on Auschwitz and Its Realities,* Améry refers to Levi respectfully and by name.[2] Levi, in turn, wrote about Améry at length in his last book, *The Drowned and the Saved.* In "The Memory of the Offense," Levi explored the nature of traumatic memory and saw it as "an injury that cannot be healed." To reinforce his point that "the memory of a trauma suffered or inflicted is itself traumatic," he quoted from Améry's powerful essay "Torture":

> It is not without horror that we read the words left us by Jean Améry, the Austrian philosopher tortured by the Gestapo because he was active in the Belgian resistance and then deported to Auschwitz because he was Jewish: "Anyone who has been tortured remains tortured. ... Anyone who has suffered torture never again will be able to be at ease in the world; the abomination of the annihilation is never extinguished. Faith in humanity, already cracked by the first slap in the face, then demolished by torture, is never acquired again."

Levi went on to note that "torture was for him an interminable death: Améry ... killed himself in 1978."[3] In light of his own death less than a decade later, these words take on a special poignancy for us today. They point if not directly to a premeditated, self-willed death, then certainly to the sense, common to both authors, that survival for those who had been in the camps could mean an intermittent death-in-life, an affliction of consciousness triggered now and again by what Levi called "the memory of the offense." Levi concluded, "Once again it must be observed, mournfully, that the injury cannot be healed; it extends through time, and the Furies, in whose existence we are forced to believe, not only rack the tormentor ... but perpetuate the tormentor's work by denying peace to the tormented."[4] While it is obviously not the case that every survivor suffers in the manner described here, there can be little doubt that Levi himself knew the Furies all too well and must have felt himself punished by them in no small measure. Memory, one of the primary sources of his genius as a writer, was also the source of much of his pain.

It was a pain that must have accumulated over many years. Although its etiology can be located precisely enough—the camp experience itself—its long period of dormancy, incubation, and eventual unfolding is not so easily charted. Out of necessity, one learns to live with such pain, to disguise it or suppress it or otherwise evade a direct confrontation with it, but these maneuvers work at best to tame the inner suffering, not eliminate it. Werner Weinberg, another keenly perceptive survivor-writer, spoke of learning "to live and function with an unexorcisable piece of the Holocaust within me."[5] Primo Levi learned to live that way as well, but at a cost to himself of a punishingly high order.

Among other things, he was troubled by a deep and lingering sense of injustice, a subject that came to the fore often in his writings and did so in an especially curious way in his reflections on Jean Améry and suicide. Levi recounted an episode from Améry's essay "On the Necessity and Impossibility of Being a Jew," in which Améry described trading blows with an aggressive Polish foreman in Auschwitz. The latter would willfully strike at Jews under his command and one day, for no apparent reason, hit Améry in the face. In a rare moment of revolt, Améry struck him back with a punch to the jaw. That blow by a rebelling Jew served to bring on a worse beating by the violent Pole, but all the same it was a deed that had to be done: Dignity demanded it. In commenting on this episode, Levi expressed appreciation for Améry's courage, but he remarked that he himself would never have been capable of striking back. "I have never known how to 'return the blow,'" he wrote. "'Trading punches' is an experience I do not have, as far back as I can go in memory." He then said something about this episode that is not at all easy to grasp. While he respected Améry's action as "a reasoned revolt against the perverted world of the Lager," he implicated it directly in Améry's suicide. Here is the crucial passage: "Those who 'trade blows' with the entire world achieve dignity but pay a very high price for it because they are sure to be defeated. Améry's suicide ... like other suicides admits of a cloud of explanations, but, in hindsight, that episode of defying the Pole offers one interpretation."[6]

Despite numerous readings of this essay, it is not at all clear to me what this "interpretation" actually is meant to reveal. Precisely what was it that Levi saw in Améry's moment of rebellion that led him to believe he had understood the nature of Améry's violent death? The American writer Cynthia Ozick, author of a lengthy essay on Levi's suicide, believes that it was rage, a perfectly understandable emotion for anyone who had been in the camps to feel but one that Levi could not readily entertain or allow himself to express. In Ozick's reading of Levi's last book, however, rage was finally and powerfully released: "*The Drowned and the Saved*," Ozick wrote, "is a book of catching-up after decades of abstaining. It is a book of blows returned by a pen on fire." In Ozick's view this long-suppressed rage was simply too much for him: "Levi waited more than forty years; and he did not become a suicide until he let passion in, and returned the blows. ... I grieve that he equated rage with self-destruction."[7]

The Drowned and the Saved is a more forceful, hard-hitting book than any Levi had published previously, but in my reading of it, it does not in fact reverberate with the clamorous tones of anger that Ozick seems to hear in it or show us the author enraged. There is an emphatic note of grievance that runs through the essays in this collection, but there is also more than a little self-criticism. Levi was hard on himself in this book—indeed, much too hard. Although he was highly critical of the Germans, he also felt the need to defend himself for his previous writings about them. "Améry," he wrote, "called me 'the forgiver.' I consider this neither insult nor praise but imprecision. I am not inclined to forgive, I never forgave our enemies of that time. ... I know no human act that can erase a crime; I demand justice, but I am not able, personally, to trade punches or return blows."[8] It is clear that Levi felt himself pressed by Améry's example of militancy and also felt the need to defend himself against Améry's accusation. As former camp inmates, both men were victims of gross injustice, but whereas Améry found ways to hit back and thereby to reclaim a measure of personal dignity, Levi held to a more characteristic restraint. The contrast must not have been an easy one for Levi to ponder. "I am the way I was made by my past," he wrote, "and it is no longer possible for me to change."[9] It was an honest way for him to account for his own relative passivity in contrast to Améry's more openly rebellious nature, but were his actions, or, more precisely, his inaction, an adequate reply to the injustices he was made to suffer? Almost certainly not. He seems to have felt himself doubly violated—first by the dehumanizing experiences of his time in Auschwitz and second by the troubling accusation, which may have been in part also a self-accusation, that he did too little to back up his demand for justice with concrete actions. What comes through in his extended reflection on Améry and suicide, therefore, has far less to do with any rage directed against his former persecutors than with intense self-criticism and, along with that, possibly a serious loss of personal dignity. These are matters that Levi regarded with the utmost seriousness and described in grave tones in writing about Améry: "In order to live, an identity—that is, dignity—is necessary. ... Whoever loses one also loses the other, dies spiritually: without defenses he is therefore exposed also to physical death."[10] Within the terms of the present argument, this passage seems ominously self-reflexive and points to a difficult moment of spiritual crisis in Levi's own life.

Werner Weinberg, already cited above, has provided insight into the inner life of the survivor that I believe is applicable here. "There are wounds that defy healing," he has written, "and the reason is that they must not be allowed to heal."[11] The reference is to spiritual wounds, memory-wounds, the very same that Primo Levi had in mind when he spoke of "the memory of the offense." Levi knew himself to be a victim of "the greatest crime in the history of humanity."[12] At the same time, as we have already seen, he understood that it was not possible to redeem such misdeeds, that "no human act can erase a crime." The tortured remain tortured, doubly so: by right of the initial act of violation against them and then, to add torment upon torment, by the unassuaged memory of the offense. Levi demanded justice, but on some very deep level he knew that justice would not be forthcoming. And so he turned in his writings to a deepening and ever more anguished analysis of the problematic itself: to an examination of the motivations and actions of those who defined, organized, and carried out unprecedented acts of injustice and to an examination of himself and others who had been in the camps, the victims of extreme injustice. At the same time, and out of a sense of increasing necessity in his latter years, he examined the quality of his own witness by looking at himself as a chronicler and anatomist of injustice. As he proceeded to think and write along these lines, his books show that he was driven to reflect more and more on the value of life itself and to ponder what it is that brings some to put an end to life through suicide.

Levi and the Germans

Prior to the war, Primo Levi had completed his formal studies in Italy, but, as he often remarked, his true university was Auschwitz.[13] Thus, in important, indeed transformative, ways, it might be said that Levi also received a "German" education. Certainly, from the age of twenty-five until the end of his life, he remained endlessly curious about Germany and the Germans. By his own count, he visited the country at least fifteen times in the postwar period,[14] spent several years studying the German language, and from his first book to his last did his best to ponder the people and the ways that constituted the German nation. He was driven to do so, as he said repeatedly, not out of hatred and not in order to exact vengeance upon his former persecutors but in an effort to figure them out.

That was to prove to be no easy task.

Levi's reflections on Germany and the Germans are dispersed throughout his writings. In addition to important sections of *Survival in Auschwitz* and *The Reawakening*, one finds observations of a telling kind in the "Vanadium" chapter of *The Periodic Table*; in the chapter entitled "Letters from Germans" in *The

Drowned and the Saved as well as elsewhere in that book; in Ferdinando Camon's collection, *Conversations with Primo Levi;* in the author's foreword and afterword to the German edition of *Survival in Auschwitz;* and elsewhere. A careful reading of this material yields numerous insights, most of which center on the author's attempts to grasp the essence of the peculiar education he had received at the hands of the Germans in Auschwitz.

It was, as he related in his first book, an education in the processes of dehumanization, or in "the demolition of a man."[15] *Survival in Auschwitz* portrays dehumanization on several different levels, but if one were to search Levi's first book for a primal scene of basic human reduction—one in which the author portrayed himself as having been the victim of a fundamental act of degradation—one could hardly do better than to return to the chapter entitled "Chemical Examination." There Levi recounted a memory of offense that showed him, as had nothing heretofore in his experience, just how vulnerable he was to the indignities and diminishments of injustice. Trained as a chemist in Turin, Levi volunteered in Auschwitz to join a chemical unit; if accepted, he could count on the relative security of an indoor job and thus hope to prolong his life a little. In order to become a member of this unit, however, he first had to pass a chemistry examination. Under ordinary conditions such an examination would have posed him no special problems, but because he was a Jewish inmate of Auschwitz, conditions were anything but normal. Here is how Levi described coming before Dr. Pannwitz, his examiner:

> Pannwitz is tall, thin, blond; he has eyes, hair, and nose as all Germans ought to have them, and sits formidably behind a complicated writing table. I, Häftling 174517, stand in his office, which is a real office, shining, clean, and ordered, and I feel that I would leave a dirty stain whatever I touch.
>
> When he finished writing, he raised his eyes and looked at me.
>
> From that day I have thought about Doktor Pannwitz many times and in many ways. I have asked myself how he really functioned as a man; how he filled his time, outside of the Polymerization and the Indo-Germanic conscience; above all, when I was once more a free man, I wanted to meet him again, not from a spirit of revenge, but merely from a personal curiosity about the human soul.
>
> Because that look was not one between two men; and if I had known how completely to explain the nature of that look, which came as if across the glass window of an aquarium between two beings who live in different worlds, I would also have explained the essence of the great insanity of the third Germany.[16]

Levi left Pannwitz not knowing if he had passed the chemistry examination (he later learned that he had), but the memory of his strange ordeal of standing in prison rags before his German examiner never left him. Although both men were scientists with academic degrees, in that place Levi could not possibly think of himself and Pannwitz as professional colleagues. Precisely who or what was he in the eyes of the other? That question, in one version or another, remained with

Primo Levi for the rest of his life. If he could have answered it, as he remarked, he would have been able to explain the essence of Nazism itself.

Levi had been taken to the chemistry examination by a *Kapo* named Alex, a *Reichsdeutscher* described as a crude, delinquent type. Once the examination was over, this same *Kapo* escorted Levi back to the camp. On the way they had to climb across some steel barriers. Alex got dirty in the process and cursed his grease-blackened hand. Here is Primo Levi's description of what followed: "Without hatred and without sneering, Alex wipes his hand on my shoulder, both the palm and the back of the hand, to clean it; he would be amazed, the poor brute Alex, if someone told him that today, on the basis of this action, I judge him and Pannwitz and the innumerable others like him, big and small, in Auschwitz and everywhere."[17]

In the large corpus of Holocaust literature, as indeed elsewhere in Levi's own writing, one can find scenes of dehumanization that are more unnerving in their depictions of human degradation than the one just quoted. It is typical of Levi's genius as a writer, however, to reveal the large offense in the ostensibly small act—in this case, to show the reduction of a fellow human being by turning him into a convenient rag. To be sure, during his time of incarceration in Auschwitz Levi was to go on to know far greater horrors, but those alluded to in "The Chemical Examination"—the disarming inequality and basic absurdity of his audience with Pannwitz and the abuse he suffered at the hands of Alex the *Kapo*—these two constituted primary acts of injustice that he never forgot. Both prompted in him a lifelong desire to understand the Germans and, as such, were at the root of his becoming a writer. Here is how he put it to his first German translator:

> I cannot say that I understand the Germans. And what one cannot understand forms a painful void; it is a thorn, a constant urge that demands fulfillment. ...
>
> When I think about my life and the various goals that I have set for myself, then I recognize only one as clearly defined and conscious, and it is this: to bear witness, to allow the German people to hear my voice, and to "answer" the Kapo who wiped his hand on my shoulder [and] Dr. Pannwitz.[18]

He was convinced, as he stated in *The Periodic Table*, that "every German must answer for Auschwitz,"[19] but the more he probed into the nature of the Nazi crimes and into what he generally regarded as a failure among Germans of the postwar period to do the same, the more forlorn he tended to become. He regarded German silence during the time of the Third Reich as inexcusable: "Most Germans didn't know because they didn't want to know. Because, indeed, they wanted *not* to know."[20] As for German silence in the years following the end of the war, "The 'I don't know' or 'I did not know' spoken today by many Germans no longer shocks us."[21] No doubt he was disappointed in the Germans, but he was also sincere when he said, as he often did, that he never harbored hatred for the German people."[22] His aim was to understand them and, through his writings, to prod them toward some necessary level of self-understanding. In both respects, he seems to have regarded his efforts as constituting more of a failure than a success.

It was a failure that he foresaw intuitively in some of his earliest writings and then went on to describe more analytically in his last book. The issue is centrally bound up with Levi's sense of his vocation as a writer—a vocation that he understood, in no small part, as implicating him as a witness to the Germans—and can be illustrated by the following passage from *The Reawakening*, his second book. In it Levi described the sensations he felt when, in October 1945, as part of his long, circuitous repatriation to Turin, he suddenly found himself in Munich. It was his first time ever in Germany:

> We felt we had something to say, enormous things to say, to every single German, and we felt that every German should have something to say to us; we felt an urgent need to settle our accounts, to ask, explain, and comment. ... Did "they" know about Auschwitz, about the silent daily massacre, a step away from their doors? ...
> I felt that everybody should interrogate us, read in our faces who we were, and listen to our tale in humility. But no-one looked us in the eyes, no-one accepted the challenge; they were deaf, blind, and dumb, imprisoned in their ruins, as in a fortress of wilful ignorance, still strong, still capable of hatred and contempt, still prisoners of their old tangle of pride and guilt.
> I found myself searching among them ... for someone who could not but know, remember, reply; who had commanded and obeyed, killed, humiliated, corrupted. A vain and foolish search; because not they, but others, the few just ones, would reply for them.[23]

The Drowned and the Saved, Levi's last book, was written some two decades later, but concludes on a similarly disconsolate note and for many of the same reasons: In Levi's view, the Germans, with only few exceptions, had chosen to remain willfully ignorant about the crimes of the Third Reich. For all of that, "Germany," he wrote, "has become 'respectable,' and in fact holds the destiny of Europe in its hands." The older generation of Germans remained by and large as he had seen them in Munich in fall 1945: deaf, blind, and dumb. As for the younger people, the memories of the survivors do not mean much to them, he lamented. Accounts such as his own seem to speak to them, if at all, of a world that is "distant, blurred, 'historical.'" A catastrophe of unprecedented dimensions had occurred, and there was nothing that guaranteed it could not reoccur. "It happened," he wrote, "therefore it can happen again: this is the core of what we have to say."[24] Who, though, was interested? Levi was generally not a cynical or fatalistic writer, but toward the end of his life he felt himself to be anachronistic and increasingly irrelevant when it came to the Germans. His final words on the subject carry uncharacteristically forceful tones of bitterness and of something approaching despair:

> Let it be clear that to a greater or lesser degree all were responsible, but it must be just as clear that behind their responsibility stands that great majority of Germans who

accepted in the beginning, out of mental laziness, myopic calculation, stupidity, and national pride the "beautiful words" of Corporal Hitler, followed him as long as luck and the lack of scruples favored him, were swept away by his ruin, afflicted by deaths, misery, and remorse, and rehabilitated a few years later as the result of an unprincipled political game.[25]

On the evidence of these words—his last on the subject of Germany—one would have to conclude that Levi had more or less given up on the Germans. His earlier hope to reach them, stir them, get them to acknowledge moral responsibility for the Nazi crimes had proven futile. In his "Letters from Germans," he reported that most of the people who wrote to him from Germany either tried to whitewash the past or expressed a sincere but helpless guilt over its worst aspects. Moreover, many responded to Levi's plea to understand the Germans by confessing that they could not understand them themselves. For all that remained unacknowledged and unresolved, however, the German nation proved enormously resilient and before long was back at the center of European power. Because Levi understood the country's rapid political recovery, though, as one unaccompanied by any fundamental spiritual transformation, he continued to look upon it as morally unrehabilitated.

Evidence of Germany's lingering ambivalence about the past surfaced in especially prominent ways in the two years leading up to Primo Levi's death. The Bitburg affair in spring 1985, for instance, was something that Levi looked upon as a personal affront to the victims of Nazism as well as a national scandal.[26] He regarded the *Historikerstreit,* which began soon after, as a troubling form of historical revisionism and sharply criticized it in print.[27] He found it alarming that German national memory was increasingly distancing itself from the worst aspects of the Hitler years, a development that he took as ominous, for the failure to comprehend the terrors of the past seemed to him to point to clear dangers for the future. "From violence only violence is born," he wrote; "many signs lead us to think of a genealogy of today's violence that branches out precisely from the violence that was dominant in Hitler's Germany."[28]

These tendencies and others like them undermined Levi's earlier hope of having some kind of honest encounter with the Germans. As becomes clear from his last book, when he first learned that *Survival in Auschwitz* was being translated into German, he had felt uneasy; but then he welcomed the prospect of a German edition, for at last, as he put it, he would be reaching "them," his work's "true recipients, those against whom the book was aimed like a gun." As a result of the translation, he wrote, "Now the gun was loaded."[29] This is an unusual, powerfully aggressive metaphor, and it highlights the strength of Levi's feelings as he anticipated his encounter with a German readership. It was an encounter long in the making and, as he saw it, would finally give him the opportunity to reestablish the proportions between him and those who had sought to diminish him. In fact, though, he came to see that the response to his book in Germany had been relatively weak, and he doubtless was disappointed that in his battle against the attenuation of historical memories of the Nazi oppression, his best shot had generated so little echo. Did he then do the desperate thing and, in keeping with the language of his metaphor, begin to anticipate a time when he might turn his loaded gun against himself?

Liberation and Self-Destruction

"Suicide," Primo Levi wrote, "is a meditated act."[30] Like all other acts of consequence, it has a history behind it, including, in the case of most writers, a literary history. A careful reading of all Primo Levi's writings, including those published under the pen name Damiano Malabaila, reveals an intermittent fascination with sudden endings, violent explosions, acts of self-destruction. Apparent as well is a concern with the psychological and spiritual components of what Levi called "the survivor's disease"—the diminution of energy, a wearing away of vitality, the heavy burdens of guilt and shame, a slow but certain collapse of the will to live. Levi did not center his major writings on such preoccupations as these, but they appear often enough in his books to signal at least an underlying concern with the possibility, if not also the desirability, of a self-willed death.

One finds explicit references to such death in Levi's expository reflections on Améry, Trakl, and Celan, but his most interesting treatment of suicide appears in the author's more imaginative writings—in the stories "Versamina" and "Westward," collected in *The Sixth Day and Other Tales;* in "Lorenzo's Return," collected in *Moments of Reprieve;* in passages of *The Periodic Table* and *The Monkey's Wrench;* and in such poems as "Pliny" and "The Girl-Child of Pompei." Reading such texts as these, one senses the stirring of awesome and destructive energies just below the surface of otherwise rationally controlled behavior.

"Pliny," for instance, portrays the dangers that accompany a fascination with the power of natural eruptions. The poem's narrator, based on Pliny the Elder, who died in A.D. 79 from venturing too close to Mount Vesuvius, is a passionate observer who will not be restrained from following his desire to investigate the explosive sources of destruction. A student of "ash," Pliny appears to be a mask for Levi himself, even as his determination to launch himself forward into the heart of danger seems at odds with the commonly held perception of Levi as a basically poised, less impulsive figure.

Pliny

Don't hold me back, friends, let me set out.
I won't go far; just to the other shore.
I want to observe at close hand that dark cloud,
Shaped like a pine tree, rising above Vesuvius,
And find the source of this strange light.

> Nephew, you don't want to come along? Fine; stay here and study.
> Recopy the notes I gave you yesterday.
> You needn't fear the ash; ash on top of ash.
> We're ash ourselves; remember Epicurus?
> Quick, get the boat ready, it is already night:
> Night at midday, a portent never seen before.
> Don't worry, sister, I'm cautious and expert;
> The years that bowed me haven't passed in vain.
> Of course I'll come back quickly. Just give me time
> To ferry across, observe the phenomena and return,
> Draw a new chapter from them tomorrow
> For my books, that will, I hope, still live
> When for centuries my old body's atoms
> Will be whirling, dissolved in the vortices of the universe,
> Or live again in an eagle, a young girl, a flower.
> Sailors, obey me: launch the boat into the sea.[31]

In contrast to the fatal impetuosity portrayed in "Pliny," caution, skepticism, and control characterize the scientific investigators of "Westward," but the compelling theme is once again self-destruction. In this story two scientists set out to study the death instinct by investigating the suicidal behavior of lemmings. As they proceed with their study, they are given to ponder the value of life itself and the option of freely choosing to put an end to life. Their dialogue is inquisitive and demanding and pushes rational inquiry to the limits: "Why would a living being want to die?" one asks. The other answers, "And why should it want to live? Why should it always want to live?"[32] As here, the questions are insistent, and the conclusions reached are often of a downcast nature: "Life does *not* have a purpose; pain always prevails over joy; we are all sentenced to death, and the day of one's execution has not been revealed; we are condemned to watch the end of those dearest to us; there are compensations, but they are few."[33] There are numerous reflections of this kind in "Westward," most of which turn on negative assessments of the ability of the life instinct to sustain itself against the inevitability of decline and the wasting power of death. The story ends with a reference to the Arunde, a people that is said to attribute "little value to individual survival, and none to that of the nation."[34] Once the members of this tribe sense the onset of decline, they freely choose death. Given the opportunity to prolong life through the aid of medicines, the Arunde declare: "We prefer freedom to drugs and death to illusion."[35]

Such a preference apparently was also Lorenzo's, as Primo Levi described it in "Lorenzo's Return." As readers of *Survival in Auschwitz* will recall, Lorenzo was a figure of crucial importance to Levi during his time in Auschwitz. An Italian civilian worker at the camp, Lorenzo faithfully brought extra food to Levi, thus enabling him to sustain hope in human goodness as well as to satisfy his physical hunger. Levi looked upon Lorenzo as a simple, thoroughly decent man, and he felt that his own survival was owing in no small measure to Lorenzo's numerous acts of kindness and generosity. In a place overwhelmed by the omnipresence of death, Lorenzo stood on the side of life. Thus it grieved Levi greatly when, at war's end, he discovered that Auschwitz had taken a far greater toll on Lorenzo than he had imagined: "I found a tired man, ... mortally tired, a weariness without remedy. ... His margin of love for life had thinned, almost disappeared. ... He had seen the world, he didn't like it, he felt it was going to ruin. To live no longer interested him. ... He was assured and coherent in his rejection of life. ... He, who was not a survivor, died of the survivor's disease."[36]

As we ponder such passages as this one and the others that have been cited above, the question inevitably presses itself upon us: Did Levi himself die of "the survivor's disease"? We shall never know for certain, but his writings point toward such a possibility. They show us an author increasingly beset by preoccupations with pain, guilt, shame, self-accusation, futility, and failure—in sum, struggling with the anguish of his own survival. This struggle finds forceful expression in Levi's last book, which is, in its mode, as painfully aggrieved a meditation on the sorrows and torments of survivorship as any in the whole corpus of Holocaust literature.

The grievance is manifold in nature and is sharply inner-directed as well as focused on forces from without. As already noted, more than a little of Levi's sense of grievance was bound up with his feelings about Germany. As a former victim of the Nazi system, Levi had sought from the Germans some show of understanding, if not also of remorse, but he discovered very little of either. He had remained tormented by traumatic memories from his time in the camp, but the people who belonged to the nation of his oppressors remained relatively untroubled in the years after Auschwitz and, in his encounters with them, gave little if any solace. Had he been able to settle his accounts with the likes of Dr. Pannwitz or Alex the *Kapo*, perhaps he might have been able to put to rest some of his more turbulent feelings, but no such settlement was to be his. Instead, the perpetuation and intensification of traumatic memories determined that he who had been tortured remained tortured.

A writer in such a condition naturally seeks refuge and relief in his work. Levi was no exception. He was fond of quoting the Yiddish saying "*Ibergekumene tsores iz gut tsu dertseylin*" ("Troubles overcome are good to tell"),[37] and there is no doubt that he looked to writing as a means of overcoming, as well as representing, his troubled past. However, although Primo Levi's writings do show a high degree of analytic precision and representational power, they generally lack cathartic effect. They are masterly in depicting the physical and moral character of the sufferings they record, but only in rare instances do they resolve such suffering or point to a less anguished future that might lie beyond it. Indeed, in writing as he did about his camp experience, Levi may have deepened his sense of trauma rather than found relief from it. In this respect he faced a dilemma of a particularly demanding and ultimately exhausting kind. Immersed as he was in memory and what he understood to be its obligations and demands on him as a writer, Levi returned time and again to the past, which was the site of his worst and also his richest experiences. Initially, he had looked upon writing as a means of inner liberation, and he had begun to write under an unusually strong compulsion, so much so that during the time of his incarceration, he had come to understand the will to survive and the will to tell as virtually one and the same. Moved to words by what he later described as "an immediate and violent impulse,"[38] he had actually begun his first book while still a prisoner in Auschwitz.[39] He saw himself at that time as a chronicler of a historic crime like none other, and, as both a victim and a witness of that crime, he had dedicated himself to assuring that others would know of its enormity. To the question posed in his first book about whether "it is necessary or good to retain any memory of this exceptional state,"[40] therefore, the only conceivable answer for the author of *Survival in Auschwitz* was an emphatic *yes*.

It is doubtful whether the older writer could have replied with such confidence in the saving powers of memory. Indeed, by the time he came to write the sometimes bitter, sometimes brooding chapters of *The Drowned and the Saved,* Levi evidently had experienced second thoughts, and he shows serious reservations about the quality of his own witness. "Have we—we who have returned—been able to understand and make others understand our experience?" he queried.[41] His answer, implicit in the question itself, is hardly affirmative: "Human memory is a marvelous but fallacious instrument," he wrote. "Even under normal conditions a slow degradation is at work, an obfuscation of outlines, a so to speak physiological oblivion, which few memories resist. … [Therefore] an apology is in order. This very book is drenched in memory; what's more, a distant memory. Thus it draws from a suspect source and must be protected against itself."[42] This is a powerful, revisionary turn, and it reveals that the young Levi who had lived, as he put it, "in order to tell"[43] is succeeded by an older, sadder author who evidently came to doubt the accuracy and efficacy of his own tellings. The sober, qualified sense of his work should be taken as both a symptom and a cause of the dejection the author felt at the end of his life, and it would seem to point darkly beyond writing to troubles that could not be completely overcome by their telling.

These troubles took on a shape in Levi's late writings that one does not find in his earlier books. The younger Levi spoke of "the liberating joy of recounting [his] story,"[44] and he narrated it with the self-confidence of an author who felt himself in full command of his expressive powers. It is true that he had serious doubts about the willingness of others to listen to his tale, but he never doubted its validity and importance or his own integrity as a storyteller. The older Levi, however, showed himself to be increasingly uneasy about the testimony of survivors and even about the reliability of memory itself. "The greater part of the witnesses," he noted, "have ever more blurred and stylized memories."[45] Moreover, in his view they have written their accounts out of only partial knowledge.

Those who knew the full horror of Nazism either did not survive their ordeals or were so incapacitated by them as to be rendered all but speechless. Thus, in his last years Levi seems to have faced the melancholy conclusion that the fundamental reality of his life—the full truth of Auschwitz itself—might never be accurately known.

Levi devoted his last book to extended analyses of the causes and implications of this disturbing prospect. The essays of *The Drowned and the Saved* exhibit a pronounced anxiety about the drift and distortion of memory and consequently about the obfuscation and falsification of the past. Levi attributed this worrisome development in part to those who would choose to forget the past or those who manipulate it in intentionally dishonest ways, but a substantial part of his worry seems to have been self-directed and points to the troubling implication that he may have come to regard himself as a compromised witness. The theme of moral ambiguity that he developed with such forcefulness and precision in "The Gray Zone" is one from which he did not absent himself, and although there is no evidence that points to Levi's complicity as an inmate of Auschwitz, he nevertheless appears to have seen himself as in some way complicit: "An infernal order such as National Socialism exercises a frightful power of corruption, against which it is difficult to guard oneself. It degrades its victims and makes them similar to itself, because it needs both great and small complicities. To resist it requires a truly solid moral armature."[46] "The Gray Zone" clearly indicates that Levi did not believe there were very many who possessed such moral defenses or who, in the depraved condition of the camps, could manage to keep them intact. "We are all mirrored in Rumkowski," he wrote; "his ambiguity is ours, it is our second nature."[47] Bravely but sorrowfully, he included himself in this judgment: "I had also deeply assimilated the principal rule of the place, which made it mandatory that you take care of yourself first of all."[48] This realization, which does not register with any substantial force at all in Levi's early books, introduces into his last writings a note of self-indictment and, with it, a burden of shame that must have been excruciating for him to bear. In *The Drowned and the Saved*, he subjected such shame to a fine moral scrutiny and set out to analyze the troubled souls of the survivors as well as the more inscrutable souls of their persecutors. As he argued in "The Gray Zone" the inmates and their overlords were frequently in close collaboration with one another in the camps, and the aftereffects of their ambiguous and often damning association could not be quieted so easily in the postwar period.

Misery, anguish, exhaustion, guilt, and shame—these were part of the legacy of the Lagers for many of those who survived them. Liberation brought physical but not necessarily psychological freedom. "One suffered," Levi wrote, "because of the reacquired consciousness of having been diminished."[49] In addition , one suffered from torturous feelings of guilt. "What guilt? When all was over, the awareness emerged that we had not done anything, or not enough, against the system into which we had been absorbed. ... [The survivor] feels accused and judged, compelled to justify and defend himself." Defend himself against what? "Self-accusation, or the accusation of having failed in terms of human solidarity, ... of having omitted to offer help, ... a human word, advice, even just a listening ear."[50] Guilt also accompanied the troubling suspicion that one survived in place of another, "of a man more generous, more sensitive, more useful, wiser, worthier of living than you. You cannot block out such feelings: you examine yourself, you review your memories. ... No, you find no obvious transgressions, you did not usurp anyone's place. ... [Nevertheless, shame] gnaws at us; it has nestled deeply like a woodworm; although unseen from the outside, it gnaws and rasps."[51] The late poem "The Survivor" expresses the agony of the former camp inmate haunted by these corrosive feelings, but their sharpest elaboration is found in the essay "Shame," from which I have been quoting. Like nothing else in Levi's work, it shows us the author turning against himself in a manner that was harsh to the point of being self-punishing:

> The "saved" of the Lager were not the best, those predestined to do good, the bearers of a message: what I have seen and lived through proved the exact contrary. ... The worst survived, the selfish, the violent, the insensitive, the collaborators of the "gray zone," the spies. ... The worst survived, that is, the fittest; the best all died. ...
> I must repeat: we, the survivors, are not the true witnesses. ... We ... are not only an exiguous but also an anomalous minority: we are those who by their prevarications or abilities or good luck did not touch bottom. Those who did so ... have not returned to tell about it or have returned mute, but they are ... the complete witnesses, the ones whose deposition would have a general significance. They are the rule, we are the exception.[52]

If one takes this passage as indicative of Levi's final sense of himself and his work, the conclusions one draws are extremely unsettling. On both moral and literary grounds, the author of *The Drowned and the Saved* seems to have called into serious question the value of the testimony offered in his earlier books. The survivors are not the true witnesses, Levi came to acknowledge, but "speak in their stead, by proxy." The story they have to tell is "a discourse 'on behalf of third parties,'" not the narrative of an experience personally lived through. Those who touched bottom remained submerged, their stories unspoken and unheard; as for those who survived and have attempted to speak for them, "I cannot see any proportion," Levi concluded, "between the privilege [of surviving] and its outcome. ... We who were favored by fate tried ... to recount not only our fate but that of the others, the drowned; but ... the destruction brought to an end, the job completed, was not told by anyone."[53]

On the evidence of these words, it seems clear that in writing his last book, Levi suffered from a belated sense of his own inadequacies as a survivor-witness. Was he moved as well to call into question the value of his survival itself? We shall never know for certain. The testimony offered by his friends is often contradictory and inconclusive. My own correspondence with him likewise cannot resolve the matter, but all the same I wish to cite it for what I believe it might tell us about one troubled side of Primo Levi's life in his last years.

In a letter to me of September 15, 1985, Levi referred to his "essay-book" in progress in these terms: "Its title will be I SOMMERSI E I SALVATI (The Drowned & the Saved), a silent quotation from Dante (Inf. xx: 3), to be understood ironically: the Saved are not the ones that deserved salvation in the theological sense, but rather the shrewd, the violent, the collaborators." Levi himself was not a brutal or cunning man and does not belong in this ironic category of the "saved," but he did manage to outlast Auschwitz and later in life came to suffer for it. The suffering took the form of intermittent depressions. When I saw him in Italy in spring 1981, he was in good spirits, but when I proposed a second visit a year and a half later, his condition had altered. In a letter of January 14, 1983, he wrote as follows:

> Your proposal to come and see me in the next months has moved me, but has caught me off-balance. I hope, I *do* hope, to be soon in a condition to meet you and to speak with you, but I am suffering now from an episode of depression (not my first one; I suppose they are a heritage from the Lager). I hope you never experienced such an alteration of the soul; it is painful and thought-hampering, it prevents me not only to write but also to drive or to travel. Naturally I am under medical care, but I cannot tell how long it will last. ... Will you excuse me? Perhaps when you are in Europe I'll be OK again, but I cannot foresee anything nor make programs.

It is generally known that Levi suffered from depressions, but I know of no other document in which he associated this affliction with his time in the camp. Precisely how he understood this connection is unclear, but it is significant that some four decades after his liberation, Levi saw Auschwitz as continuing to have such an overwhelmingly negative, debilitating effect on his life.

Whatever the benefits of the medical treatment he received, the condition of lassitude and creative paralysis that Levi described did not pass quickly. On April 23, 1983, he wrote me: "My condition of general tiredness has slightly improved, but I am not yet satisfied. I experience a difficulty in concentrating, and especially in writing. Rarely did I wish something so intensively as to recover quickly my normal condition." This particular episode of depression lasted for some seven months and then, at the end of May, lifted. He wrote me on August 3, 1983: "One feels as [if] re-born! Although I live now quite normally, I am short of ideas, and for the moment my activity is reduced to a desultory collaboration with the local newspaper."

Shortly afterward Levi began writing the essays that would constitute *The Drowned and the Saved*. He worked well and by September 1985 had completed six of the ten or twelve essays he had originally scheduled for the book (letter of

September 15, 1985). He added two more pieces (the published volume was to include a total of eight essays) and on January 16, 1986, wrote me in generally buoyant spirits, "Exactly today I have handed to Einaudi my book of essays." Levi originally intended this book as a sociology of camp life (letter of May 8, 1985), but however we may value that aspect of it, we are moved to read his last book today in other terms—as a profound self-portrait of a Holocaust survivor as well as testimony of the author's farewell to writing. In the same letter in which he mentioned that he had just submitted the manuscript to his publisher, Levi typed out for me an English translation of his poem "The Survivor." The opening lines, from Coleridge's *The Rime of the Ancient Mariner*, stand as an epigraph to *The Drowned and the Saved*:

> Since then, at an uncertain hour,
> That agony returns:
> And till my ghastly tale is told,
> This heart within me burns.

There is no doubt that Levi identified with the figure of the Ancient Mariner and saw himself under a similar compulsion to tell his tale. The figure of the spectral storyteller who searches about passionately for listeners epitomized for him the writer as a survivor-witness bound to recount his experience of extraordinary events. The syndrome of the survivor who is a compulsive narrator, however, is a highly problematic one, for it repeatedly returns the storyteller to the memory of his traumatic past without relieving him of it. It also exposes him to the peril of urgently telling a tale that others may not want to hear. Such a writer faces a triple jeopardy: through his tellings and retellings, he may exhaust the propellant charge of his narrative impulse; or he may become exhausted by its demands on him; or he may suffer the rebuff that comes with the sense that he is not reaching his intended listeners. To some degree, Levi suffered at the end of his life from all three of these consequences. In addition, he suffered from a guilt that only other survivors can properly understand—a guilt that finds relentless expression in the concluding lines of "The Survivor":

> Once more he sees his companions' faces
> Livid in the first faint light,
> Gray with cement dust,
> Nebulous in the mist,
> Tinged with death in their uneasy sleep.
> At night, under the heavy burden
> Of their dreams, their jaws move,
> Chewing a non-existent turnip.
> "Stand back, leave me alone, submerged people,
> Go away. I haven't dispossessed anyone,

Haven't usurped anyone's bread.
No one died in my place. No one.
Go back into your mist.
It's not my fault if I live and breathe,
Eat, drink, sleep and put on clothes."[54]

Levi must have written *The Drowned and the Saved* at least in part to quiet these dead, but they were not to be quieted. He thought he had written a "harsh" book and did not expect it would reach a broad audience (letter of June 30, 1986), but in fact it found a sizable and receptive readership in Italy. Nevertheless, Levi was disquieted by what he took to be the futility of his efforts. As he wrote his friend Dan Vittorio Segre, "The trouble is that the people who read and understand this book don't need it and those who need it don't understand." In contemplating these words after Levi's death, Segre thought that "his end, the manner of his end, came either because he could not speak anymore, or could not be understood."[55]

There were other complicating factors—too many to bear up under easily. He described some of these to me in a letter of July 30, 1986: "Our family situation has suddenly worsened. Last Monday my mother had a stroke, and now she is in hospital …; unfortunately she is fully conscious, but she has speaking difficulties. The future is completely obscure, but, at her age (91) the hopes of a recovery are practically null." He concluded the letter with these words: "Forgive my brevity. Hope to be more tranquil and extensive next time, if things clear."

Things did not clear but, on the contrary, evidently worsened. Several months passed without any further word from Italy. Then came the following letter, dated March 29, 1987:

Dear Alvin,
  Thank you for your letter of March 13, and for the fine essay enclosed. Yes, in fact we have been out of touch for a while: it is my fault, or at least mine was the missing link. My family has been struck twice, and things at home are going pretty badly: my mother, 92, is in a bed paralyzed for ever, I came home yesterday from a hospital where I underwent a serious surgical operation; but mainly, as a consequence of all the above, I am suffering from a severe depression, and I am struggling at no avail to escape it.
  Please forgive me for being so short; the mere fact of writing a letter is a trial for me, but the will to recover is strong. Let us see what the next months will bring to all of us, but my present situation is the worst I ever experienced, Auschwitz included.
  Best wishes for your summer trip in Europe, and warmest regards to all your dear family and to you.

Primo

This letter arrived on April 9, 1987. Two days later I learned that Primo Levi was dead.

Some Final Reflections

The death of a great writer leaves a gap in consciousness that we do not know how to fill. We pay tribute to the dead and offer other forms of personal testimony and public respect, but whatever the ceremonial and therapeutic value of these gestures, we recognize that they do not suffice. When, as in this case, the death appears to have been self-inflicted, we are moved as well to search for explanations. Primo Levi anticipated such a move and, in *The Monkey's Wrench*, provided a cautionary warning against it: "When a person dies ... afterward everybody says they saw it coming. ... After the disaster they all had to speak their piece.... Obviously, if a person dies ... there has to be a reason, but that doesn't mean there was only one, or if there was, that it's possible to discover it."[56]

During his lifetime Primo Levi accumulated a surplus of pain, and it would be unwise to attribute his death to any single cause. There is no doubt that as a result of his wartime experiences he suffered the torment of traumatic recollections and that through his writings he sought both clarity and relief. It is evident today that he found more of the former than the latter. In terms of his literary achievements, the results of his efforts were enormous. In terms of the cost to his spiritual and psychic well-being, there are few among us with imaginations large enough to understand the extent of his inner suffering. In the end, the pain and anguish of his life were simply too great and apparently overwhelmed him. His books remain—an unmatched record of troubles encountered and overcome and of still other troubles too profound for the survivor to withstand.

Notes

1. Primo Levi, "Afterword: The Author's Answers to His Readers' Questions," trans. Ruth Feldman, *Survival in Auschwitz and the Reawakening: Two Memoirs*, trans. Stuart Woolf (New York: Summit, 1986), p. 276.

2. Jean Améry, *At the Mind's Limits: Contemplations by a Survivor on Auschwitz and Its Realities*, trans. Sidney Rosenfeld and Stella Rosenfeld (Bloomington: Indiana University Press, 1980), p. 3.

3. Primo Levi, *The Drowned and the Saved*, trans. Raymond Rosenthal (New York: Summit, 1988), pp. 24, 25.

4. Ibid.

5. Werner Weinberg, *Self-Portrait of a Holocaust Survivor* (Jefferson, N.C.: McFarland and Company, 1985), p. 10.

6. Levi, *The Drowned and the Saved*, pp. 135, 136.

7. Cynthia Ozick, "Primo Levi's Suicide Note," in *Metaphor and Memory* (New York: Alfred A. Knopf, 1989), pp. 47–48.

8. Levi, *The Drowned and the Saved*, p. 137.

9. Ibid., pp. 137–138.

10. Ibid., p. 128.

11. Weinberg, *Self-Portrait of a Holocaust Survivor*, p. 82.
12. Levi, *The Drowned and the Saved*, p. 14.
13. Ferdinando Camon, *Conversations with Primo Levi*, trans. John Shepley (Marlboro, Vt.: Marlboro Press, 1989), p. 61.
14. Ibid., p. 37.
15. Levi, *Survival in Auschwitz*, p. 26.
16. Ibid., pp. 105–106.
17. Ibid., pp. 107–108.
18. Primo Levi, "Aus einem Brief Primo Levis an den Übersetzer," in *Ist das ein Mensch? Erinnerungen an Auschwitz* (Frankfurt: Fischer, 1979), pp. 8–9.
19. Primo Levi, *The Periodic Table*, trans. Raymond Rosenthal (New York: Schocken, 1984), p. 223.
20. Levi, afterword to *Survival in Auschwitz*, p. 381.
21. Levi, *The Drowned and the Saved*, pp. 19–20.
22. Ibid., p. 174.
23. Levi, *The Reawakening*, pp. 370–371.
24. Levi, *The Drowned and the Saved*, p. 199.
25. Ibid., p. 203.
26. Primo Levi, "Questions and Answers at Indiana University," *Midstream* 32 (April 1986), pp. 26–28. For more on the Bitburg affair, see Geoffrey Hartman, ed., *Bitburg in Moral and Political Perspective* (Bloomington: Indiana University Press, 1986).
27. Primo Levi, "The Dispute Among the Historians," in *The Mirror Maker*, trans. Raymond Rosenthal (New York: Schocken, 1989), pp. 163–166.
28. Levi, *The Drowned and the Saved*, p. 200.
29. Ibid., p. 168.
30. Ibid., p. 76.
31. Primo Levi, "Pliny," in *Collected Poems*, trans. Ruth Feldman and Brian Swann (London: Faber and Faber, 1988), p. 33.
32. Primo Levi, "Westward," in *The Sixth Day and Other Tales*, trans. Raymond Rosenthal (New York: Summit, 1990), p. 128.
33. Ibid., p. 129.
34. Ibid., p. 132.
35. Ibid., p. 135.
36. Primo Levi, *Moments of Reprieve*, trans. Ruth Feldman (New York: Summit, 1986), pp. 159–160.
37. Levi uses this Yiddish proverb as an inscription to *The Periodic Table* and also quotes it elsewhere.
38. Author's preface to *Survival in Auschwitz*, p. 9.
39. Levi, afterword to *Survival in Auschwitz*, p. 375.
40. Levi, *Survival in Auschwitz*, p. 87.
41. Levi, *The Drowned and the Saved*, p. 36.
42. Ibid., pp. 23, 24, 34.
43. Primo Levi, "Beyond Survival," *Prooftexts* 4 (January 1984), p. 13.
44. Levi, *The Reawakening*, p. 373.
45. Levi, *The Drowned and the Saved*, p. 19.
46. Ibid., p. 68.

47. Ibid., p. 69.
48. Ibid., pp. 78–79.
49. Ibid., p. 75.
50. Ibid., pp. 76–78.
51. Ibid., pp. 81–82.
52. Ibid., pp. 82–84.
53. Ibid., pp. 83–84.
54. Levi, "The Survivor," in *Collected Poems*, p. 64.
55. "A Romantic Grows Up," an interview with Dan Vittorio Segre, *Jerusalem Post International Edition* (September 5, 1987).
56. Primo Levi, *The Monkey's Wrench*, trans. William Weaver (New York: Penguin, 1987), pp. 118–119.

8

Elie Wiesel and Primo Levi

Richard L. Rubenstein

I cannot begin this essay without acknowledging my enormous indebtedness to Raul Hilberg. I can think of no better way to do this than to cite the statement that I wrote in 1974 to introduce the notes to *The Cunning of History:*

> I wish to express my especial indebtedness to Raul Hilberg, whose indispensable and magisterial work, *The Destruction of the European Jews,* contributed more to making this book possibly than the work of any other scholar. Those acquainted with the literature on the Holocaust will recognize the extent of my indebtedness to Hilberg, a debt I acknowledge with much gratitude.[1]

That statement holds true of everything I have ever written about the Holocaust.

On this occasion I propose to explore the subject of Elie Wiesel and Primo Levi: the victim as witness, with special reference to the theological significance of their testimony. Wiesel has written, "The Holocaust is a sacred realm. One cannot enter this realm without realizing that only those who were there can know. But the outsider can come close to the gates. One can never know and yet one must try."[2]

Those who did not enter the "kingdom of night" cannot possibly understand what those who did were compelled to endure. To the extent that we have any inkling of their experience, it is largely through what the survivors have communicated to us. Preeminent among the witnesses to the kingdom of night are Elie Wiesel and Primo Levi. Nevertheless, if we have had only hints of what the victims endured, we have been able to learn a great deal about the world of the perpetrators. As Raul Hilberg has observed, "The Germans demonstrated once and for all how quickly even large groups, numbering in the millions, could be annihilated."[3] Moreover, Hilberg has shown that whatever the personal sentiments of individual Germans, the process of mass extermination ultimately fed "upon the resources of the entire community" and thus the "machinery of destruction was the organized community in one of its special roles."[4]

In 1961 Hilberg wrote, "We saw how the Nazis built upon the experiences of the past. Now there are means which will allow still others to seize upon the Nazi experience, so that it in turn may yet become a precedent for the future."⁵ This was long before the Pol Pot genocide in Kampuchea, Saddam Hussein's threat to gas half of Israel with German-made gas, and the destruction he has visited upon perhaps 3 million Kurds to achieve his long-held objective of ridding Iraq of a troublesome minority by terror-induced flight if not outright genocide. No one would voluntarily repeat the experience of even those victims who survived: The same cannot be said of the perpetrators.

In the preface to the 1961 edition of *The Destruction*, Hilberg observed that "only a generation ago, the incidents described in this book would have been considered improbable, infeasible, or even inconceivable. Now they have happened. The destruction of the Jews was a process of extremes. That, precisely, is why it is so important as a group phenomenon. That is why it can serve as a test of social and political theories."⁶ I would add that the Holocaust also serves as a test of deeply and profoundly held religious beliefs. The testimony of Elie Wiesel and Primo Levi is of supreme importance largely because both witnesses to the kingdom of night confronted the issue of God and the Holocaust, each in his own way.

Elie Wiesel has confronted this issue directly or indirectly in everything he has written. He does not address the agonizing question of God and the Holocaust by attempting to create an elaborate philosophical or theological system but as a storyteller, undoubtedly the most important Jewish storyteller of the twentieth century. Nevertheless, Wiesel's role as a storyteller does not diminish his stature as a religious thinker.⁷ On the contrary, it is one of the two authentic modes of expression of Jewish religious thought, a tradition that encompasses Scripture, Midrash, Aggadah, and the tales of the Hasidim, the other being that of the rational philosophical system such as the *Moreh Nebuchim* of Maimonides.⁸

In the first edition of *After Auschwitz*, published in 1966, I wrote that the "theologian is really closer to the poet or the creative artist than to the physical scientist."⁹ I did not have Elie Wiesel in mind, but I believe he fits the description. I therefore begin my discussion of Elie Wiesel not with abstract analysis but with a few stories, stories of my own initial encounters with Wiesel and his writings.

I first met Elie Wiesel on October 31, 1968, when he came to Pittsburgh to lecture. After the lecture, my wife, Betty, and I invited him to our home. He accepted. I had been deeply moved by reading *Night*, but what struck me most was the enormous spiritual authority he conveyed by his presence. An indispensable element in that authority was, of course, that he had survived the Holocaust. Nevertheless, having survived Auschwitz was not sufficient to account for his personal charisma. Few if any other Holocaust survivors seemed to convey a comparable spiritual authority.

When I heard Elie Wiesel speak that evening, I recalled how I had spent the wartime years, especially the period from September 1942 to June 1945.¹⁰ Like Wiesel until he was deported with the Jews of Sighet in April 1944, I, too, studied the classical texts of Judaism at a Jewish institution. Unlike Wiesel, I concurrently studied the history of Western philosophy at a nearby university. There were, obviously, other differences in our circumstances. Elie studied Talmud by day and Kabbalah by night, and he and two friends—*chaverim* is the more appropriate term—were convinced that with the right words and gestures, they could bring about the messianic redemption of Israel and all humanity.[11] I had more modest religious ambitions. My institution, located in the American heartland, prepared its students to be gentlemanly religious functionaries who would serve upper-middle-class communities; it offered its pupils a life-style few had known before. While millions of Jews far more knowledgeable and observant than we were starved and obscenely abused before being murdered, we were served tasty, plentiful meals by white-jacketed black waiters. We also enjoyed the use of excellent tennis courts, a well-equipped gymnasium, and a heated swimming pool. Even in wartime our summer vacations were long. The institution was the Hebrew Union College in Cincinnati, Ohio.

I wish I could testify that the worst catastrophe in all of Jewish history was uppermost in the minds of our teachers or of the majority of the student body. It wasn't. There were, of course, exceptions among both students and faculty, such as Abraham Joshua Heschel and Samuel Atlas, a Lithuanian-born Talmudist. Nevertheless, the faculty that counted politically, the Hebrew Union College alumni, tended to regard Nazi anti-Semitism as a temporary interruption in humanity's upward march toward enlightenment, progress, and rationality. Even as news of the Holocaust began to trickle in from Europe, most of the faculty, led by President Julian Morgenstern, remained uncompromisingly anti-Zionist. With the defeat of national socialism and fascism, we were told, Europe's Jews should not go to Palestine but should return to their homes to make their contribution to the creation of a truly democratic postwar world.

The happy optimism of wartime Reform Judaism came to an end for me on the eve of Rosh Hashannah in 1944. As I prepared to act as the student rabbi for the small Reform congregation in Tupelo, Mississippi, news arrived that the advancing Russian armies had captured the Polish town of Madjdanek and had found a huge Nazi death camp nearby. Reality had outstripped even the most darkly paranoid imagination. As terrible as were the numbers murdered by the Nazis, the image that made the most permanent impression on me was the discovery at the camp of 600,000 pairs of ownerless shoes.

In *Night* Elie Wiesel has told us about his inability to pray on Rosh Hashannah after immersion into the world of Auschwitz. In the relative security of a small southern town, I had a similar experience. The dissonance between the Rosh Hashannah liturgy I was obliged to recite and the cold-blooded slaughter I had just learned about could under no circumstances be reconciled. I could no longer accept Reform Judaism's faith in progress and human perfectibility. Nor could I praise God for having chosen Israel as the people with whom he had entered into a covenant. In the months that followed, as the Russian troops marched westward toward Auschwitz and beyond, as Elie Wiesel and his father were forced to undertake the death march from Auschwitz to Buchenwald, I followed the events in Europe as if they were happening to me personally. Indeed they were, for the life of every Jew was irrevocably changed by the Holocaust. By spring 1945 the worst facts had finally been made public in America. Overwhelmed by that terrible knowledge, I could no longer believe in a just and righteous creator who had chosen Israel and would ultimately weigh and judge the deeds of men and women.

My wartime experience, so different from that of Elie Wiesel and Primo Levi, is not irrelevant to my second meeting with Elie Wiesel at the first International Scholars' Conference on the German Church Struggle and the Holocaust, which took place at Wayne State University in Detroit in February 1970. Both Wiesel and I had been scheduled to speak. I spoke first, stressing the logic of the theology of covenant and election that has been at the heart of Jewish belief from biblical times to the present. Just as Hilberg saw the Holocaust as a test of social and political theories, I saw the Holocaust as a test of Israel's traditional faith. I argued that if one takes the belief that God has chosen Israel with the seriousness it deserves, one must either affirm that Israel's destiny is unconditionally dependent upon fidelity to the divinely bestowed covenant or one must reject the idea of the God of the covenant altogether. I hasten to add that this is not atheism. There are many ways of believing in God, but after Auschwitz it seemed to me that the idea of a God of history who protects Israel when it is faithful to his Law and punishes Israel when unfaithful is not one of them.

I also argued that there is no credible intellectual basis for affirming the existence of *human rights in the abstract*. On the contrary, no matter how much it offends our sense of decency, as it certainly does mine, the only rights possessed by an individual are those he or she has by virtue of his or her membership in a political community that has the *power* to guarantee those rights. When the Jews were wholly defenseless and were regarded as an alien presence, they lost even the right to life itself when the cover of war permitted the practice of extreme behavior unthinkable in peacetime. One of the Holocaust's most important lessons is that power and human rights are inseparable.

The lessons I had derived from the Holocaust were not those Elie Wiesel was prepared to accept. He had been scheduled to speak on Holocaust literature but decided instead to address himself largely to the issues I had raised. As is his manner, he began by telling stories. He told the story of Moishe, a shammes somewhere in Russia during the Shoah.[12] This was not Moche the Beadle of *Night* who returned to Sighet in late 1942 after miraculously escaping an *Einsatzgruppen Aktion* to warn the Jews of what was in store for them. Moche spoke the truth, but people took him for a madman. Moishe the Beadle *was* mad, and in his madness he would come to the synagogue every day, ascend the *bima,* and say to God, "*Ribbono shel Olam,* Master of the Universe, I want you to know that we are still here." The transports came regularly to take away the town's Jews until only mad Moishe was left. This time when he ascended the *bima,* he declared, "Master of the Universe, I want you to know, I am still here." And then he stopped, only to murmur: "But you—where are you?"

There is an absolutely fundamental difference between crying out, "Where are you, God?" and concluding that the idea of a God who chooses Israel lacks credibility. Those Jews who come to the latter conclusion are no longer troubled or agonized about God and the Holocaust. They do not demand that God stand in judgment for what he has done to Israel nor do they feel the slightest sense of revolt against God. Rebellion is, after all, an indirect statement of belief. They believe the world is the way it is. They also believe the Jewish problem is how to survive in the world the way it is.

Elie Wiesel explicitly rejected such a view. Here are his words: "Those who came out with the so-called God is dead theology, not one of them had been in Auschwitz. Those who had never said it. I have my problems with God, believe me. I have my anger and I have my quarrels and I have my nightmares. But my dispute, my bewilderment, my astonishment is with men. I didn't understand how men could be so 'barbarian.' ... I still don't understand."[13] Wiesel went on to tell a story of how he survived the shock of going straight from a yeshiva in Sighet to carrying rocks in Birkenau. When the man with whom he carried rocks, whose face he had not seen, asked him what he did at home, Elie told him that he was a yeshiva *bochur*. The man asked him the tractate of the Talmud and the page he was studying before being taken away. Here are Wiesel's words concerning what happened when he told him: "He said 'Let's continue.' I said, 'Are you mad? Here? Without books, without anything and why?' He said, 'We must continue. That is the only way.' And believe it or not, we continued. He was a famous ... head of a famous Yeshiva Talmudic school in Galicia. ... We studied Talmud to the very end."[14]

Thus, in Detroit Wiesel reminded us that the Germans wanted to destroy the Jews spiritually as well as physically. That is why it was impossible for him to deny the God of Israel no matter how difficult belief had become. I had spoken of the difficulty of living in a world without God. Wiesel corrected me: "You say it is more difficult to live today in a world without God. NO! If you want difficulties, choose to live *with God*. Can you compare today the tragedy of the believer to that of the non-believer?! The real tragedy, the real drama, is the drama of the believer."[15]

Sixteen years later, on December 11, 1986, Wiesel returned to the same theme in his Nobel lecture delivered in Oslo, Norway: "And to me, a Jew who comes from a deeply religious background, there was the question of questions: *Where was God in all this?* It seemed as impossible to conceive of Auschwitz with God as to conceive of Auschwitz without God. The tragedy of the believer is much greater than the tragedy of the nonbeliever."[16]

Of course he was right about the tragedy of the believer, both in Detroit and in Oslo. I had ceased to believe in the traditional God because I could not stand the incessant inner psychic warfare between what I was expected to believe and preach and what I had learned about the Holocaust and the world in which a Holocaust could take place.

Wiesel had known the godless world of radical destructiveness both experientially and intellectually. He could deny neither the terrible facts of his experience nor the God of Israel. "To be a Jew," he told us in 1970, "is to have all the reasons in the world not to have faith in language, in singing, in prayers, and in God, but to go on telling the tale, to go on carrying on the dialogue, and to have my own silent prayers and quarrels with God."[17]

A month after the Detroit conference, I left active service in the rabbinate and began my academic career. I had made the journey from a religious career within the Jewish community to a scientific career in a publicly supported state university. Judaism and Jewish history continued to be of fundamental interest to me, but it was now my vocation to investigate religion as a humanly produced phenomenon. Insofar as my profession was concerned, my personal belief and practice were now strictly private matters.

In this new environment, I went through a period of impatience with Wiesel's writings. Why, I asked myself, does he go to such convoluted and tortuous efforts to maintain some kind of relationship with his God when he, of all people, knows about Auschwitz? Even when Michael Berenbaum wrote his doctoral dissertation on Elie Wiesel at Florida State University (which became his exceptionally fine book, *The Vision of the Void: Theological Reflections on the Works of Elie Wiesel*), I could not understand nor could I sympathize with Wiesel's efforts to reconcile his experience with our people's faith and tradition. I encouraged my students to read Wiesel, but I was far more likely to tell them about *Night* than about *The Trial of God*.

Of especial importance to me was the passage in *Night* depicting the brutal shattering of Elie's world of faith: "Never shall I forget that night, the first night in camp, which has turned my life into one long night, seven times cursed and seven times sealed. ... Never shall I forget those flames which consumed my faith forever. ... Never shall I forget those moments which murdered my God and my soul and turned my dreams to dust."[18] In the language of sociology, this passage describes the collapse of Elie's symbolic universe, by which we mean "the matrix of *all* socially objectivated and subjectively real meanings" that provide order for the individual's subjective apprehension of his or her biographical experience.[19] A symbolic universe performs the same function for the institutional order.[20] Should the symbolic universe collapse, both the individual and the group are likely to dissolve into a collection of disconnected atoms for whom life has lost all meaning and no set of norms remain to structure individual or group relationships. Sociologists call that condition anomie and argue that it is more threatening to human beings than death itself. This can be seen in the willingness of a convict, unlike a cornered animal, to play his proper role at his own execution.

A symbolic universe is likely to disintegrate when its legitimations are radically disconfirmed.[21] By legitimations I mean the reasons a society accepts as normative why its institutions and interpersonal relations are structured as they are. The ultimate legitimation of Wiesel's pre-Auschwitz world was that things are or should be in accordance with God's will. Neither Elie nor most other Jews could conceive of Auschwitz as in accordance with God's will.

The collapse of Elie's symbolic universe is further described in a scene that many of us regard as the most memorable in *Night*, the one in which the camp inmates are forced to witness the excruciatingly long death by hanging of a young boy. As Elie watches, he hears someone behind him ask, "Where is God? Where is He?" When the boy finally dies, a voice within Elie answered, "Where is He? Here He is—He is hanging here on this gallows."[22]

Not only does Elie tell of the collapse of his own symbolic universe but also that of some of his fellow inmates. For example, initially Akiba Drummer attempts desperately to maintain the integrity of his symbolic universe. He declares: "God is testing us. He wants to find out whether we can dominate our base instincts and kill the Satan within us. We have no right to despair. And if He punishes us relentlessly, it's a sign that He loves us all the more."[23] Nevertheless, when Drummer becomes a victim of the selection, his desperate faith collapses. He is only able to repeat to whoever will listen that he has neither strength nor faith left. A Polish rabbi also loses faith. Before his world collapses, he prays unceasingly and recites "whole pages of the Talmud from memory." Then one day he tells Elie, "It's the end, God is no longer with us."[24] In Elie's case, in spite of everything that conspires to destroy his symbolic universe, the destruction is never total. Elie cannot deny God. "I did not deny God's existence," he says, "but I doubted His absolute justice."[25]

I believe that Elie's refusal to deny God prevented his descent into anomie and contained the germ of his later restoration to wholeness. Wiesel has written that the Orthodox, the Zionists, and the Communists had the best chance of surviving.[26] That is because their respective symbolic universes were never wholly destroyed. Neither was Wiesel's.

Insofar as any book can, *Night* encapsulates the Jewish experience at Auschwitz. Wiesel is witness not only to what the Germans did to the Jews and to what the Jews endured physically and psychologically but to what happened spiritually to the Jewish world. In addition to its radical honesty and absence of any hint of false emotion, the total scope of this slender book as paradigmatic of the Jewish experience gives it its enduring power.

Nevertheless, for many years I found myself drawn closer to Primo Levi than to Elie Wiesel. Although Levi was a person of towering importance in his native Italy—Italian schoolchildren study his writings—he never achieved the unique and distinctive status accorded to Wiesel either by the world Jewish community or by many thoughtful Christians.[27] Levi and Wiesel came from radically different Jewish backgrounds. Levi was neither a student of Talmud nor of Kabbalah. He was a highly assimilated Italian Jew who had received his doctorate in chemistry two years before he was deported to Auschwitz.

Moreover, even in the most extreme situations, Levi steadfastly refused the consolations of religious tradition. Levi has described the one and only moment in which he experienced "the temptation ... to seek refuge in prayer." In October 1944, as he stood naked, waiting for an SS "commission" to glance at him and instantaneously decide whether to condemn him to be gassed or permit him to continue working as an Auschwitz slave, Levi felt the need for "help and asylum," but he immediately overcame it: "Despite my anguish, equanimity prevailed: you do not change the rules of the game at the end of the match, nor when you are losing. A prayer under these conditions would have been not only absurd ... but blasphemous, obscene, laden with the greatest impiety of which a non-believer is capable. I rejected that temptation: I knew that otherwise were I to survive, I would have to be ashamed of it."[28]

Levi could never have said, as has Wiesel, "If I told you I believed in God, I would be lying; if I told you I did not believe in God, I would be lying."[29] Nevertheless, much of Wiesel's unique ability to speak to and on behalf of thoughtful religious believers, both Jewish and Christian, lies precisely in his profound theological ambivalence.[30]

Unlike Wiesel's, Levi's cultural background was fundamentally the literature of his native language, Italian, and its classical sources in Greco-Roman civilization. His experience at Auschwitz instilled in him a strong curiosity about and an appreciation for the culture of Eastern European Judaism. Nevertheless, he tells us, "it was not my culture."[31] As a young man Levi was far more conversant with Dante Alighieri's *Divina Commedia* than with any work of either biblical or rabbinic Judaism. According to critic Clive James, "Levi often echoes Dante."[32] Indeed, as James points out, one of the difficulties in reading Levi in translation is that the allusions to Dante, taken for granted in Italian, are lost in English. No one would ever worry about allusions to Dante being lost in translating Wiesel.

The reader will recall that in his Detroit response, Wiesel told of a *Rosh Yeshiva* with whom he studied the Talmud. Levi tells a similar story of studying a classical text from memory, not the Talmud but Dante's *Divine Comedy*. One of the chapters of *Se questo e un uomo,* known in English translation as *Survival in Auschwitz,* is titled "The Canto of Ulysses." In the chapter Levi describes how Jean, the twenty-four-year-old Alsatian *Pikolo* of his *Kommando,* asks the author to teach him Italian. Levi tries to teach him some passages from the *Divine Comedy*. One passage in particular is strikingly appropriate:

> Think of your breed; for brutish ignorance
> Your mettle was not made; you were made men
> To follow after knowledge and excellence.[33]

Levi tells us that it was as if he were hearing the passage for the first time: "like the blast of the trumpet, like the voice of God. For a moment I forget who I am and where I am." It was natural for both Elie and the *Rosh Yeshiva* to study the Talmud from memory. It was equally natural for Levi to study the greatest poetic work of the Christian Middle Ages from memory. Nevertheless, this cultural difference may go a long way in explaining the difference in the reception accorded to their work within the Jewish world.

Levi has described his family background in the first chapter of his book *The Periodic Table*. Each chapter is given the name of a chemical element that Levi employs as a metaphor for a particular human characteristic or experience. The chapter describing his personal background is entitled "Argon," an inert gas. According to Levi, argon is one of three gases that are "so inert, so satisfied with their condition, that they do not interfere in any chemical reaction, do not combine with any other element, and precisely for this reason have gone undetected for centuries."[34] Levi tells us that his ancestors and their descendants were like that gas. Hard workers, "they were inert in their inner spirits, inclined to disinterested speculation, witty discourses, elegant, sophisticated, and gratuitous discussion. ... All the deeds attributed to them ... have in common a touch of the static, an attitude of dignified abstention, of voluntary (or accepted) relegation to the margins of the great rivers of life."[35] Using the metaphor of an inert gas, Levi offers a succinct description of the apolitical way of life of a merchant and professional class separated from the indigenous majority in both belief and origin.

"They were never much loved or hated," Levi writes, but there was enough mutual suspicion to have kept them distinct from the rest of the population until late in the nineteenth century. Although Levi had a bar mitzvah, his sense of Jewishness was minimal until the racial laws of 1938. As Levi has written,

> Like most Jews of ancient Italian descent, my parents and grandparents ... had thoroughly assimilated the language, customs, and ethical attitudes of the country. Religion did not count much in my family. ... Nevertheless, both in my family and among Jews in general, the sense that we were Jewish was not entirely lost. It was manifest in the observation of a number of family rituals (especially the holidays of Rosh Hashannah, Passover, and Purim).[36]

Levi himself was born in 1919 in the industrial city of Turin. His motives for studying chemistry were very different from those of his Roman Catholic classmates. The study of chemistry and physics was for Levi the key to understanding the universe, a kind of substitute religion. For Rita, a Christian student with whom Levi had with difficulty become friends, "the university was not at all the Temple of Knowledge: it was a thorny and difficult path that led to a degree, a job, and regular pay." By contrast, science and the Enlightenment, not religion, were at the heart of Levi's symbolic universe.

With the enactment of Mussolini's anti-Semitic racial laws in 1938, Levi came to understand how different he was from his classmates. Levi describes his growing awareness of his Jewish identity in the chapters of *The Periodic Table* entitled "Iron" and "Zinc." In "Zinc" Levi describes his personal response to the atmosphere in Italy during the period when the racial laws were enacted. There was much Fascist propaganda about racial purity and of the Jews as impurities in the pure body of the Italian people.[37]

Levi writes that zinc is capable of reacting with acids only if certain impurities are present in it. If it is too pure, no reaction takes place. Impure zinc became for Levi a metaphor for his Jewish identity:

> I am the impurity that makes the zinc react, I am the grain of salt or mustard. Impurity, certainly, since just during those months the publication of the magazine *Defense of the Race* had begun, and there was much talk about purity, and I had begun to be proud of being impure. In truth, until precisely those months it had not meant much to me that I was a Jew: within myself and in my contacts with my Christian friends, I had always considered my origin an almost negligible but curious fact, a small amusing anomaly, like having a crooked nose, or freckles. A Jew is one who does not put up a tree at Christmas; who should not eat salami, but who eats it all the same; who learned a bit of Hebrew at thirteen years of age, and then forgot it. According to the magazine mentioned before, a Jew is stingy and astute. But I was not particularly stingy nor astute; nor had my father been.[38]

Elsewhere, Levi has written that this passage reflected accurately the state of mind of most Italian Jews at the time.[39]

When Mussolini's racial laws went into effect, neither Levi's teachers nor his classmates were overtly hostile. However, Levi recalls, "I could feel them withdraw and, following an ancient pattern, I withdrew as well: every look exchanged between me and them was accompanied by a minuscule but perceptible flash of mistrust and suspicion. What do you think of me? ... The same as six months ago, your equal who does not go to Mass, or the Jew who, as Dante put it, 'in your midst laughs at you'?"[40]

Although Levi felt increasingly isolated, he became friends with Sandro Delmastro, a Christian student whose family had been tinkers and blacksmiths for generations. Hence, the title "Iron" for the second chapter describing Levi's life. Sandro was also a loner. This was originally the basis of their bond. Unlike Levi, Sandro had decided on a career in chemistry because he wanted "a trade that dealt with things one can see and touch."[41] But Levi's enthusiasm for both literature and science proved contagious, and Sandro became a voracious reader. In the course of one conversation, Primo told Sandro that chemistry and physics are the "antidote to Fascism ... because they were clear and distinct and verifiable at every step, and not a tissue of lies and emptiness, like the radio and newspapers."[42] Levi's commitment to that which is "clear and distinct and verifiable at every step" was to remain an enduring characteristic of his life and work. It constitutes a fundamental difference between his testimony and that of Elie Wiesel, who is capable of great clarity and precise expression but for whom ambiguity and paradox are essential, especially when addressing the theological issues present in the Holocaust.

Levi's capacity for dispassionate analysis contributed materially to his survival in Auschwitz. The same quality is always present in his writing. He never sensationalizes; he almost never lets his own feelings intrude on the cool accuracy of his descriptions of many of the most degrading, antihuman experiences to which men and women have ever been subjected. Refraining from anger, Levi shifts the burden of anger and indignation to his readers, for whom it is inescapable. Levi has stated that he deliberately refrained from formulating judgments in *Survival in Auschwitz* because he felt it was wrong for the witness to take the place of the judge. Nevertheless, he tells us, although he suspended explicit judgments, "his implicit judgments are clearly there."[43]

Levi's entrance into the kingdom of night was different from Wiesel's. He was a member of Giustizia e Liberta, Italy's non-Marxist, anti-Fascist organization. When captured by the Fascists, he was interned at Fossoli, a large camp 18 miles north of Modena. Conditions at Fossoli deteriorated when the SS took over. On February 21, 1944, 650 Jews were transported in boxcars to Auschwitz. Primo Levi was one of them. Only twenty-three returned.[44]

Like Wiesel, when Levi arrived at Auschwitz, he was chosen for slave labor rather than immediate death. Overnight, he was transformed into one of the phantomlike prisoners he had seen on arrival. Levi describes the transformation:

> Imagine now a man who is deprived of everyone he loves, and at the same time of his house, his habits, his clothes, in short, of everything he possesses: he will be a hollow man, reduced to suffering and needs, forgetful of dignity and restraint, for he who loses all often easily loses himself. He will be a man whose life and death can be lightly decided with no sense of human affinity, in the most fortunate cases on the basis of a pure judgment of utility. It is in this way that one can understand the double sense of the term "extermination camp," and it is now clear what we seek to express with the phrase: "to lie on the bottom."[45]

We have noted Elie Wiesel's description of his entry into the same world in his memorable declaration, "Never shall I forget that night." Both writers offer overpowering descriptions of the dehumanizing abuse to which they were subjected. Nevertheless, the horror Elie had to endure was even worse than Primo Levi's. Levi was ten years older when he entered Auschwitz as a single man with a scientific education. His symbolic universe did not collapse. On the contrary, his symbolic universe, the world of the Enlightenment, scientific rationality, and the classical tradition of Western culture, enabled him to survive. Elie entered Auschwitz with his family before his fifteenth birthday. Immediately upon arrival, he heard the order, "Men to the left! Women to the right!" which separated him from his mother and sister forever. Levi describes the brutal, initial assault on his sense of self. In contrast, when Elie describes his first encounter with Auschwitz, he does not tell of the indignity to his person but of the loss of his world and his God. Levi experienced no comparable loss.

Levi had become *Häftling* (prisoner) 174517, the number indelibly tattooed on his left arm. Apart from the indispensable ingredient of luck, survival depended on his ability to learn how to cope with an artificially created obeisant state of nature, an incessant war of all against all.

Levi has given a brief description of those who failed the test of survival, the *Muselmänner*. His description is also one of the best and most terrifying of individuals who have sunk wholly into anomie:

> To sink is the easiest of matters; it is enough to carry out all the orders one receives, to eat only the ration, to observe the discipline of the work and the camp. Experience showed that only exceptionally could one survive more than three months in this way. All the mussulmans who finished in the gas chambers have the same story, or more exactly, have no story; they follow the same slope down to the bottom, like streams that run down to the sea. On their entry into the camp, through basic incapacity, or by misfortune, or through some banal incident, they are overcome before they can adapt themselves; they are beaten by time, they do not begin to learn German, to disentangle the infernal knot of laws and prohibitions until their body is already in decay, and nothing can save them from selections or from death by exhaustion. Their life is short, but their number is endless: they, the *Muselmänner*, the drowned, form the backbone of the camp, an anonymous mass, continually renewed and always identical, of non-men who march and labour in silence, the divine spark dead within them, already too empty to really suffer. One hesitates to call them living: one hesitates to call their death death, in the face of which they have no fear, as they are too tired to understand. ... If I could enclose all the evil of our time in one image, I would choose this image which is familiar to me: an emaciated man, with head dropped and shoulders curved, on whose face and in whose eyes not a trace of a thought is to be seen.[46]

I know of few if any writings that convey the immeasurable harshness and horror of what passed for life in the camps as effectively as does the above. In his pitiless honesty and his undeviating commitment to factuality, Levi describes how those incorporated into the Nazi camp system could survive only by becoming in some measure part of the system. Inside the Lager the Germans had created a society of total domination, an intensified version of the hierarchical structure of the totalitarian state. At each level of the hierarchy, with members of the SS at the top and below them the various ranks of prisoner-collaborators with derivative authority or specialized functions, the domination of those above was always absolute over those beneath. In the camps as outside, there were "grey, ambiguous persons ready to compromise."[47]

Levi calls these prisoner-collaborators "grey-zoners." He contemptuously rejects the irresponsible and malicious statement of Liliana Cavani, the director of the film *The Night Porter:* "We are all victims or murderers, and we accept these roles voluntarily." Levi cites as an extreme case of collaboration the *Sonderkommandos,* who consisted largely of Jews assigned the task of maintaining order among the new arrivals about to be gassed, taking away the corpses, then removing the gold teeth and hair from the dead, collecting their clothing, cremating the bodies, and disposing of the ashes. The SS would periodically murder the whole group and create a new squad with fresh replacements recruited as they stepped off the freight trains at Auschwitz, disoriented and exhausted from the journey. At that point, they had no will to resist.

Levi holds that creating these squads was "National Socialism's most demonic crime." Apart from any pragmatic motives, Levi discerns an attempt to shift the burden of guilt from the perpetrators to the victims, who were "deprived of even the solace of innocence." According to Levi, the existence of the *Sonderkommando* contained a message. The Germans were saying to their victims: "We, the master race, are your destroyers, but you are no better than we are; if we so wish and we do so wish, we can destroy not only your bodies but also your souls, just as we have destroyed ours."[48]

Yet if the creation of the *Sonderkommando* was a demonic crime, Levi nevertheless insists that we must suspend judgment in considering the behavior of the *Sonderkommando*. He asks his readers to consider why these men were under a *Befehlnotstand*, a compulsion to obey orders:

> I would invite anyone who dares pass judgment to carry out upon himself, with sincerity, a conceptual experiment: let him imagine, if he can, that he has lived for months and for years in a ghetto, tormented by chronic hunger, fatigue, promiscuity and humiliation; that he has seen die around him, one by one, his beloved; that he is cut off from the world, unable to receive or transmit news; that, finally, he is loaded on to a train, eighty or a hundred people to a boxcar; that he travels towards the unknown, blindly, for sleepless days and nights; and that he is at last flung inside the walls of an indecipherable inferno. This, it seems to me, is the true *Befehlnotstand*.[49]

When Levi reflected upon human nature after his Auschwitz experience, he expressed the belief that when every civilized institution is removed, humans are not fundamentally brutal or egoistic. Nevertheless, "in the face of driving necessity and physical disabilities many social habits and instincts are reduced to silence."[50]

Levi's own survival was in part made possible because he had taught himself enough German to obey commands and was a trained chemist who, after months in the camp, came to be regarded as useful to IG Farben in manufacturing Buna (synthetic rubber). His scientific training also enabled him to grasp his human and social environment as it was rather than as he might have wished it to be. Above all, he refused to fabricate his own truths as did so many others. Chemists deal with elements whose laws must be obeyed rather than invented. Levi's capacity for dispassionate scientific analysis was also a factor in his survival.

Yet another factor was friendship, namely, his friendship with two Italians, Alberto, a fellow *Häftling*, and Lorenzo, an Italian civilian worker at the Buna installation whom Levi met by chance. Levi was assigned to Alberto's block after a two-week stay in the *Ka-Be,* the *Krankenbau* that passed for an infirmary. Levi and Alberto shared rations and supported each other in their quest for survival. Lorenzo's friendship was of even greater importance. Lorenzo became Levi's protector and brought him a piece of bread and what was left of his ration every day for six months. Lorenzo's conduct was atypical of the civilian behavior toward the *Häftlinge* in the camp; most civilians believed the degraded and disfigured slaves deserved their fate even though they threw them potatoes or bread. Lorenzo treated Levi as a human being, and it was that treatment that Levi says kept him alive: "I believe that it was really due to Lorenzo that I am alive today; and not so much for his material aid, as for his having constantly reminded me by his presence, by his natural and plain manner of being good, that there still existed a just world outside our own ... a remote possibility of good, but for which it was worth surviving."[51]

There was yet another reason why both Levi and Wiesel survived: sheer chance. Philippe de Saint Charon, a French writer, asked Wiesel in an interview whether he might have been saved for some higher providential purpose. Wiesel insisted that his survival was the result of chance rather than providence. In reality, he could hardly have said anything else without seeing those who perished as the objects of either divine providence or indifference. In Levi's case, he came down with scarlet fever on January 11, 1945, and was sent to the infirmary, such as it was. A week later the Germans evacuated the entire camp except those in the infirmary. Levi estimates that there were about 20,000 people on the evacuation march, almost all of whom, including Alberto, died. Levi survived because of his illness.

According to Levi, most of the people he describes in the Lager, from the SS down to the indifferent slave *Häftlinge,* are hardly human: "All the grades of the mad hierarchy created by the Germans paradoxically fraternize in a uniform internal desolation."[52] Nevertheless, Lorenzo was a man of whom Levi could say, "Thanks to Lorenzo, I managed not to forget that I myself was a man." Lorenzo was the slender thread connecting Levi to humanity. I believe he was also connected to humanity by his intact symbolic universe.

As we know, God is absent from Levi's symbolic universe. The question of God and the Holocaust never agonized Levi as it does Wiesel. He has written that he entered the Lager as a nonbeliever and that he remained a nonbeliever throughout his entire life. The experience of the Lager prevented him from "conceiving of any form of providence or transcendent justice."

On at least one occasion, Levi regarded a fellow inmate's prayer as obscene. By October 1944 the Lager had become overcrowded with 2,000 extra "guests" inhabiting the huts. The Germans had a simple solution to the overcrowding, a *Selekcja,* in which the physically fit or those otherwise useful would remain and the others would be gassed. The entire camp was made to file naked past an SS subaltern who by an instantaneous glance made the decision for life or death. It took no more than three or four minutes to decide the fate of 200 men in a hut and the 12,000 inmates of the Lager in an afternoon. Levi survived the *Selekcja*. After it was over, Levi noticed another prisoner, Kuhn, swaying and praying aloud, thanking God that he was not chosen to be gassed. Levi was infuriated. He asked himself how Kuhn could offer thanks when next to him Beppo the Greek knew that he would be gassed in two days. Levi asked: "Does Kuhn not understand that what has happened today is an abomination, which no propitiatory prayer, no pardon, no expiation by the guilty, which nothing at all in the power of man can ever clean again? *If I was God, I would spit at Kuhn's prayer"* (italics added).[53] I can understand Levi's anger, but I believe it is possible to be more charitable concerning the terrorized Kuhn, who expressed his relief in the only manner he knew.

Even before Auschwitz Levi saw no reason to believe in a providential God of Israel. In January 1941 he came together with a group of friends in the gym of the Turin Talmud Torah to study the Bible. Through their study they came to recognize in Ahasuerus and Nebuchadnezzar the oppressors of the Jewish people of their own time. Nevertheless, they could not find the God of the Bible:

> But where was *Kadosh Barukhu*, "the Holy One, Blessed be He," he who breaks the slaves' chains and submerges the Egyptian chariots? He who dictated the Law to Moses, and inspired the liberators Ezra and Nehemiah, no longer inspired anyone; the sky above us was silent and empty: he allowed the Polish ghettos to be exterminated, and slowly, confusedly, the idea was making headway in us that we had no allies we could count on, neither on earth nor in heaven.[54]

Elie Wiesel could have written those words. Nevertheless, he responded to the same question in a very different way. After the war, when Levi returned to Italy, a friend who was a believer visited him and told him that his survival was not a matter of chance or fortunate circumstances but of providence, just as Philippe de Saint Charon had implied by his question to Wiesel. According to his friend, Levi, the nonbeliever, was one of the elect, touched by grace, saved by God to bear witness by writing about Auschwitz.

As Levi recollected this encounter almost forty years later, the following dialogue took place with Ferdinando Camon:

> *Levi:* ... And this, I must confess, seemed to me like a blasphemy, that God should grant privileges, saving one person and condemning someone else. I must say that for me the experience of Auschwitz has been such as to sweep away any remnant of religious education I may have had.
> *Camon:* Meaning that Auschwitz is proof of the nonexistence of God?
> *Levi:* There is Auschwitz and so there cannot be God.

That, however, was not quite Levi's final word. On the typescript of Camon's manuscript, he added "I don't find a solution to this dilemma. I keep looking, but I don't find it."[55]

On April 11, 1987, two days before Passover, Primo Levi either fell or threw himself to his death down the stairwell of the apartment house in Turin in which he had lived his entire adult life. Some of those closest to Levi have been unable to believe that Levi could have committed suicide. Rita Levi Montalcini, his friend for forty years, protested that such an act was impossible because it would have contradicted the message of courage to be found in all of his books.[56] Risa Sodi, who knew Levi and interviewed him shortly before he died, argues that he did in fact commit suicide and that the key to his action is to be found in his last book, *The Drowned and the Saved*. Concerning the book, Sodi writes, "Scrupulously honest, it is written with singular equanimity. But it also betrays the slow-burning rage of a man who sees detachment in the world's reaction to the Holocaust, who sees justice unfulfilled."[57] Sodi's opinion is shared by critic Clive James, who cites Levi's quotation, in *The Drowned and the Saved*, of his friend Jean Améry, who was tortured by the Gestapo and committed suicide decades later: "Anyone who has been tortured remains tortured ... never again will be able to be at ease in the world, the abomination of annihilation is never extinguished. Faith in humanity, already cracked by the first slap in the face, then demolished by torture is never acquired again."

James argues that Levi's vocation as witness both kept him sane and continually threatened to undo him. He lived by a continuous act of will. All that it took to unhinge his will to survive was a bout of depression induced by recent surgery. He had never absorbed the pain and had never found consolation for a gratuitous violence that could never be forgotten. James finds part of Levi's greatness as a writer in that he warns us "against drawing up a phony balance sheet."[58]

James's analysis is not inconsistent with Sodi's. Beneath the equanimity of Levi's cool style, the demand for justice and the rage at justice unfulfilled are inescapable. To the extent that Levi remained a believer, it was in the possibility that the witness who gave, as did he, honest testimony renders the only justice possible to the victims. His suicide, if such it was, leaves us with the agonizing question of whether he finally despaired of even that belief.

As stated above, for many years I found myself drawn to the works of Primo Levi more than to those of Elie Wiesel. I was committed more or less to the same symbolic universe. I do not refer to the literature of Dante or Greco-Roman antiquity but to the culture of dispassionate research and scientific rationality that had enabled Levi to survive in Auschwitz. Unlike Levi, I did not acquire that culture as a student of the hard sciences but as a student at the Hebrew Union College, the Jewish Theological Seminary, and the doctoral program in the history and philosophy of religion at Harvard. That is a far more devastating entrance into the culture of scientific rationality than the hard sciences, for in the process many things held sacred throughout the ages are transformed into that which is utterly profane, at least for the purposes of study and research.

In the aftermath of the Holocaust, religious Jews needed the assurance that the traditions the Germans had sought to destroy retained their integrity. For some, that assurance eventually came through radical messianism, which saw the Holocaust, the founding of the state of Israel, and the recapture of the whole land of Israel as divinely ordained steps culminating in the final messianic climax of Jewish history. I cannot enter into detail here, but the ideology of the ultranationalist Gush Emunim in Israel can be seen as potentially one of the most important and dangerous Jewish religious responses to the Holocaust. Another response was to assert that God was in truth punishing the Jews or, alternatively, to assert with Akiba Drummer that God was testing his people. For most Jews, however, such responses stretched credibility too far. What was required was a Jewish response rooted in tradition that took account of the unprecedented ordeal, in other words, a new Midrash.

In the Holocaust generation, the author of such a Midrash could only be an Eastern European survivor, either a Hasidic Jew or one deeply influenced by Hasidism, who had *not* been trained in the scientific, historical analysis of religious texts and the social scientific analysis of religious behavior and institutions. Only a person for whom some vestige of the traditional Jewish symbolic universe remained intact could credibly create the new Midrash or retell the old stories with a hint of their old sacrality. Elie Wiesel was that person.

No Midrash ever told by a religious Jew was as blasphemous as Wiesel's Midrash on the verse, "No man shall see me and live" (Ex. 33:20). It is the story of Sarah, a prostitute, in *The Accident*. In the novel Eliezer tells of meeting her in Paris and taking her to a room. There he learns that, as a twelve-year-old, she had been forced to service German officers with a preference for young girls in a special barracks. After liberation, she had been so devastated by the experience that she could take up no other way of life.

Hearing her story, Eliezer cannot make love to her—not, as she thinks, because she is no longer twelve but because he sees God in her eyes:

> The God of impotence made her eyes flame. Mine too. I thought: I am going to die. It is written in the Bible. I have never quite understood that: why should God be allied with death? Why should He want to kill a man who succeeded in seeing Him? Now everything became clear. God was ashamed. God likes to sleep with twelve-year-old girls. And he doesn't want us to know. Whoever sees it or guesses it must die so as not to divulge the secret. Death is the only guard who protects God, the doorkeeper of the immense brothel that we call the universe.[59]

Only the creator of such a Midrash could offer a credible post-Holocaust Midrash. Nevertheless, in spite of the blasphemy, this Midrash, like all of Wiesel's Midrashim that question and contend with God, is an affirmation of God's existence. The telling of the tale transmutes the horror of Auschwitz into the beginning of a new divine-human relationship.

Wiesel's authority rests largely on the nature of his vocation. He had no interest in storytelling as entertainment or diversion. He tells us, "I did not want to be a philosopher, or a theologian. The only role I sought was that of witness. I believed that, having survived by chance, I was duty-bound to give meaning to my survival."[60] He has done so by serving as an "emissary" of the dead to the living. "I owe the dead my memory. I am duty-bound to serve as their emissary, transmitting the history of their disappearance, even if it disturbs, even if it brings pain. Not to do so would be to betray them, and thus myself. I simply look at them. I seem them and write."[61] At the end of this essay, he asks rhetorically, "Why death?"[62] As witness-emissary, Wiesel could never say, as did Levi, "There is Auschwitz and so there cannot be God."

We cannot enter into the details of Wiesel's literary transmutation save to note that Wiesel's thought is a contemporary expression of the Jewish mystical conviction, expressed most insistently in Lurianic Kabbalism, that the created order is deeply flawed, not only as a result of the separation of God and human beings but even more profoundly because of an inner division in the Godhead itself. It is thus not in God's power wholly to prevent evil. If evil is to be overcome, it will be as a result of human acts of *Tikkun*, the restoration of God, so to speak, to God, through Israel's and humanity's fidelity to his word.

Nevertheless, if Elie Wiesel speaks for the dead and their symbolic universe, he does so with enormous ambivalence. Let us recall his 1970 response: "To be a Jew is to have all the reasons in the world not to have faith … in God, but to go on telling the tale, to go on carrying on the dialogue, and to have my own silent prayers and quarrels with God." Wiesel's ambivalence expresses that of the contemporary Jewish world and carries with it the authority of both his roots in the world of traditional Judaism and his distinctive role of survivor-witness. It is not only Wiesel but every religious Jew who finally cannot say either yes or no to the God of Sinai. In the face of the most demonic assault in all of history against Judaism, few Jews are prepared to say that the religion for which they and their ancestors have suffered so much was built upon a foundation wholly lacking in credibility.

That, however, is precisely the theological import of Primo Levi's message as a witness. No one who reads Levi's professions of unbelief can doubt his honesty or his lucidity. Moreover, the message of unbelief is expressed implicitly in almost every word he ever wrote about his experience. Thus, although Levi wrote as a Jewish witness, it is Wiesel rather than Levi who is the preeminent Jewish witness to the Shoah. There are hints of consolation in the corpus of Wiesel's writing; Levi remained inconsolable to the very end.

Nevertheless, both witnesses are very precious indeed. Levi's works can be seen as wholly committed to communicating the manifest events. There is little if any place for fantasy, and the unmanifest is excluded. By contrast, in the face of so radical a trauma, Wiesel makes manifest the full range of the feelings, yearnings, and fantasies we normally hide from ourselves, even the blasphemous responses of Jews to the trauma. He also gives expression to their desperate yearning for a Parent who is loving and caring even if incapable of protecting his children against the harsh depredations of the natural and human environment. This is evident in so many of Wiesel's stories of his search "for the child" he once was, his attempts to make the dead live again by being their "emissary," his imagined conversations with family members, his exploration of the possibilities of acting out in response to trauma, and, above all, in his contentions with the imagined all-powerful Parent. Nevertheless, Wiesel is ultimately as committed to the reality principle as is Levi, for only by giving expression to the radical trauma in all of its dimensions and thereby mastering the unconscious can life be made whole again. Although it is hard to offer a judgment in these matters, I would conclude that while both witnesses are necessary, Wiesel goes somewhat further in helping both Jews and Christians to master the trauma of Auschwitz than does Levi.

Notes

1. Richard L. Rubenstein, *The Cunning of History* (New York: Harper and Row, 1975), p. 98.

2. Ellen Fine, "Dialogue with Elie Wiesel," *Counterpoint* 4:1 (Fall 1980), pp. 19–25.

3. Raul Hilberg, *The Destruction of the European Jews* (Chicago: Quadrangle Books, 1961), p. 639.

4. Ibid., p. 640.

5. Ibid., p. 760.

6. Ibid., p. v.

7. Among those who have explicitly recognized Wiesel's stature as a theologian are Jeanmarie Cardinal Lustiger, Michael Berenbaum, Emil L. Fackenheim, and John K. Roth. Cardinal Lustiger has written, "He is one of the greatest theologians of our century." See Jean-Marie Lustiger, "Night: The Absence of God? The Presence of God? A Meditation in Three Parts," in Carol Rittner, ed., *Elie Wiesel: Between Memory and Hope* (New York: New York University Press, 1990), p. 188. See also Michael Berenbaum, *The Vision of the Void: Theological Reflections on the Work of Elie Wiesel* (Middletown, Conn.: Wesleyan University Press, 1979). Berenbaum's title testifies to his view of the importance of Wiesel's contribution as a theologian. Fackenheim has written about Wiesel, "His writings are forcing Jewish theological thought in our time into a new dimension"; Emil L. Fackenheim, *God's Presence in History* (New York: New York University Press, 1970), p. v. See also John K. Roth, *A Consuming Fire: Encounters with Elie Wiesel and the Holocaust* (Atlanta: John Knox Press, 1979).

8. See Berenbaum, *Vision*, p. 42, and Byron L. Sherwin, "Wiesel's Midrash: The Writings of Elie Wiesel and Their Relationship to Jewish Tradition," in Alvin H. Rosenfeld and Irving Greenberg, eds., *Confronting the Holocaust: The Impact of Elie Wiesel* (Bloomington: Indiana University Press, 1978), pp. 117–132.

9. Richard L. Rubenstein, *After Auschwitz* (Indianapolis: Bobbs-Merrill, 1966). p. 246.

10. The story of those years is told in somewhat greater detail in Richard L. Rubenstein, *Power Struggle: An Autobiographical Confession* (New York: Scribner's, 1974), pp. 57–76.

11. Elie Wiesel, "A Celebration of Friendship," in Elie Wiesel, *From the Kingdom of Memory: Reminiscences* (New York: Summit Books, 1990), pp. 81–82.

12. Elie Wiesel, "Talking and Writing and Keeping Silent," in Franklin H. Littell and Hubert G. Locke, eds., *The German Church Struggle and the Holocaust* (Detroit: Wayne State University Press, 1974), p. 270.

13. Ibid., pp. 271–272.

14. Ibid., pp. 272–273.

15. Ibid., p. 274.

16. Elie Wiesel, "The Nobel Lecture," in Wiesel, *From the Kingdom of Memory,* p. 242.

17. Wiesel, "Talking and Writing and Keeping Silent," p. 277.

18. Elie Wiesel, *Night,* in Elie Wiesel, *Night Dawn Day* (Washington: B'nai B'rith, 1985), p. 43.

19. Peter L. Berger and Thomas Luckmann, *The Social Construction of Reality: A Treatise in the Sociology of Knowledge* (Garden City: Anchor Books, 1967), pp. 96–97.

20. Ibid., p. 102.

21. Peter Berger, *The Sacred Canopy: Elements of a Sociological Theory of Religion* (Garden City: Anchor Books, 1969), pp. 29–51.

22. Wiesel, *Night,* pp. 71–72.

23. Ibid., p. 53

24. Ibid., p. 83.

25. Ibid., p. 53.

26. Ibid.

27. Even in his native land, Levi never received the Portico d'Ottavia Literary Prize awarded biannually for the best work published in Italy expressing the "Hebraic spirit." This is especially puzzling to me, as I was the 1977 recipient of the prize. If any writer deserved the prize, it was Levi.

28. Primo Levi, *The Drowned and the Saved,* trans. Raymond Rosenthal (London: Sphere Books, 1988), p. 118.

29. See Richard L. Rubenstein and John K. Roth, *Approaches to Auschwitz: The Holocaust and Its Legacy* (Atlanta: John Knox Press, 1987), p. 285.

30. For an informed exploration of the theological significance of Wiesel, see Berenbaum, *Vision.* See also Roth, *Consuming Fire.* For an interesting Christian interpretation of Wiesel, see Graham B. Walker, Jr., *Elie Wiesel: A Challenge to Theology* (Jefferson, N.C.: McFarland, 1988).

31. Primo Levi, "Beyond Survival," *Prooftexts,* vol. 4, 1984, p. 19.

32. Clive James, "Last Will and Testament," *New Yorker,* May 23, 1988, p. 89. This is a review essay of Levi's last book, *The Drowned and the Saved.*

33. Primo Levi, *Survival in Auschwitz: The Nazi Assault on Humanity,* trans. Stuart Woolf (New York: Collier Macmillan, 1978), p. 103.

34. Primo Levi, *The Periodic Table,* trans. Raymond Rosenthal (London: Sphere Books, 1986), p. 3.

35. Levi, *The Periodic Table,* p. 4.

36. Levi, "Beyond Survival," pp. 9–10.

37. Imitating Goebbels, the Fascists initiated the publication of a viciously anti-Semitic newspaper, *La Difesa della razza* (Defense of the race), in August 1938. It was published nationally every two weeks until Italy's capitulation to the Allies in July 1943. See Susan Zuccotti, *The Italians and the Holocaust: Persecution, Rescue, Survival* (New York: Basic Books, 1987), p. 34.
38. Levi, *The Periodic Table*, pp. 35–36.
39. Levi, "Beyond Survival," p. 12.
40. Levi, *The Periodic Table*, p. 40.
41. Ibid., p. 41.
42. Ibid., p. 42.
43. Ferdinando Camon, *Conversations with Primo Levi*, trans. John Shepley (Marlboro, Vt.: Marlboro Press, 1989), p. 13.
44. Zuccotti, *The Italians*, p. 180.
45. Levi, *Survival in Auschwitz*, p. 23.
46. Ibid., p. 82.
47. Levi, *The Drowned and the Saved*, p. 118.
48. Ibid., p. 37.
49. Ibid., p. 43.
50. Levi, *Survival in Auschwitz*, p. 79.
51. Ibid., p. 111.
52. Levi, *Survival in Auschwitz*.
53. Ibid., p. 118.
54. Levi, *The Periodic Table*, p. 52.
55. Camon, *Conversations with Primo Levi*, pp. 67–68.
56. Rita Levi Montalcini, "Non si e suicidato," *Panorama*, May 3, 1987, p. 62. I am indebted for this reference to Risa Sodi, "The Memory of Justice: Primo Levi and Auschwitz," *Holocaust and Genocide Studies*, vol. 4, no. 1 (1989), p. 90.
57. Sodi, "Memory of Justice."
58. Clive James, "Last Will," p. 91.
59. Wiesel, *Day*, p. 291.
60. Elie Wiesel, "Why I Write," in Rosenfeld and Greenberg, *Confronting the Holocaust*.
61. Elie Wiesel, "Why I Write," in Wiesel, *From the Kingdom of Memory*, p. 16. The text in this later version is somewhat different from the original in Rosenfeld and Greenberg.
62. Wiesel, *From the Kingdom of Memory*, p. 21.

9

Raul Hilberg's "Minutiae": Their Impact on Philosophical and Religious Inquiries After Auschwitz

John K. Roth

I pray to the God within me that He will give me the strength to ask Him the right questions.

—Moshe, in Elie Wiesel's *Night*

In April 1991 a major symposium honored one of the University of Vermont's retiring faculty members. It paid tribute to an extraordinary professor of political science. His research—including especially a monumental book called *The Destruction of the European Jews*—arguably has made Raul Hilberg the world's preeminent scholar of the Holocaust.

Among the many distinguished persons who honored Hilberg was the brilliant and unrelenting filmmaker Claude Lanzmann, whose epic *Shoah* is a cinematic counterpart to Hilberg's monumental writing. Hilberg plays an important part in Lanzmann's film. In a segment on the Warsaw ghetto, for example, he discusses the dilemmas faced by Adam Czerniaków, the man who headed the Jewish Council in that place. Czerniaków documented his role in the diary he kept until he took his own life on July 23, 1942, the day after the Germans began to liquidate the Warsaw ghetto by deporting its Jews to Treblinka. Hilberg knows the details of Czerniaków's life because he helped to translate and edit the Czerniaków diary, which survived the Final Solution.

In another segment of Lanzmann's *Shoah*, Hilberg studies a different kind of document: *Fahrplananordnung* 587. This railroad timetable scheduled death traffic. Conservative estimates indicate that *Fahrplananordnung* 587, which outlines a few days in late September 1942, engineered some 10,000 Jews to Treblinka's gas chambers.

Raul Hilberg has spent his life detailing how such things happened. Thus, in his first appearance in the Lanzmann film, he observes, "In all of my work, I have never begun by asking the big questions, because I was always afraid that I would come up with small answers; and I have preferred to address these things which are minutiae or details in order that I might then be able to put together in a gestalt a picture which, if not an explanation, is at least a description, a more full description, of what transpired."[1]

Big Questions

Hilberg's opening statement in *Shoah* warns about "big questions." He does not deny that the Holocaust raises them—first and foremost the question *why*. Contrary to much human expectation, however, because a question can be asked does not mean that it can be answered well, if at all, particularly when the questions are "big," fundamental and sweeping ones of the kind that characterize philosophical and religious inquiries. So Hilberg concentrates on details instead. Those minutiae, however, are much more than minutiae. Their particularity speaks volumes and forms a terribly vast description. So full of life distorted and wasted, its accumulated detail makes the big questions less easy and simple to raise but all the more important, too.

Put into perspective by work like Hilberg's, the big questions become what Elie Wiesel's teacher, Moshe, called the "right questions," and thus they command the respect they deserve. That respect enjoins suspicion about "answers" that are small—inadequate for the facts they must encompass. That same respect also focuses awareness that the big questions raised by the Holocaust nonetheless need to be kept alive. For the political scientist's detail and the historian's minutiae, far from silencing the big questions, ought to intensify wonder about them. Otherwise we repress feeling too much and deny ourselves insight that can only be deepened by asking the right questions.

Note that *insight* and *answer,* at least as used here, are not identical terms, for if a question does not lead to an answer, as that word is conventionally understood, it does not mean that the question is not right. On the contrary, especially when they are grounded in and provoked by work like Hilberg's, questions are often as "right" as they are "big" just because they do not have conventional answers but instead produce awareness and understanding that can come in no other way than through inquiry, reflection, and meditation about them.

We will not get final answers to the Holocaust's big questions—indeed, we should be suspicious if we think we have. Pursuit of those questions, however, has important awareness to give. Those insights may not be the same for everyone, but they may be shared, and in the sharing we may better discern the differences between what is true, right, and good and what is not. Justification for such claims, of course, is not self-evident. It invites testing. In fact, that is the point. So to test these suggestions, turn to the heart of the matter.

Surely two of the biggest Holocaust questions are, *Where was God?* and, an issue sometimes posed as a rejoinder to the first, *Where was humanity?* When explored in that order, the intent is usually to avoid underemphasizing humanity's responsibility, which could happen by overemphasizing God's. That concern makes sense. It may be served even better, however, by asking—as I suggest we do—where God was after considering where humanity was. Whatever the order, though, direct and immediate answers to those questions are likely to be small. So, resisting that approach, try inquiring, reflecting, and meditating about them by attending to some details, some minutiae that are not minutiae at all.

Where Was Humanity?

David Rousset, who spent much of his career as a journalist, was born in Roanne, France, in 1912. After completing his formal education, he wrote on politics and economics for publications such as *Time* and *Fortune* and also taught philosophy in a Parisian school. Adamantly opposed to fascism, he became active in the Resistance when France fell to Germany in World War II.

The Gestapo arrested Rousset in Paris on October 16, 1943. He endured German concentration camps at Buchenwald, Neuengamme, and Helmstedt, where he worked in the mines for a year. A solid man, more than 200 pounds, he weighed less than 120 when he returned to Paris at the war's end. Soon he began to write *L'Univers concentrationnaire*. One of the first studies of the Nazi concentration camps, Rousset's book—translated as *The Other Kingdom* (1947)—appeared in France in 1946. In restrained and understated prose, Rousset offered a series of brief, hard-hitting essays that start with an ironic epigraph: "There exists a decree issued by Göring protecting frogs."[2]

Rousset's epigraph referred, of course, to Hermann Göring. A key leader in the Third Reich, Göring did much to create "the other kingdom," which denied protection to every human being imprisoned within it. Its victims included between 5 and 6 million Jews—more than 1 million of them children—who were killed by Nazi Germany and its collaborators in what came to be called "the Final Solution of the Jewish question."

"The existence of the camps," wrote Rousset, "is a warning."[3] Part of that warning is the most memorable statement from his book: "Normal men do not know that everything is possible."[4] Rousset warned the unsuspecting against their own optimism. Even after the Holocaust, he worried that people would imperil themselves by forgetting or ignoring how terribly destructive human life can be.

Rousset's warning and the worry that prompted it remain on target. The worst that has been and can be done by human beings must have the attention it deserves. But Rousset's warning, at least implicitly, goes further than that. Warnings exist not merely *against* but also *for* something. Their best purpose is to protect and encourage what is good. Hence it is important to underscore that before the Holocaust too many people disbelieved such a thing could happen. During the Holocaust too many people disbelieved that such a thing was happening. After the Holocaust too many people still disbelieve what has happened and that repetitions of it are possible.

True, some people were ignorant about Auschwitz—how it arose and what it produced. There are those who remain ignorant about those realities even now. But disbelief and ignorance are not the same, and ignorance was not at the heart of disbelief about the Holocaust. The testimony of Jan Kozielewski, a witness better known as Jan Karski, helps to make the case.

A Polish Catholic who taught for many years at Georgetown University in Washington, D.C., and who is honored as a "righteous Gentile" at the Yad Vashem memorial in Jerusalem, Karski resisted the German occupation of his homeland during World War II.[5] Only in his mid-twenties at the time, he served as a courier for the Polish underground and government-in-exile. Captured and tortured by the Gestapo, he managed to escape and continued to carry out one dangerous mission after another.

Toward the end of September 1942, Karski was headed for London to convey important messages to the Polish government-in-exile. Shortly before his departure, two Jewish underground organizations inquired whether he would be their courier, too. Specifically, they asked Karski to make known that the Germans were implementing their intention to destroy all Jews and to stress that only direct intervention by the Allies could stop the Final Solution. Although Karski agreed to spread this word abroad, one of the Jewish leaders, fearing that Karski might not be believed, pressed on. It would help to disarm disbelief, he argued, if Karski saw firsthand what was happening to European Jewry. Thus it was that arrangements were made for Karski to enter both the Warsaw ghetto and a camp where Jews were being murdered. Although Karski might prefer not to speak about those explicit experiences, he confesses that "I saw horrible, horrible things." He is much more outspoken, however, about the disbelief he encountered when trying to convince the Allies to acknowledge the Holocaust's reality and to take direct action to alleviate Jewish plight. He met with President Franklin D. Roosevelt and Foreign Minister Anthony Eden of Britain. He testified to leading American Jews as well; Rabbi Stephen Wise and Supreme Court Justice Felix Frankfurter were among them. But *futile* is one of the words Karski would use to sum up his private diplomacy on behalf of the Jewish people.

It was not primarily ignorance, contends Karski, that produced the heartless abandonment of the Jews and thereby made the Nazis' genocidal aims all the easier to achieve. Self-imposing disbelief to dismiss inconvenient evidence, too many Allied leaders knew what was happening and yet were unconvinced and unmoved. They acted—or failed to act—accordingly. Granted, the Allies eventually crushed the Third Reich and in that process the Holocaust was brought to an end. The ending was anything but complete, however, because Karski—and he is far from alone—remains haunted that "six million Jews perished. Six million totally helpless, abandoned by all. No country, no government, nobody, nothing."

Not all of the disbelief Karski encountered had the same texture. He recalls, for example, his meeting with Frankfurter. Asked to describe what was going on in Poland, Karski obliged in detail. Frankfurter listened intently until Karski had no more to say. When the justice broke the silence that followed, he said, "Mr. Karski, a man like me talking to a man like you must be totally frank. So I am unable to believe you." Clarifying his point, Frankfurter underscored that he did not think Karski was lying. "I am unable to believe you," the justice insisted; "there is a difference."

Why was Justice Frankfurter unable to believe Jan Karski? Karski himself finds that the question still unsettles him. Even though we live knowing all too well that the Holocaust did happen, that question should unsettle us, too, because we may not yet have come to terms with Richard L. Rubenstein's disturbing proposition in a work called *The Cunning of History*. In this brief book about the Holocaust, a volume no less hard-hitting than Rousset's *Other Kingdom*, Rubenstein writes that "the Holocaust bears witness to *the advance of civilization*."[6] That proposition is loaded with ominous portents that require us to find strength to pursue the right questions.

Note that in 1933, the year in which Adolf Hitler took power in Nazi Germany, the Chicago World's Fair celebrated what its promoters optimistically hailed as "A Century of Progress." As Rubenstein goes on to point out in *The Cunning of History*, "the theme of the fair was expressed in the slogan: 'Science Explores; Technology Executes; Mankind Conforms.'"[7] Cast in those terms, the Holocaust bears witness not only to the tragically cunning and ironic elements of "progress" but also acts as a warning about what could—but should not—lie ahead for humanity.

The Holocaust did not result from unplanned random violence. Instead, it was ultimately a state-sponsored program of population elimination made possible by modern technology, political organization, and highly educated intelligence. As Nazi Germany became a genocidal state, its antisemitic racism required a destruction process that needed and got the cooperation of every sector of German society. The killers and those who aided and abetted them directly—or indirectly as bystanders—were, for the most part, civilized people from a society that was scientifically advanced, technologically competent, culturally sophisticated, and efficiently organized. For the most part, those who permitted or carried out the orders were ordinary, even "decent" folk not so different from us.

Teachers and writers helped to till the soil where Hitler's virulent antisemitism took root; their students and readers reaped the wasteful harvest. Lawyers drafted and judges enforced the laws that isolated Jews and set them up for the kill. University administrators curtailed admissions for Jewish students and dismissed

Jewish faculty members. Bureaucrats in the Finance Ministry handled confiscations of Jewish wealth and property. Postal officials delivered mail about definition and expropriation, denaturalization and deportation. Driven by their eugenic imperatives and biomedical visions, physicians were among the first to experiment with the gassing of "life unworthy of life." Scientists performed research and tested their racial theories on those whom German science had branded sub- or nonhuman. Business executives found that Nazi concentration camps could provide cheap labor; they worked people to death, turning the Nazi motto *Arbeit Macht Frei* (Work Makes One Free) into a sardonic truth. Stockholders made profits from firms that supplied Zyklon B to gas people and from companies that built crematoria to burn the corpses. Radio performers were joined by artists, such as the brilliant film director Leni Riefenstahl, to broadcast and screen the propaganda that made Hitler's policies persuasive to so many. Engineers drove trains, factory workers modified trucks so that they became deadly gas vans, city policemen became members of squadrons that made murdering Jews their specialty.[8] The list could go on and on.

It was no accident that the Holocaust broke out in one of the most scientifically advanced, technologically competent, philosophically sophisticated, and even theologically steeped cultures of all human history. The Nazis saw what they took to be a practical problem: the need to eliminate unwanted people and to find enough labor for a state whose destiny spelled expansion. Then they moved expeditiously to solve it. How efficiently and rationally they did so—using those terms in Max Weber's sense of "the methodical attainment of a definitely given and practical end by means of an increasingly precise calculation of adequate means"—is still becoming clear as research about the Holocaust's history continues.[9]

Several months before the United States Holocaust Memorial Museum opened in Washington, D.C., in April 1993, that fact was driven home for me when Michael Berenbaum, then the museum's project director, showed me the exhibits he had helped to coordinate. One of them especially caught my eye because it made me think of a comment in Rubenstein's *Cunning of History*. Reflecting on the deadly efficiency of the process of destruction unleashed by the Germans, Rubenstein had remarked that "the Nazis didn't even have computers."[10]

The particular exhibit that drew my attention then (and I have always paused before it when I have visited the museum since) is one that calls Rubenstein's passing remark into question. The exhibit shows that although primitive by today's standards, computers were in fact part of the Nazis' bureaucratic arsenal. Much more than disputing Rubenstein's judgment about the Nazis' computer capabilities, this particular exhibit amplifies support for his claim that "the Holocaust bears witness to *the advance of civilization.*"

Systematically to identify, isolate, target, and eventually destroy people, one needs to know how many there are, what they can do, and where they live. Statisticians and census takers therefore played a critical role in Nazi Germany's plans.

Experts in those fields naturally look for means to make their work more accurate and speedy. Such means typically entail machines—in this case machines known as Holleriths.[11]

The Hollerith machines took their name from a German-American inventor and U.S. Census Office employee named Herman Hollerith. In the late nineteenth century, Hollerith devised the first punch-card counting machine; it was used in the 1890 U.S. census. Hollerith founded a company to produce the machine but sold the enterprise to a firm that became known in the mid-1920s as IBM. Included in IBM's holdings were 90 percent of the stock in a German company identified by the acronym DEHOMAG. This Deutsche Hollerith Maschinen Gesellschaft had been licensed to produce Hollerith machines in Germany, but financial straits during World War I and its aftermath led to DEHOMAG's becoming the German Hollerith subsidiary of IBM.

We do not yet know all the details about the use and abuse of these early computers in the Holocaust, but it is known that with considerable Nazi fanfare, DEHOMAG opened a new data-processing facility in Berlin-Lichterfelde on January 8, 1934. On that occasion, the founder and director of the company, Willy Heidinger, gave a major address that contained the following point of view:

> We are recording the individual characteristics of every single member of the nation onto a little card. ... We are proud to be able to contribute to such a task, a task that makes available to the physician of our German body-social the material for his examination, so that our physician can determine whether, from the standpoint of the health of the nation, the results calculated in this manner stand in a harmonious, healthy relation to one another, or whether unhealthy conditions must be cured by corrective interventions. ... We have firm trust in our physician and will follow his orders blindly, because we know that he will lead our nation towards a great future. *Heil* to our German people and its leader![12]

Consonant with the content and tone of Heidinger's speech, these additional clusters of facts have been documented: (1) Holleriths functioned in German census taking after the Nazis came to power, and their data made possible a national card catalog about Jews. (2) Contributing to that data were German churches. After the Nürnberg racial laws were passed in 1935, the Nazi government instructed the churches to prepare demographic data that could be processed by the Hollerith machines. Church officials complied, and the accumulated information helped to identify those who were Christian and those who were not. The churches were further required to identify members who had converted from Judaism to Christianity. Although the Final Solution was not yet under way in 1935, the cooperation of the churches implicated them in Nazi Germany's segregation, persecution, and destruction of the Jews. (3) Although it remains unclear whether the Holleriths were used directly to compile deportation lists, the information the machines processed provided the raw material for such plans. These advances were especially developed during and after the 1939 German census, when explicit racial categories based on the Nürnberg laws were included in the census forms for the first time. (4) Many institutions in the Third Reich—including banks, railroads, and the SS Racial Office—either leased or owned Holleriths. (5) The Gestapo Political Section in several concentration camps, including Mauthausen and Ravensbrück, used Hollerith machines to classify inmate data.

In sum, while the exact ways in which these machines may have functioned to help identify and dispatch the Holocaust's victims are less than crystal clear, it is unmistakable that pivotal players in the destruction process did possess and use them. There is more to learn about the Holleriths, but suffice it to say that the Nazis took population statistics with deadly seriousness. The faster and more efficiently the counting could be done the better. Compared to current computer technology, the Holleriths were primitive. Much human labor—usually provided by German women—was required to enter raw data into the Holleriths' punch cards. But once those entries were made, the machines' electrical contact brushes could aggregate, store, and retrieve the information relatively quickly. The Holleriths were an advance in civilization. That advance helped to spell death Holocaust-style. To reflect on such details, on minutiae that are not minutiae, leads one to wonder not only, Where *was* humanity? but also, Where is it *now*?

Where Was God?

Religion was not a sufficient condition for the Holocaust, but it was a necessary one. What happened at Auschwitz is inconceivable without beliefs about God held first by Jews and then by Christians. But what happened at Auschwitz also makes religious affirmations more difficult and problematic than they were before. To see how, begin with some details about a Jew from Turin, Italy, who took his degree in chemistry from the university there in 1941. Two years later, at the age of twenty-four and with the greater part of his native Italy under Nazi Germany's control, Primo Levi was arrested for resisting fascism. At first Levi's Jewish identity was undetected by his captors, but under questioning he acknowledged it and was sent to a detention camp at Fossoli, near Modena. Deported to Auschwitz in February 1944, he ended up in Monowitz, one of the main camp's many forced labor satellites.[13] After his liberation in late January 1945, Levi eventually found his way back to Italy, resumed his career as a chemist, and became an acclaimed author who wrote about the Holocaust with honesty that few others have matched. In what was probably suicide, a fall down a stairwell in April 1987 cost him his life.

Primo Levi's best-known book about the Holocaust is *Survival in Auschwitz*. It is a classic memoir about his year there, which Levi called "a journey toward nothingness."[14] Although Levi's writings speak about many things, rarely do they say much directly about God. *Survival in Auschwitz,* however, contains a striking exception to that rule. What led to this exception was an Auschwitz "selection" on a Sunday afternoon in October 1944.

All the prisoners in Levi's part of the camp were ordered to their barracks. As in all of them (Levi's hut was number 48 out of 60), everyone in Levi's quarters received "a card with his number, name, profession, age and nationality" and obeyed the order to "undress completely, except for shoes."[15] Levi and his comrades then waited for the "selection." It would sentence some to the gas chambers. Others would be reprieved to work a while longer.

When the SS "inspectors" reached hut 48 to process Levi's group, the procedure was as random and capricious as it was quick and simple. One by one, each prisoner ran a few steps and then surrendered his identity card to an SS man who, in turn, passed the card to a man on his right or left. "This," wrote Levi, "is the life or death of each of us. In three or four minutes a hut of two hundred men is 'done,' as is the whole camp of twelve thousand men in the course of the afternoon."[16] Not quite "done," however, because in Levi's part of the camp it usually took two or three days before those "selected" actually went to the gas.

Meanwhile the prisoners could figure out whose cards went left, whose went right, and what the difference meant. Thus, Levi continued by noting what he observed after the meager portion of soup had been devoured on that postselection evening and how he felt about what he saw and heard:

> Silence slowly prevails and then, from my bunk on the top row, I see and hear old Kuhn praying aloud, with his beret on his head, swaying backwards and forwards violently. Kuhn is thanking God because he has not been chosen.
>
> Kuhn is out of his senses. Does he not see Beppo the Greek in the bunk next to him, Beppo who is twenty years old and is going to the chamber the day after tomorrow and knows it and lies there looking fixedly at the light without saying anything and without even thinking any more? Can Kuhn fail to realize that next time it will be his turn? Does Kuhn not understand that what has happened today is an abomination, which no propitiatory prayer, no pardon, no expiation by the guilty, which nothing at all in the power of man can ever clean again?
>
> If I was God, I would spit at Kuhn's prayer.[17]

Some forty years after that October night in Auschwitz, and less than a year before his own death, Primo Levi checked the typescript of a series of interviews he had granted to Ferdinando Camon. At the end of one of the interviews, Levi had said, "No, I have never been [a believer]. I'd like to be, but I don't succeed. ... I must say that for me the experience of Auschwitz has been such as to sweep away any remnant of religious education I may have had." Camon sought clarification about those reflections: "Auschwitz," he asked Levi, "is proof of the nonexistence of God?" To that big question Levi gave a simple reply but not a small answer: "There is Auschwitz," he said, "and so there cannot be God."

In those few words, Levi's response seemed done. Not quite done, however, because when Camon received back the corrected typescript for the interview, he saw that Levi had penciled a margin note beside his not-quite-final comment: "I don't find a solution to this dilemma," Levi had added; "I keep looking, but I don't find it."[18]

Looking ... not finding ... looking some more: When the question is whether Auschwitz is proof of the nonexistence of God, when the dilemma is that there is Auschwitz and so there cannot be God, does that rhythm make sense? By no means would everyone say yes, but Levi, who was not a believer, still sensed that those big questions were among the right ones. So does Elie Wiesel, whose Holocaust-based reflections are never far removed from the question, Where was God?

With reference to his comment that "if I was God, I would spit at Kuhn's prayer," Primo Levi and Elie Wiesel together might make us consider that "the right questions" include: Did God spit at Auschwitz? In particular, did God spit at a prayer of thanks offered by one who, like Kuhn for the moment, "has not been chosen"? To those questions others might be added: If God did spit at Auschwitz, if God did spit at a prayer of thanks offered by one who "has not been chosen," did God do more than spit? And if, in either case, God failed to spit, did God do anything else instead?

Care should be taken before one even considers responding to such questions. Replies to them may be disorienting, impossible, or both—even for God. Elie Wiesel suggests as much in one of his many gemlike dialogues. Following death traffic scheduled by another *Fahrplananordnung*, following another Auschwitz selection, Wiesel invites meditation on some last words between a mother and her daughter:

Where are we going? Tell me. Do you know?
I don't know, my little girl.
I'm afraid. Is it wrong, tell me, is it wrong to be afraid?
I don't know; I don't think so.
In all my life I have never been so afraid.
Never.
But I would like to know where we are going. Say, do you know? Where are we going?
To the end of the world, little girl. We are going to the end of the world.
Is that far?
No, not really.
You see, I am really tired. Is it wrong, tell me, is it wrong to be so tired?
Everybody is tired, my little girl.
Even God?
I don't know. You will ask Him yourself.[19]

Could Albert Camus, the French philosopher, have been thinking about such defenseless mothers and daughters—the Final Solution destroyed so many of them—when he underscored that humanity is responsible but added that "man is not entirely to blame; it was not he who started history"?[20] Who or what did start history, that arena of human consciousness and activity that Hegel—a nineteenth-century, pre-Holocaust, German philosopher—so aptly called "the slaughter-bench at which the happiness of peoples, the wisdom of states, and the virtue of individuals have been sacrificed"?[21] Maybe God started history, but maybe not, because the French novelist Stendhal may have been correct when he suggested that God's only excuse is that God does not exist. And yet, remaining aware of Stendhal's observation, what, if anything, should we ask God after Auschwitz? And what, if anything, would be the point of such asking?

Two areas of questioning could involve freedom and suffering. The point of raising issues about them would not be to shirk our responsibilities by blaming God. On the contrary, the point would be to probe honestly the tension between despair and hope so that resistance against the abuse of freedom and compassion for those who suffer are both increased.

With those points in mind, consider that most people want a totally good God or none at all. In religious circles, then, it usually has not been popular to put God on trial. For centuries human beings have taken themselves to task—and not without reason—in order to protect God's innocence. Life is simpler that way. Nevertheless, it is irresponsible to assign responsibility inequitably. If God exists, God's responsibility is located in that God is the one who ultimately sets the boundaries in which we live and move and have our being. True, since we are thrown into history at our birth, we appear in social settings made by human hands, but finally those hands cannot account for themselves. To the extent that they are created with the potential and the power to be dirty, credit for that fact belongs elsewhere. "Elsewhere" may be God's address.

Do not take lightly what God's, as well as humanity's, responsibility entails. It must reckon, for example, with minutiae about a Jewish carpenter named Jankiel Wiernik, who once said, "Perhaps some day I shall know how to laugh again."[22] When those words were published in 1944, Wiernik was unsure. Deported by the Germans from Warsaw to Treblinka on August 23, 1942, Wiernik would escape from that death camp in the prisoner revolt that occurred a year later on August 2. But prior to that time, he went through experiences that made him say: "My life is embittered. Phantoms of death haunt me, specters of children, little children, nothing but children. I sacrificed all those nearest and dearest to me. I myself took them to the execution site. I built their death chambers for them."[23]

The point is not that God predestined or caused such events directly. On the contrary, human freedom brought them about, and that freedom enabled Nazi Germany and its collaborators to force Jankiel Wiernik into the positions of choiceless choice to which his lamentation about sacrifice and building refers so poignantly. But human freedom—much as some defenders of God would like—does not remove God from the dock.

Using freedom as a defense for God is a well-known strategy. Moving from the idea that freedom is a good, the argument has usually been that God gave freedom to human life in innocence. The gift, to be sure, did include a capacity for self-perversion. God knew that and perhaps even that liberty would be abused. Still, the apology continues, God's gift is justified. Only with the freedom we were given can men and women truly be God's children.

For big questions raised by the minutiae of experience like Wiernik's, such an answer is too small, because freedom is more problematic for both God and humanity than it admits. Human freedom constitutes an insufficient defense for God. It does so because our freedom is both too much and too little—too much because human freedom fueled the Holocaust's consuming fire; too little because once that power was unleashed, humanity's countervailing energy, individual or collective, could not halt it before millions perished. Human freedom, enfeebled and empowered, wastes so much life. We are responsible for that freedom but, as Camus reminds us, not entirely. Human freedom raises big questions about God's responsibility, too.

Those questions, some of God's defenders say, can be answered by acknowledging that God's gift of human freedom involves limitations on God's power. Thus, they add, the claim that God is totally benevolent can be preserved as well. In effect, then, this answer provides the alibi that God is always doing the best God can. Originally, this perspective could contend, God brought order out of chaos and fashioned a world of beauty and richness. Within that setting, God lured humanity into existence, endowing it with freedom to choose. But if God's authority can minimize the confusion that we produce with our liberty, it is also true that God cannot both intervene directly and still retain the integrity of free human creatures. What God can do, this view often goes on to emphasize, is to suffer with those, like Wiernik, whose lives are shattered by the destructive uses of human power.

Where was God? Where is God? Is suffering with the abused and defenseless the best that God can do once the problematic gift of human freedom is bestowed and runs amok? If the answer to that question is yes, the affirmation is too small, because the God it defends is too small as well. God's responsibility, indeed God's guilt, can be reduced to the extent that God lacks power. But to the extent that God lacks power, God may also be ineffectual. Short of no God at all, what we have to ask religiously, therefore, is whether we should settle for an innocent but ineffectual God or whether we should run the risks of relating to a God who is really master of the universe but less than perfectly good by any standards that we can comprehend.

Infinite Yearning

Incomplete and perhaps unending, these inquiries about a few of the philosophical and religious implications of some Holocaust questions began with Raul Hilberg: "In all of my work," he reflected, "I have never begun by asking the big questions, because I was always afraid that I would come up with small answers." To protest against small answers—specifically to do so, as I have shown here, by attending to what Hilberg calls "minutiae or details"—proves worthwhile. It does so by suggesting how the big questions—Where, for example, was humanity? Where was God?—remain fundamental to our humanity as we try to struggle with them constructively. That insight, I believe, was one that Elie Wiesel's teacher wanted to impart to his young student when he responded to Wiesel's big question, "And why do you pray, Moshe?" by saying, "I pray to the God within me that he will give me the strength to ask Him the right questions."[24]

By pursuing Moshe's insight, Wiesel came to see something else. It can work with Raul Hilberg's emphasis on "minutiae or details." Instead of answers to big questions, especially if the answers are destined to be small, a story may have much more to say. So, taken from the conclusion of Wiesel's novel *The Town Beyond the Wall*, here is a story to end on for now. It complements Hilberg's attempt—and mine—"to put together in a gestalt a picture which, if not an explanation, is at least a description, a more full description, of what transpired."

> Legend tells us that one day man spoke to God in this wise:
>
> "Let us change about. You be man, and I will be God. For only one second."
> God smiled gently and asked him, "Aren't you afraid?"
> "No. And you?"
> "Yes, I am," God said.
>
> Nevertheless he granted man's desire. He became a man, and the man took his place and immediately availed himself of his omnipotence: he refused to revert to his previous state. So neither God nor man was ever again what he seemed to be.
> Years passed, centuries, perhaps eternities. And suddenly the drama quickened. The past for one, and the present for the other, were too heavy to be borne.
> As the liberation of the one was bound to the liberation of the other, they renewed the ancient dialogue whose echoes come to us in the night, charged with hatred, with remorse, and most of all, with infinite yearning.[25]

Notes

1. See Claude Lanzmann, *Shoah: An Oral History of the Holocaust* (New York: Pantheon Books, 1985), p. 70.

2. David Rousset, *The Other Kingdom*, trans. Ramon Guthrie (New York: Reynal and Hitchcock, 1947), p. 27.

3. Ibid., p. 172.

4. Ibid., p. 168.

5. The information about Jan Karski, including the quotations, comes from an interview with Karski conducted by Ken Adelman. See "Seeing Too Much," *The Washingtonian* 23 (July 1988): 61–67. For additional information about Karski, see Walter Laqueur, *The Terrible Secret: Suppression of the Truth About Hitler's "Final Solution"* (Boston: Little, Brown, 1980), pp. 229–237, and David Engel, "Jan Karski's Mission to the West, 1943–1944," *Holocaust and Genocide Studies* 5 (1990): 363–380.

6. Richard L. Rubenstein, *The Cunning of History: The Holocaust and the American Future* (New York: Harper Torchbooks, 1987), p. 91.

7. Ibid., p. 78.

8. Christopher R. Browning tells the story of Reserve Police Battalion 101 from Hamburg, which became involved in the mass murder of Polish Jewry. See his *Ordinary Men: Reserve Police Battalion 101 and the Final Solution in Poland* (New York: HarperCollins, 1992). For a briefer account, see Browning's essay, "One Day in Józefów: Initiation to Mass Murder," *Lessons and Legacies: The Meaning of the Holocaust in a Changing World*, ed. Peter Hayes (Evanston: Northwestern University Press, 1991).

9. See Max Weber, "The Social Psychology of the World Religions," *From Max Weber: Essays in Sociology*, trans. and ed. H. H. Gerth and C. Wright Mills (New York: Oxford University Press, 1976), p. 293.

10. Rubenstein, *The Cunning of History*, p. 77.

11. For information about computers and the Holocaust, I am indebted to Sybil Milton, David M. Luebke, and Peggy Olbrecht from the United States Holocaust Memorial Museum, Washington, D.C., as well as Michael Berenbaum, whose book *The World Must Know: The History of the Holocaust as Told in the United States Memorial Museum* (Boston: Little, Brown, 1993) contains important information about the Hollerith machines (see pp. 42–43). See also Götz Aly and Karl Heinz Roth, *Die restlose Erfassung: Volkszählen, Identifizieren, Aussondern im Nationalsozialismus* (Berlin: Rotbuch Verlag, 1984).

12. David M. Luebke of the United States Holocaust Memorial Museum kindly shared with me his translation of this portion of Willy Heidinger's speech. The source for the speech is "Festrede des Gründers, Generaldirektor Willy Heidinger," *Denkschrift zur Einweihung der neuen Arbeitsstätte der Deutschen Hollerith Maschinen Gesellschaft m.b.H. in Berlin-Lichterfelde am 8. Januar 1934* (Berlin, n.d.), p. 39. The quoted portion of this speech can also be found in Berenbaum, *The World Must Know*, p. 42.

13. At Auschwitz, Levi reports, the identifying number 174517 was tattooed on his left arm. See Primo Levi, *Survival in Auschwitz: The Nazi Assault on Humanity*, trans. Stuart Woolf (New York: Macmillan, 1961), p. 23. Levi's identification number enables one to place his arrival at Auschwitz in late February 1944. See Danuta Czech, *Auschwitz Chronicle 1939–1945*, trans. Barbara Harshav, Martha Humphries, and Stephen Shearier (New York: Henry Holt, 1990), p. 589. Czech's book documents what happened at Auschwitz day by day. Its entry for February 26, 1944, states: "650 Jewish men, women, and children from the Fossoli camp arrive in an RSHA transport from Italy. After the selection, 95 men, given Nos. 174471–174565, and 29 women, given Nos. 75669–75697, are admitted to the camp. The remaining 526 people are killed in the gas chambers."

14. Levi, *Survival in Auschwitz*, p. 13.

15. Ibid., p. 116.

16. Ibid., pp. 116–117.

17. Ibid., p. 118.

18. See Ferdinando Camon, *Conversations with Primo Levi*, trans. John Shepley (Marlboro, Vt.: Marlboro Press, 1989), pp. 67–68. See also Alexander Stille, "Primo Levi and the Jews of Piedmont," *Present Tense* (September–October 1989): 50–53.

19. Elie Wiesel, *A Jew Today*, trans. Marion Wiesel (New York: Random House, 1978), pp. 144–145.

20. Albert Camus, *The Rebel*, trans. Anthony Bower (New York: Vintage Books, 1956), p. 22.

21. G.W.F. Hegel, *Reason in History*, trans. Robert S. Hartman (Indianapolis: Bobbs-Merrill, 1953), p. 27.

22. Quoted from Jankiel Wiernik, "One Year in Treblinka," *The Death Camp Treblinka*, ed. Alexander Donat (New York: Holocaust Library, 1979), p. 149.

23. Ibid., p. 148.

24. Elie Wiesel, *Night*, trans. Stella Rodway (New York: Bantam Books, 1986), p. 3.

25. Elie Wiesel, *The Town Beyond the Wall*, trans. Stephen Becker (New York: Avon Books, 1970), p. 190.

PART THREE

Personal Tributes

10

Raul Hilberg, Actor in *Shoah*

Claude Lanzmann

At this very moment of paying homage to a man I admire and to whom I owe much, I have before my eyes my own copy of the American edition of *The Destruction of the European Jews,* marked and scarred throughout, the copy that has been my companion during my years of research and of filming *Shoah,* and to which I have constantly referred. No other book will ever be, by my hand, annotated to such a degree. Other editions, more complete and less stark in their presentation on the page, have been published since, but it is this one, the first American printing, that will remain forever *princeps* in my heart.

I remember that luminous afternoon of the summer of 1974 in Jerusalem when I had in hand for the first time the Hilberg that had been sent to me from New York. I studied it with a reverential dread: 800 pages of close printing in double columns, shot through with synoptic tables, supported by an impressive critical apparatus, rich with thousands of names, mainly German names, that I felt I would have to learn and memorize all to the point where they would be perfectly familiar to me, without even knowing which ones belonged to the living and which to the dead, and unable to imagine really how much reading this book would change my life, into what insane pursuit it would thrust me.

I read Hilberg for months, I reread some chapters year after year, not for the purpose of storing knowledge but in the pursuit of a concrete goal, with the perspective of a work to be realized or in the process of being realized. That is the only way to learn. And since Hilberg had fed his thinking and his theoretical constructs on countless written documents, generated and preserved by the Nazi bureaucracy, by each one of those cogs in the German administrative machine, his book was, at least as far as Germany was concerned, my privileged source.

Translated from the French original by Susan M. Whitebook, assistant professor of French, University of Vermont.

But this is about a unique book, a beacon of a book, a breakwater of a book, a ship of history anchored in time and in a sense beyond time, undying, unforgettable, to which nothing in the course of ordinary historical production can be compared.

Its power derives first from the principles of organization of the work, from the author's choice of a vertical structure that, by breaking chronology and cutting straight through the denseness of twelve years of persecution and of extermination, lets one take in with a single look, as in a geological section, each of the constituent elements of the process of destruction; to follow, in time and in space, the major lines; to espouse the patience, the rehearsals, the hesitations, the trials and errors, the advances, the stunning and irreversible leaps forward. How does one pass in less than two years, unfathomable mystery of the Final Solution, from an official policy of emigration or expulsion to the large-scale murderous operations executed by mobile killing units, then to the first gassings of Polish Jews in the trucks at Kulmhof?

The vertical structure, with its central divisions ("Definition," "Expropriation," "Concentration," "Mobile Killing Operations," "Deportations," "Killing Center Operations," and so on), which organize in an impressive architecture the enormous mass of documents examined by the author—documents that are not mere written traces of facts but are themselves artifacts: they were orders, letters, reports, and thus caused actions—shows relentlessly how, as far as Germany alone is concerned (to say nothing of the rest of the world), the process of destruction could not have been put into place and carried out without a grounding in the almost entire consent of the German nation. The annihilation of millions of Jews was an undertaking of tremendous difficulty and complexity that presented the killers with many huge problems: Carrying it out required the unflinching participation of the entire administrative apparatus of a large modern state. But the bureaucrats were perpetually up to their task. They never backed off, never turned back. If it ever happened that they were stumped, they quickly improvised an effective and innovative solution; they always, as Hilberg notes with his dry irony, did more than was expected of them.

The dryness, the absence of pathos, the refusal of all idealism, the tireless confrontation of the sole question of the how of the destruction, the refusal to ask the question of the why, which would only condemn the thought to pufferies that reflect nothing but themselves, these are other virtues of this great book, shot through with passion.

I met Hilberg for the first time in New York, in 1975, some months after reading him, at a colloquium on the Holocaust (we didn't say "Shoah" in those days) that I was attending as an observer. This was before my first investigation in Germany, and I was intent on meeting him, in a way to affirm my own sense of purpose. For three days I had listened, unbelieving, to scholarly and sterile papers, where I could see nothing of the horror that inhabited me, and which alone seemed to me worth transmitting.

Hilberg took the floor on the evening of the third day, and I knew immediately that he would figure in the film I wanted to make. He stood out against the others: by what he said; by his voice, metallic and warm; by the way he carried his body. His body itself spoke. Hilberg literally embodied and accepted the essential dare that the Holocaust makes to all who seek to bring it back to life.

He appears in *Shoah* three times. His function, in the first and second appearances, is to consider sorrowfully what he knows rather than to transmit it magisterially. When he comes back, the third time, he has taken the place of a dead man. He is, entirely, Adam Czerniaków, the chairman of the Jewish Council of Warsaw who committed suicide on July 23, 1942. His voice, heard "off" over the snows of his Vermont, over the foliage of the Jewish cemetery of Warsaw, resurrects the dead.

But this was another task.

11

"Inescapable, and the Best": Tribute to Raul Hilberg

Herman Wouk

Let me say at the outset that I rather wonder at my inclusion in this symposium of distinguished scholars. You may recall that Leo Tolstoy, after his famed religious conversion, wrote confessions in which he repudiated his novels as bad art because they didn't meet his revised moral and philosophical standards. His objection to such works as *Anna Karenina* and *War and Peace* was that he had written them merely to entertain his readers. Now I must own that harsh impeachment myself, though I would strike out "merely." In all my work I've been entertaining my readers, or at least trying to, for in my view the fiction art requires it, whatever deeper freight a novel may be said to carry. Nor in that sense have I undergone a conversion. Therefore, when Professors Pacy and Wertheimer graciously invited me to deliver one of the learned lectures, I did not feel quite at home with the notion. However, I wanted very much to be here and to pay tribute to my old friend Raul Hilberg. So when they suggested, instead, that I speak at this dinner and give a personal tribute, I was grateful. I will speak very personally, and I trust you will find at the end that this is not a self-indulgence but rather the way I must say the few simple things I want to convey tonight.

Air schedules are such that I could not fly in one day to Burlington from Palm Springs, where I live. Since I don't travel on Shabbat, I was compelled to spend the weekend with my widowed sister on the south shore of Connecticut—not an onerous expedient at all; I loved it—so as to be able to arrive in Burlington this morning. On Saturday, browsing in her library, I came upon *The Destruction of the European Jews,* a faded copy of the first Quadrangle paperback. I took it down, curious about the inscription I'd written for my sister. Here was what I found scrawled on the flyleaf: "Irene—not pleasant, this book, but inescapable, and the

---

Mr. Wouk spoke extemporaneously and began by thanking Professor James Pacy for his "mercifully brief" introduction.—Eds.

best." I realized that in this inscription I had a summary of what I want to say to you tonight. Twenty-five years later I would not change a word of it.

"The best ..."

What better evidence of it than this symposium of stellar personalities in the academic world who have gathered to pay tribute to Raul Hilberg?

"Inescapable ..."

Raul calls the book in his introduction a first step in the understanding of a difficult subject. To this day his book is the inescapable first step for anyone who seeks even to begin to comprehend, to deal with, or to work on what happened between 1941 and 1945 to the European Jews.

"Not pleasant ..."

Well, there you have Hilbergian understatement at its purest. When something has happened that is so horrifying and the emotions that are stirred are so deep that words are inadequate, then all one can do is use the simplest, plainest, least colorful words. And so, yes, *The Destruction of the European Jews* is not pleasant. But it is inescapable, and it is the best.

Let me tell you how I met Raul. Back in 1961 I came upon a review by Professor Trevor Roper of his book, and at once I obtained a copy, and I read it, flipping the pages eagerly—I won't say like a Stephen King but surely like a Trollope. Then I fired off a letter to Raul, asking if I could meet him. I was then working on, or more correctly fighting off, an impulse, a mad impulse, to write a book that would throw a rope around World War II. I estimated that it would be 1,000 pages long and would take five years. Little did I know that I was letting myself in for two books, each 1,000 pages long—a task that would take me sixteen years, with three added years for bad behavior (working on two miniseries).

But which of us among the symposium members who knew in advance what he was getting into when he started a book would go ahead? You experience an irresistible impulse, and you follow it to the end.

Well, in the material I was reading, there was a dark void at the center of World War II, and that was the Germans, the Germans and what they had done to the Jews. To me, at the time, the Germans were either the bestial monsters of caricature, the horrible villains of the thriller movies or—another caricature I find even more offensive to this day—the comic bunglers who wore swastikas and did lots of funny, clumsy, unsuccessful things. What the Germans really were like, what they had done, why they had done it, I could not come to grips with. That was why I wanted to see Raul Hilberg.

He wrote back a very gracious letter. I came to see him here in Burlington, and we talked for three days. As you who know him may well believe, that meant we walked for three days. Up and down and back and forth in Burlington we walked, discussing my project; and you can imagine what three days with Hilberg meant to me at that time in clarifying my task.

He said two things that I never forgot. One was, "You've got to go to Germany." I objected, "I've all but taken a vow that I will never set foot on that bloodstained and cursed ground as long as I live." He replied, "I understand that, but you've got to go to Germany."

The other thing he said was, "You have to find a structure. It seems to be a war of two disconnected parts, the Pacific and Europe, with the Jewish problem at the heart of it, but there is a structure and you must find it." We talked a lot about that structure.

I went to Germany. There I obtained, by talking to publishers, to politicians, to newspaper people—whoever I talked to—a liberating, illuminating, and appalling insight, which was that they're human beings like us. Once I grasped that somber reality, I could begin to deal with the whole thing, because I can write only about real people, as I comprehend them. And as for structure, I went back and wrestled with the interconnection of the Pacific war, the European war, and the war against the Jews until I found an organic narrative that would pull them together, such as my gifts granted me. You understand then, or start to understand, something of my debt to Raul Hilberg.

Now let me talk a little bit about his work. In the first instance, his book certainly stands with a few key classics, without which you cannot write or think about World War II: with Churchill's six volumes, with Sherwood's *Roosevelt and Hopkins*, with Bullock's *Hitler: The Study of Tyranny*, and with Morison's sixteen volumes on the naval war. It has in common with those books the distinction of defining one theme within the war so masterfully that thereafter it is impossible to deal seriously with that theme without reading the work.

But I see more in Raul's monumental book. I find that it equals, at least in grasp—I don't speak of stature, for stature is a function of time—but it holds a place, for me, in world literature with Gibbon and with Tocqueville. In the same way it seizes on a mighty theme of human experience, a unique theme, and plumbs it. Much has been written about the rise and fall of Rome—books come out every year—and Gibbon in some respects is said to be dated. But who can write about Rome without knowing Gibbon? Similarly, there are torrents of books about America, its people, its character, its politics, but there is no serious work to done about the United States without at some point digesting Tocqueville's *Democracy in America*. Such is Raul's work on the destruction of the European Jews.

And there is yet another dimension to it, the Jewish dimension, which comes into my area of special concern. We have in Jewish literature a large body of poetry—elegies, threnodies, cries of anguish—about the recurring tragedies of the Jewish people, transmuted into restorative art, much of it stemming from the times of the Crusades and the Spanish expulsion but going back to the destruction of the First Temple. The peak, the *locus classicus*, of such works, is of course the Book of Lamentations, by tradition ascribed to the prophet Jeremiah. Whatever else *The Destruction of the European Jews* is—as a work of political science, as a work of social history—it is at heart a Jewish lamentation, all the more powerful because not a word of grief escapes from its 1,000 pages line by line; and yet between every line there is the grief, the prophetic grief, of a Jew mourning for his people. It is that grief that drove the author to write those 1,000 riveting pages.

Perhaps you have noticed that in speaking to you tonight, I have never yet used the word *Holocaust*. I don't object to the word, and if I did, it would make no difference. It is embedded in the language, the culture, inescapably, irrevocably. Holocaust studies, Holocaust memorials, Holocaust literature, Holocaust films! *But what happened was not a "Holocaust."* The word *holocaust* is a figure of speech. It's a metaphor, and a handy one. What happened was the massacre of the European Jews; my own family; more than 1 million of them children who would have, alive today, been making the extraordinary contributions that rise from the Jewish genius to enrich human society. That was what really happened. It is an abiding glory of Raul Hilberg that he searched out the truth and called it by its right name for all time: *The Destruction of the European Jews*.

Let me conclude, as we do in reading the Torah, with a word of hope. The Masoretes many centuries ago cut up each *sedra*, each weekly reading of the Pentateuch, into seven sections, and they saw to it that each section ended with a line of upbeat, of hope, of promise of something good happening. If there is an event in the century that matches in its might and depth and mystery what happened to the European Jews, it is this: that as one generation walked, duped victims of a cruel hoax, into gas chambers to their annihilation, the very next generation rose and found in its genes the warriors of Joshua, and the Jews marched back to the Holy Land from which they had been exiled for eighteen centuries. It is the paradox of the century that this people, of all peoples, who gave the United Nations its slogan, "They shall beat their swords into plowshares," and to the world the word "Nation shall not lift up sword against nation, neither shall they learn war any more"; that this tiny crushed nation rose again and learned war, because all other ways to defend itself that Raul lists in his structured tale—submission, accommodation, compliance, bribery, flight—all had failed. And so the next generation stood up and learned to make war and to fight for its life.

And now I speak in faith: There is in the air today a coming of a time when, as the Midrash predicts, Ishmael and Isaac will be reconciled at the tomb of Abraham, and our people will live in peace; when the law "Nation shall not lift up sword against nation, neither shall they learn war any more" will become the law of the nations; and by the grace of God, that law will go forth from Zion.

Raul, God bless you! May your greatest years lie ahead. I can never repay my debt to you. Still, I came here to lay this poor tribute at your feet, my old friend, the humblest great man that I have known.

About the Contributors

Yehuda Bauer is the Jona M. Machover Professor of Holocaust Studies and academic chairperson of the Institute of Contemporary Jewry at the Hebrew University of Jerusalem. He is the author of *A History of the Holocaust, The Holocaust in Historical Perspective, The Jewish Emergence from Powerlessness,* and other works.

Christopher R. Browning is professor of history at Pacific Lutheran University, Tacoma, Washington, and lists among his books, *Fateful Months, The Final Solution and the German Foreign Office, Ordinary Men: Reserve Police Battalion 101 and the Final Solution in Poland,* and *The Path to Genocide.*

Peter Hayes is professor of history and German and Alfred W. Chase Professor of Business Institutions at Northwestern University. His publications include *Industry and Ideology: I.G. Farben in the Nazi Era, Lessons and Legacies: The Meaning of the Holocaust in a Changing World,* and a coedited work, *Imperial Germany.*

Eberhard Jäckel is professor of history at Stuttgart University in Germany. Professor Jäckel has authored *Hitler in History* and *Hitler's World View: A Blueprint for Power,* as well as books in German.

Claude Lanzmann is producer and director of the universally acclaimed *Shoah,* a documentary film about the Holocaust. He is also the director of the publication *Les Temps Modernes.*

Alvin H. Rosenfeld is professor of English and director of Jewish studies at Indiana University. His books include *Confronting the Holocaust: The Impact of Elie Wiesel, A Double Dying: Reflections on Holocaust Literature,* and *Imagining Hitler.*

John K. Roth is the Russell K. Pitzer Professor of Philosophy at Claremont McKenna College in California. Some of his books are *Memory Offended: The Auschwitz Convent Controversy, A Consuming Fire: Encounters with Elie Wiesel and the Holocaust,* and *Different Voices: Women and the Holocaust.*

Richard L. Rubenstein, the Robert O. Lawton Distinguished Professor of Religion at Florida State University, has written *After Auschwitz: History, Theology and*

Contemporary Judaism, Spirit Matters: The Worldwide Impact of Religion on Contemporary Politics, and *The Cunning of History.*

George Steiner is professor of English and comparative literature at the University of Geneva, and Extraordinary Fellow of Churchill College, Cambridge University. His numerous books include *Antigones, The Death of Tragedy, Martin Heidegger,* and *Proofs and Three Parables.*

Robert Wolfe, National Archives specialist of captured German records and editor of *Captured German and Related Records,* has written several essays on the Holocaust, including "Putative Threat to National Security as a Nuremberg Defense for Genocide" and "To Embellish the Truth of the Holocaust Is Unnecessary."

Herman Wouk is an internationally known author whose novels *The Winds of War* and *War and Remembrance* deal extensively with the destruction of the European Jews.

About the Book and Editors

This volume brings together original historical, literary, and philosophical analyses of the Holocaust by some of the world's leading scholars, including Yehuda Bauer, Christopher R. Browning, George Steiner, Alvin H. Rosenfeld, Richard L. Rubenstein, Robert Wolfe, Eberhard Jäckel, Peter Hayes, and John K. Roth. The essays cover topics as diverse as Nazi-Jewish negotiations, corporate involvement in the Holocaust, and the writings of Primo Levi and Elie Wiesel. The book also contains personal tributes by Claude Lanzmann (*Shoah*) and Herman Wouk.

Both **James S. Pacy** and **Alan P. Wertheimer** are professors of political science at the University of Vermont–Burlington.